More Praise for *Business as War*

"Having attended Navy Officer Candidate School in 1956 followed by three years of active duty and now with 44 years of experience in the investment industry, I applaud Ken Allard for the superb job he does in combining military philosophy with that of how a business should be run. His anecdotes and straight talk send messages that should be an example for many of us."

> —Lee Kopp
> President and CEO, Kopp Investment Advisors

"*Business as War* is especially relevant for managers in fast-moving, technology-intensive industries, where winner-take-all payoffs accrue to first movers who can outmaneuver their rivals and focus their firepower on the right targets. Allard explains that the modern U.S. military shares these priorities, and its successes stem from the tight alignment of strategy and organizational processes. The military has learned how to audit its performance, gather intelligence and share it rapidly, give strategic plans real teeth, inculcate values, and promote cooperation across unit boundaries. Managers know that this 'soft stuff' is crucial, and hard stuff to master. *Business as War* shows how to make it happen."

> —Tom Eisenmann
> Assistant Professor, Harvard Business School

"Colonel Ken Allard was one of the pioneers who showed the military how to use information as a weapon of war. His television audiences have come to rely on his pungent, hard-hitting analyses of international conflict. With *Business as War,* he combines those perspectives into a powerful new message for corporate America—from value-centered leadership to the predatory use of information. If globalization and dramatically increased competition are affecting your business, then you owe it to yourself to read this path-breaking new book."

> —Admiral William A. Owens
> United States Navy (Retired)

BUSINESS

★★ AS ★★

WAR

BUSINESS
☆☆ AS ☆☆
WAR

☆ ☆ ☆ ☆ ☆ ☆ ☆ ☆ ☆ ☆ ☆ ☆

Battling for
Competitive Advantage

KENNETH ALLARD

WILEY

John Wiley & Sons, Inc.

Published by John Wiley & Sons, Inc., Hoboken, New Jersey.
Published simultaneously in Canada.

For general information on our other products and services please contact our
Customer Care Department within the United States at (800) 762-2974, outside the
United States at (317) 572-3993 or fax (317) 572-4002.

Wiley also publishes its books in a variety of electronic formats. Some content that
appears in print may not be available in electronic books. For more information about
Wiley products, visit our web site at www.wiley.com.

Library of Congress Cataloging-in-Publication Data:

Allard, C. Kenneth (Carl Kenneth), 1947–
  Business as war : battling for competitive advantage / by Kenneth Allard.
    p. cm.
  Includes bibliographical references and index.
  ISBN 0-471-46854-1 (CLOTH)
  1. Leadership. 2. Business ethics. 3. Strategic planning. 4.
Competition. 5. Business intelligence. 6. Business
enterprises—Security measures. I. Title.
HD57.7.A619 2004
658.4—dc22

                                                  2003020607

10 9 8 7 6 5 4 3 2 1

Acknowledgments

My most interesting experience writing acknowledgments came in late 1992, when I was helping direct a congressionally mandated survey of the nation's procurement laws. It had been a massive effort, lasting more than two years, covering some 600 separate statutes and producing a report of over 1800 pages. Editing all of that was one of my main tasks, made more difficult by the fact that anyone on the advisory panel, as well as our support staff, was free to make changes. The last thing I did before sending the report to the printers was to double-check our introductory volume one last time, but not in anticipation of any problems since I had written most of it. It was a good thing I did, because although most of the wording was just as I had left it, the heading was now different. Some anonymous zealot with more military bearing than proper English usage had changed "Foreword" to "**Forward!**" No one ever admitted making that change, and I was sorely tempted to leave it just like that—but, alas, conventions had to be observed.

The lady who prevented similar recurrences in this book was my editor at John Wiley and Sons, Pamela Van Giessen, who not only deserves credit for her skills at untangling various errors of syntax and willful violations of political correctness—but also for having the patience of Job. She does what an editor is supposed to do and makes me a better writer—although you, dear reader, will have to be the ultimate judge of how well she did. Right up there with Pamela is my agent Lynn Johnson, who in addition to being my teacher and mentor into the strange folkways of commercial publishing, is also annoyingly patient. In equal parts cheerleader and confidante, she was also my envoy to the world of business literature.

So was Florence Stone: As someone who really does know the science of business and business literature, she provided not only expert knowledge but encouragement. My many indiscretions here should in no sense be charged to her account. Two of my Georgetown graduate students—Mike Lynch and Pete Sickle—provided valuable assistance in the writing of my chapters on business intelligence and enterprise security. So grateful thanks to Florence, Pete, and Mike for all their help.

I simply would not have had the time to complete this book at all, if not for the flexibility and understanding of my MSNBC colleagues, Mike Tanaka and Mark Effron, who, during its writing, allowed most of my network "hits" to take place from Washington rather than Secaucus, New Jersey. Jeremy Gaines, of the MSNBC production staff lent valuable assistance in our production as well; and my military analyst colleague, retired Marine Lieutenant General Bernard "Mick" Trainor, a distinguished author in his own right about the first Iraq war, was generous in sharing his insights about the most recent one. Several CNBC colleagues—Ron Insana, Chris Whitcomb, and Alan Murray—were equally generous in offering support and encouragement.

General John M. Keane, United States Army, who concluded a distinguished military career in 2004 after serving as the Army's 29th Vice Chief of Staff, generously offered support and advice. He was particularly helpful in arranging interviews with several of the Army's top combatant commanders, several of whom were still serving in combat zones. My friend Evan Gaddis, a former Army brigadier general and now a distinguished association executive, offered valuable comments and advice on the manuscript.

Several CEOs deserve credit—though not of course any of the blame—for having educated me about their respective leadership challenges. Lee Kopp, head of Kopp Investments, who, as noted in Chapter 1, provided an early and courageous call for a return to corporate accountability. Tom Petrie, CEO of Petrie-Parkman, is an expert on energy matters as well as corporate leadership, and generously shared that information with me. David Rothkopf, CEO of Intellibridge, fully shares my faith about corporate intelligence—and provided much helpful information about that area for this book. Admiral Bill Owens—while in uniform a prophet and practitioner of the revolution in military affairs, and thereafter a distinguished corporate leader in his own right—has taught me many valuable lessons over the years about both business and war. My sincere thanks to all four gentlemen.

Thanks as well are due the publishers of *CIO Magazine* for their kindness in granting permission to publish the short extract from my article in the September 2003 edition of their periodical that appears in Chapter 7.

But probably the most significant debt of gratitude is due my beautiful wife, Debby, who provided not only the inspiration for this book but of course had a far better sense of where it needed to go—and what I really needed to say. Most of all: During the writing of this book, I underwent a serious illness. Deb stuck by me, encouraged me, and kicked my butt until things came together again. (More about that in our next book—promise!) But for now: Without her the book wouldn't be here and neither might I. So thanks Debby: as they said at the end of *A Beautiful Mind*, "You're all my reasons."

Which reminds me of my favorite story—which Pamela, Lynn, and Debby all agreed had no place whatsoever in this book. And because it didn't seem especially relevant to any of the chapters that follow, I had to agree. Until now.

So a priest is sitting there in the confessional and the penitent begins:

Penitent: "Bless me, Father for I have sinned."

Priest: "What is this sin, my son?"

Penitent: "Father, I'm a ninety-year-old man and last night I made love to a beautiful, twenty-year-old girl."

Priest: "When did you last confess?"

Penitent: "I've never confessed. I'm not even Catholic."

Priest: "Then WHY are you telling me this?"

Penitent: "I'm telling EVERYBODY!!"

Me, too. So read on. And enjoy!

C. K. A.

McLean, Virginia
September, 2003

Contents

1

★ ★ Introduction ★ ★

air warning: This book is meant to be dangerous. Provocative. Arresting. Like a brick thrown through the plate-glass window of the CEO's office, the meeting room of the board of directors, or the faculty club of the business school that hits you up all the time for alumni contributions. I argue that today's competitive environment for the business leaders is sufficiently hazardous and uncertain that you are better off thinking of it not as business but as war. To help you cope, or even to survive, you need to understand the secrets of the warrior—things that probably were not a part of either your professional business education or all that other stuff you like to put on your resume. So fasten your seat belt, because we're in for a rough ride—but an interesting one. And leave those other business books right there on the shelf where they are: Not only do they not have the right answers, the authors aren't even sure what the right questions are.

But you may have noticed that already because business thinkers typically attempt to solve individual problems—which they will then publish with overwrought titles suggesting breakthrough solutions. Or even better, they propound the absurd notion that strategy is nothing more difficult than conjuring up some "big hairy audacious goals" at your next corporate outing. (More about that later—I promise.) If you have a penchant for silly ideas—often dulled by some characteristically bad writing—then be my guest. However, you may occasionally notice that those approaches in effect leave you intellectually disarmed in a changing environment that does not lend itself to such facile solutions—essentially slogans masquerading as dynamic new approaches to some much more fundamental problems of the business environment.

The only thing weaker than such easy diagnoses is their curious inability to relate some things to other things, so let's try connecting the dots. Does your competitive universe look anything like this?

- Has heightened security in the face of terrorism heightened your feeling that all these precautions may not make a difference?

- Do you have an uneasy sense that business security—in all its aspects—is no longer something that business leaders can take for granted? From terrorists to power blackouts?

- Forget about uneasiness: Do you have a pervasive, gnawing worry that your electronic assets are all at risk, that the hackers, crackers, phreakers, and cyber-wackos are engaging you every day in a game you barely understand?

- Do you agree with this statement: We have never had access to so much data? And we have never been as confused as we are now?

- Have you tried to conceive or execute a business strategy either to: (1) fail or (2) partly succeed but make everything worse.

If you answered "yes" to one or more of these questions, then welcome to the exciting world of business as war. (If you did not, then please give my best to your fellow inmates there in the joint—especially those from Enron, WorldCom, Tyco, and many Wall Street investment houses who obviously received this message too late.)

Even if you are willing to concede that your new competitive environment may be challenging, you may not yet be willing to accept that it's closer to war than business. It's been years, but I first made that connection—or rather had it explained to me—while teaching on the West Point faculty. I ran a lecture series funded by one of the wealthier alumni classes, and as a courtesy, we invited the donors to visit with our cadets. One of the donors had done his obligatory payback period with the Army after graduation and had then made it big in the west Texas oilfields when there was a lot of money there to be made. Now in a gorgeous

Armani suit and cowboy boots, he squinted out at the cadets and allowed as how they were lucky to be at West Point, especially in the company of such distinguished professors, who could teach them all kinds of things that would be useful inside the Army and out. (An oilman, he obviously knew how to grease up his listeners.) "Of course," he drawled, "ah hope that they gonna' teach yew boys a lesson ah din't learn until years after ah left West Point—namely that the military is really jest a VAH-lent form of economics." A violent form of economics is not really a bad way to think about the military—but it was years until I realized that some of the skills we had absorbed as warriors could be translated into the business world as well.

One of them was strategy, which had been a more or less continuous counterpoint throughout my military career, but had become particularly interesting toward the end of it. Sure we had won the Cold War and Desert Storm—but now there were whole new classes of international problems to deal with. I had written a book about one of them—our operations in Somalia—and several years later found myself on the ground in the middle of another one—Bosnia. There were all kinds of lessons to learn there but maybe the best one was on my first day in Sarajevo, which gave a whole new meaning to the casual phrase *war-torn*. Now, armed and in combat gear, I was being guided around the city's more notorious hot spots when I felt someone touch the American flag combat patch on my right shoulder. Startled, I now found myself looking down at an old Bosnian man, who reached up again, touched the combat patch and simply said, "Senk you." My admiration for peacekeeping duty has remained under firm control since then, but the human dimension of strategy I learned that day has stayed with me as well.

There were more heart-wrenching scenes throughout my time in Bosnia, especially when seeing painfully thin children or the remnants of a mass gravesite, but one of the lessons learned from Somalia seemed appropriate: Beware the temptation to do too much. Strategy is a matter of balance and sometimes that's tough: choosing between two equally unpalatable alternatives, for example, or calibrating what you may be forced to do one day against your original motivation—or for that matter your ultimate objectives. While I had plenty of experience worrying about such things while in uniform, leaving the Army in 1997 brought with it my first chance to try translating those insights into the commercial world. I tried business intelligence, strategic planning, enterprise security, defense projects and any number of freelance consulting assignments. Although I didn't recognize it as such at the time, by the end of my five-year post-Army apprenticeship, I knew what it was like to compete for and lose a contract; win one and wish I hadn't; get stiffed by a deadbeat employer; and know how to stretch out payments to make ends meet. Painful lessons sometimes, but all of them useful.

As the owner and sole employee of my own consulting firm, I considered it strategic marketing at first—but my occasional forays on television were beginning to look promising—and their checks didn't bounce. Based on my writings on Somalia, I became the technical advisor for what turned out to be a highly acclaimed PBS special called "Ambush in Mogadishu." Because American military power was constantly being flexed as the situation with Saddam's Iraq deteriorated—I was regularly being asked for commentary on Fox, CNN, and increasingly MSNBC. Well, the more you do, the more you seem to do—and the MSNBC gig was becoming a second home. The people there were (and are) great, and MSNBC seemed to be running an apprenticeship program of their own. I worked with talented anchors like Brian Williams (before he became Tom Brokaw's designated successor at NBC); Soledad O'Brien (before she went first to NBC News and then to CNN); and John Gibson (now a star and stalwart at Fox News, along with many other MSNBC alums). All were gracious, patient, and taught me a lot.

By the time we went to war in Kosovo, I had an exclusive arrangement with MSNBC that meant being available for in-studio appearances whenever breaking news so demanded. That happened pretty frequently, because even after Kosovo was settled, the continuing topics included the constant back-and-forth-ing on Iraq; terrorism and the impotent U.S. response to attacks on our embassies and the USS Cole; Middle East unrest; and preparations for the supposed Y2K computer meltdowns. It got to be so bad that, every time I ran into bureau chief Tim Russert at the NBC studios in Washington on my way to a network "hit," he would recoil in mock alarm and ask, "Oh no! If you're here, then something, somewhere must be terribly wrong." And on September 11, 2001, it was.

Only weeks before, I had participated in an MSNBC special that had predicted exactly this sort of attack, culminating in the destruction of the Twin Towers, but now it was no easier to deal with the real thing. At such a moment, thoughts become indistinguishable from emotions. My own were that this was probably not the best moment to be a retired soldier, when so many terrorists were out there who clearly required some serious killing. Knowing so many senior officers who were still on active duty, I wondered if there was a chance of getting back in uniform. But despite the jammed phone lines, my fiancée (now my wife) somehow reached me at that moment. A beautiful, smart, and thoroughly tough woman, Debby had been through the IRA bombing campaigns while working as lawyer in London—and she now offered some very good advice. "Look: Americans have never been through anything like this before and it is now our turn in the barrel. Other people out there are doing what needs to be done. What you need to do is to get your emotions under control, get on TV and tell the viewers as clearly as you can that this is a time for courage. Forget all that stuff about the people in World War II being *The Greatest Generation:* this is our moment. So tell your audience as well that there is a reason why we have a strong military—and that everything is eventually going to be okay."

Great advice, of course, but tough to do—especially as the Twin Towers came down and our coverage showed the carnage there and at the Pentagon. Mostly I just gulped hard—and spent most of that terrible day struggling to put events into some sort of reasonable context. The emotions came out only once—when Tom Brokaw asked me how long it might be before the terrorists were brought to justice. A sensible enough question—and from our top guy. But I had heard that phrase just one time too many. In fact, it had been used consistently throughout the Clinton administration, which seemed curiously unable to grasp that *fatwas* (Islamic declarations of holy war) followed by repeated attacks against our embassies and warships were not crimes—they were acts of war requiring a concerted military response. So my response was probably a little over the top for a supposedly objective analyst: "Tom, we don't need to bring these people to justice at all. We need to send them to hell."

The days and months that followed became a marathon of long hours in front of the cameras as we struggled to inform a suddenly energized

TV audience that craved an understanding of their military and its ability to fight the new kind of war that everyone knew was coming. Probably the ultimate honor—like being hanged—was becoming a regular on the Don Imus program, simulcast by MSNBC as well as reaching a national radio audience of over twenty million listeners. I had been a fan of "the I-man" for years, and it was somewhat startling to realize that one of the toughest interviewers in the business now expected me to have something worthwhile and somewhat amusing to say to him and his audience—often at 0630 in the morning. One of our first conversations involved the forthcoming war in Afghanistan. From somewhere I recalled a quote usually attributed to Machiavelli, who once described France as "Easy to conquer but impossible to govern." It seemed like an apt comparison—in both directions.

Momentous as the events of 9/11 were, it still took time to understand that what had really happened is what social scientists call a "paradigm shift"—a kind of earthquake in human events that has a lasting impact on our emotional and physical landscapes. And a personal one as well. Not only was I living much of my life back and forth between TV studios, but there also were changes in my increasingly frequent speeches to business audiences. I had given lots of speeches before 9/11—but mostly to academic and think-tank sponsored conferences. They didn't pay particularly well and their conclusions usually suggested the need for more conferences. But in a post-9/11 world, I was now being asked to give speeches for some very nice fees. These speeches were basically the same material and covered much of what I had said before for free—but now with much better PowerPoints and travel arrangements. Organized under the general heading of "Business as War," these talks usually covered three topics: the war abroad, the war at home, and what these changes meant to the specific interests of the business audiences.

And suddenly there were all kinds of audiences: real estate, insurance, finance, construction, even pharmaceutical manufacturers. Much of what I had to tell them drew on my 26-year military career as well as my more recent experience as a business consultant, especially those engagements featuring enterprise security and business intelligence. My apprenticeship as a consultant had demonstrated the validity of the business axiom that if you are too far in front of the power curve, you starve.

Part of my education involved struggling to make the case to business leaders that they needed to understand these new disciplines—and to make the human and financial investments to capitalize on them. In one memorable instance, I made my pitch to the senior vice president of a Fortune 100 telecommunications company in subzero temperatures during a fire drill outside his Chicago headquarters. The argument was one of my best: that Chicago had learned the hard way in the nineteenth century about fire prevention and that business intelligence was a sensible investment in preventing competitive disasters in the twenty-first century. But the neurons must have been cold, too: No sale.

However the reactions of my audiences now suggested that business leaders in the aftermath of the terrorist attacks were beginning to get the message. Increasingly I began to link the business-as-war themes to the overriding need for new and better leadership at the CEO level—essential if these new disciplines were ever to become standard in corporate America. And at precisely this point, our country experienced the second major disaster to befall it in six months: the collapse of Enron and the ensuing waves of corporate governance scandals that persisted throughout 2003. The corporate disasters also became personal when MSNBC mixed its coverage of the war on terror with the human costs of the Enron tragedy, sending my MSNBC anchor buddy Rick Sanchez to Houston to interview former Enron employees. Rick's interviews were compelling. Some of those former Enron employees—in addition to being jobless—had lost all or most of what they had saved for the rainy day—and that rain had turned into a Texas-size downpour. The reality was so grim that one kept expecting former Enron officials and their lawyers to start speaking Arabic and triumphantly pulling out *fatwas*. Lives hadn't been lost—but livelihoods had been.

No matter how compelling, any major event has a certain shelf life before media attention inevitably turns elsewhere. But the Enron story turned out to be the bow wave of a series of corporate scandals that became a virtual catalog of wrongdoing: insider trading, questionable or downright false accounting standards, and the systematic looting of some companies by the very executives charged with their survival and well-being. The problems had become pervasive—how much so became evident when I spoke to an investment conference in Minneapolis organized by Lee Kopp—the head of a nationally ranked investment firm where the minimum account is $250,000. One of the few nonmillionaires in the room, I listened respectfully as Lee gave his investors a brutally honest prognosis. Returns on investment were no more exempt from the sluggish economy than any other business: But what was making matters far worse was the "malignant greed" with which business leaders were systematically weakening the American corporation and all who depended on it. In fact, Lee called it a corporate cancer fed by greed and a lack of effective corporate governance. He summed up the major flaws: excessive executive pay, weak leadership, corrupt analysts, complacent boards of directors, and questionable accounting practices.

Which pretty much covered it—except for the heartfelt note that came at the end of Lee's remarks and was specifically addressed to the CEO of a company in which the Kopp Group was among the largest investors. Decrying the generous options program currently in effect at this company, Lee pointed out that it was stockholders, rather than the option-wielding executives, who actually had money at risk—and it was to these investors that the board was ultimately accountable. "Like your employees, the shareholders are real people. They are professionals, retirees, young couples and single parents. They are not a vast mass of wealthy institutions."[1]

Ordinary Americans were being shortchanged by people who were already getting paid a lot of money to look out for their interests. It could hardly have been a better introduction for me had Lee Kopp simply stood up and waved a red flag. In what became (according to most observers) a fairly impassioned speech, many of the themes explored in this book emerged for the first time. Basically, these corporate scandals involved leadership. And having spent most of a professional lifetime in the military, I had some reason to know what leadership was—and what it was not. So I hit the basics. CEOs had to be leaders above all else, and if they couldn't lead, then they shouldn't be in the job. The same thing goes double for every member of the board of directors—and every member of the leadership team from corporate officers to line or project managers. There are lots more elaborate ways to say it but what it comes down to is that, to be a real leader, vision and competence are prerequisites: But the defining characteristic is to put everyone else's interest ahead of your own. And in business, those interests include the shareholders, the employees, the customers, and even the firm itself. Or simply get the hell out of Dodge.

Seemed like pretty basic stuff to me. But the reactions of all the people who came up to me afterward suggested nothing less than that a nerve had been hit. As things turned out, in the year between that speech and the writing of this book, our nerves were in for a wild ride. The panoply of corporate neglect and wrongdoing has become a sad constant of American life, so much a staple of network TV news and newspaper reporting that we are in serious danger to becoming desensitized to how pervasive and insidious this problem is.

Two examples will suffice: the indictment of Martha Stewart, an American icon, role model and former board member of the New York Stock Exchange, in June 2003, for obstruction of justice (basically, lying); and in April 2003, the forced resignation of American Airlines CEO Don Carty.

The Carty resignation, in particular, was a watershed event because sheer public embarrassment led to the resignation of a CEO. It seems as if Carty, while trying to save American from bankruptcy, was most publicly identified with jawboning his flight attendants, mechanics, baggage handlers, and pilots to take pay cuts of up to 23 percent—all under the guise of responsibility and cost cutting. At the same time, he himself had an annual salary of $1.6 million that was not tied to the airline's performance and naturally was not cut at all. Worse yet, Carty turned out to be one of the principal administrators of a special pension trust created for the top executives that could not be touched by any bankruptcy proceeding. These deals were kept secret even as American's unions were agreeing to concessions to help stave off bankruptcy. But once the truth was known, all bets were off and Carty was forced to resign.

Reflecting on American's difficulties, Robert J. Samuelson noted that overcompensation was becoming characteristic of the CEO culture in the United States. "Sprinkling so much money over so few people has created a new sense of entitlement. The upper echelons of corporate America have come to believe that they shouldn't simply do well. They deserve to become rich, perhaps fabulously so . . . The CEO conceit is that everyone near the top of the corporate staircase should become a multimillionaire several times over."[2]

So pervasive has this culture of CEO greed and selfishness become that *Fortune* magazine highlighted CEO salaries in a cover article titled "Oink"—illustrated with the head of a pig imposed over a blue pinstripe suit. To stress the point of "high pay, rotten returns," *Fortune* profiled 12 CEOs "whose companies' returns lagged the S&P last year—but whose comp topped $22 million." And to bolster its point, that "the CEO only rises," *Fortune* showed that the pay of CEO and Board Chairmen was up 32 percent (2000 to 2002) while the compensation of top marketing and sales executives was down 13 to15 percent. Most strikingly, there was also an excerpt from the employment contract of 3M CEO James McNerney; it provided that potential reasons for firing him could not include either negligence or bad judgment. "Screwing up doesn't qualify. Would a felony conviction do the trick? Maybe."[3]

Once nearly unheard of, felony convictions are not all that far-fetched since increasing numbers of CEOs and their principal officers have taken the "perp walk" into law enforcement custody as the various accounting scandals, insider trading allegations, and corporate looting inevitably progress from investigation to indictment. Quite beyond the personalities involved, what we are really hearing in these endless waves of corporate scandals is pure and simple bad leadership—the natural end product of a self-centered mentality that starts at the top and quickly comes to pervade an organization. Leadership is about planning and direction, but it is also about setting an absolute moral and ethical standard that puts the greater good before any individual, in any position.

The paradigm shift of a world at war, the continuing war on terrorism, and the lack of leadership in many sectors of American business are the rationales for this book, as well as what we need to do about these things— beyond issuing the usual platitudes. The tragedy of 9/11 was clearly a clarion call to Americans to stand up and be counted in the international arena. As conservative columnist Jed Babbin put it: "The Afghanistan campaign began on October 5, 2001, less than a month after 9/11. The application of focused military power literally shook the mountains where the Soviet army had come to grief a decade earlier. Soon after, Toby Keith sang about how 'soon as we could see clearly through our big black eye, we lit up your world like the Fourth of July.' That song was an enormous hit, and should have tipped the world off about America's mood swing."[4] In the same way, the sorry examples of Enron and all the rest should have tipped off corporate America that they simply aren't living right, that they need to spend less time and money on their lawyers, lobbyists, and lackeys and more in leading their organizations. They are doing much less than what is expected of them if they fail to return to the values of leadership, selflessness, and giving back that have been the hallmark of the American way—and American greatness.

The primary purpose of this book is to explain why CEOs, senior managers, and other business leaders need to understand and apply some truths not covered during their MBA education or executive experiences. While I focus on major changes prompted by war and terrorism, the points presented here also serve as a practical guide for what business leaders need to do to survive and prosper in a competitive environment that has become much more intense—and in which even some of the basic rules have changed. Ultimately, this book is about leadership—and why business leaders need to draw some important practical and philosophical lessons from their warrior counterparts. The reasons those worlds are so different are explored later on in greater depth, but for now consider only this basic distinction: Business schools train managerial survivors. The military trains leaders.

In fact, the military is at heart a system in which leadership and the values surrounding it are firmly planted, enriched through a graduated series of educational and operating experiences, and which—as they are embodied in the development of leaders—finally form the basis for advancement and promotion. The objective is to produce what one historian has called "A Genius for War," in which leadership and warrior skills are seamlessly transferred from one generation to the next. Think of it as a system consciously set up to bring about not profits, nor even great efficiencies, but victories over the nation's enemies. There are lots of ways of saying it, but what leadership comes down to is character. Although character can be defined in many ways, my favorite is the one my pastor taught me many years ago: The real test of character is what you do when no one is looking.

An excellent example of what someone does when no one is looking—and of applied character and leadership—was seen by an audience of millions of Americans who tuned in on May 24, 2003, to watch the National

Memorial Day Concert from Washington, D.C. Amidst the patriotic songs and celebrations, they heard actor Ossie Davis tell the story of Captain Lincoln D. Leibner—and what he did on 9/11. Captain Leibner, a 40-year old former infantryman, looked trim in his green uniform but was visibly uncomfortable at being distinguished before the audience on the Capitol Grounds and on national television.

As Ossie Davis's narrative continued, it became apparent why this young soldier had been singled out. Assigned to a later shift, Captain Leibner had not been at his Pentagon desk on the morning of 9/11 when the first two airliners hit the World Trade Center. But, when they did, his first instinct was to report to the Pentagon, little imagining that he would become a full participant in the third attack of that dreadful day. As he left his car in an adjacent parking lot, Captain Leibner was startled by the sound of a high-speed jet engine. He looked up just in time to see the last four seconds of Flight 77 before it plowed into the northwest wall of the Pentagon and exploded in a ball of flame and smoke. He remembers staring at the crash site for several seconds before being propelled toward a building that other people were rapidly fleeing. As he recalled later: "I ran toward the building because that was what I was supposed to do."

Just inside the Pentagon, he made his first rescue of the day, a burned and dazed woman whom he led outside to safety. As he returned the second time, he heard people sobbing and asking for his help. Moving debris, dodging the smoke and flames, he helped two more to escape before lowering a number of others from the blown-out windows on what was left of the second floor. At this point, everyone was ordered to leave the building because fire, smoke, and structural strains were creating the third potential building collapse of the day. Shortly after leaving the building and being placed on oxygen support, Captain Leibner watched as the entire façade of the Pentagon came down. Briefly treated at a nearby hospital, Captain Leibner determined that his duty was elsewhere. He returned to the still burning Pentagon and to his office—which is part of the personal staff of the Secretary of Defense. In fact, Captain Leibner may have been the first person to tell Secretary Donald Rumsfeld that they had been hit not by a cruise missile or a car bomb but by a commercial airliner—hijacked and flying on the final leg of a murderous suicide mission.[5]

Gripping as it was, Captain Leibner's story was not all that different from the many tales of heroism the nation witnessed on 9/11—from New York City firefighters, policeman, and ordinary citizens. But it touched me deeply for two reasons. It filled in some critical information that I had wondered about ever since that fateful September day when I saw the Pentagon under attack, but reluctantly realized that my wife Debby had been right when she said that my place was now in a TV studio and that other people—the police, the firefighters, and the military—would step up and do what had to be done. She had been right—and Captain Leibner had been one of those seemingly ordinary people performing magnificently in extraordinary circumstances.

But there was another reason as well: Until that Memorial Day telecast, I had not seen Captain Leibner since he graduated from my National Securities Studies class at Georgetown University two years earlier. In that class and in a military career that included service as a Green Beret from Bosnia to Panama, he had distinguished himself, so his performance on 9/11 was deeply gratifying—but it came as no surprise. Far from it: Knowing him, knowing how he was trained, and knowing above all the military culture that had helped to shape his character, I could have expected nothing less.

If you are looking for a quick way to sum up the difference between business and war, there could not be a more direct contrast between this young Army leader and his counterparts in the business community. Forget about the fact that there is an income discrepancy of at least $100,000, that one wears an off-the-rack polyester uniform from the post exchange while the other gets his suits at Nordstrom's. Social scientists point out that each represents a system—defense and commerce—created by society to do some things well—but not all things and inevitably with some by-products as well. The young MBA comes from an increasingly globalized free market system that produces the largest number of goods and services, at the lowest price, and for greatest number of consumers—possibly the most efficient economic machine in all of recorded history. The problem is, this system has some underlying fault lines that sometimes produce unfortunate by-products along with economic success—lately including this rogue race of greedy, power-tripping CEOs who lead their companies only in the sense that a Judas cow leads its cohorts down the path to destruction. Now the defense institution—at least in the United States—is also organized for and produces certain things, military victories being at the top of the list. Like its commercial counterpart, the defense institution also produces certain by-products: higher than normal taxes and a military-industrial complex that requires enormous oversight and regular injections of defense appropriations. But it also routinely produces such outstanding young officers as Captain Lincoln Leibner, the kind of people who, on their own initiative, run into burning buildings and rescue people because that is what they think they are supposed to do. This stark, stunning contrast should be a wake-up call for anyone concerned with the future of American business. It has been more than year since *BusinessWeek*—hardly known for its Marxist leanings—noted that business leaders have rarely been held in such low esteem—and quoted with approval a candid speech by one of them, Goldman-Sachs CEO Henry M. Paulson: "In my lifetime, American business has never been under such scrutiny. To be blunt, much of it is deserved."[6] Noted business analyst Joseph Nocera was undoubtedly correct when he observed in *Fortune* that what ailed corporate America was a "system failure."[7]

When faced with system failure, there is an oft-repeated pattern in the business cycle: Boom leads to bust, which leads in turn to an inevitable quest for new laws and regulations intended to solve old problems. That is an approach that Charles Colson—who, after all, has some reason to know—has specifically warned against: "What fools we are when we think we can legislate away human immorality . . . I stand as living proof that the cure comes not from laws and statutes but from the transforming of the human heart. . . . The real hope for corporate America lies in cultivating conscience, a disposition to know and do what is right. And I have surveyed business school curriculum and found that hardly any teach ethics."[8]

Exactly. Which takes us back to the basics and the need—before looking at new laws and regulations—to search for new models. In this case, those models include not only applied behavioral standards, but new tools for competitive excellence in the twenty-first century. The main issue this book examines is, What are the moral and professional lessons that today's businesspeople and tomorrow's business leaders can learn from their warrior counterparts?

WAR PLAN

MISSION OBJECTIVES

CEOs, senior managers, and other business leaders need to understand and apply some truths not covered during their MBA education or executive experiences up until now:

★ Strategy is a matter of balance, and sometimes that's tough: choosing between two equally unpalatable alternatives, for example, or calibrating what you may be forced to do one day against your original motivation—or, for that matter, your ultimate objectives.

★ CEOs have to be leaders above all else, and if they can't lead, then they shouldn't be in the job. The same thing goes double for every member of the board of directors—and every member of the leadership team, from corporate officers to line or project managers.

★ To be a real leader, vision and competence are prerequisites: but the defining characteristic is to put everyone else's interest ahead of your own. And in business, those interests include the shareholders, the employees, the customers, and even the firm itself. Or simply get the hell out of Dodge.

★ What we are really hearing in these endless waves of corporate scandals is pure and simple bad leadership—the natural end product of a self-centered mentality that starts at the top and quickly comes to pervade an organization.

★ Leadership is about planning and direction, but it is also about setting an absolute moral and ethical standard that puts the greater good before any individual, in any position.

★ The sorry examples of Enron and all the rest should have tipped off corporate America that its leaders simply aren't living right, that they need to spend less time and money on

(continued)

their lawyers, lobbyists, and lackeys and more in leading their organizations.

★ Today's business leaders are doing much less than what is expected of them if they fail to return to the values of leadership, selflessness, and giving back that have been the hallmark of the American way—and American greatness.

★ What leadership comes down to is character; and although character can be defined in many ways, my favorite is the one my pastor taught me many years ago: The real test of character is what you do when no one is looking.

PART

I

☆☆ Business as War ☆☆

2

☆ ☆ Worlds Apart? ☆ ☆

It may be startling to the average business reader to equate business with war. After all, not many business leaders will ever find themselves facing anything like the Normandy landings as so grippingly illustrated in *Saving Private Ryan*. But the point of this book is that many of the military principles demonstrated from Normandy to Iraq apply to business as well as war. Giving the matter some urgency is the undeniable fact that corporate America faces today a chaotic, ever-changing competitive environment filled with enemies who learn lessons—and who don't always believe our press notices. As we shall see in later chapters, that changing, dog-eat-dog landscape requires new sets of leadership and management skills not offered in traditional MBA programs.

However, the conventional view of business and war—uncritically maintained by business leaders, warriors, and the more cloistered variety of academics—is that they are indeed worlds apart. Hence, a confession is in order right at the outset. Were you to attend the opening sessions of my Georgetown University seminars, you might have to endure a lecture on the fact that the worlds of business and war are reverse images of each other. One of my favorite texts for these sermons is from Edward Luttwak's book, *Strategy: The Logic of War and Peace*, which begins by stressing that war itself is a paradox: When the Romans said all those years ago, *Si vis pacem, para bellum* (If you want peace, prepare for war), they understood that these two worlds exhibited two peculiar and fundamentally different systems of logic.[1]

19

Much of the work of the businessperson involves, for example, getting goods to market in the most direct and cost-effective way. In the world of peace, that usually involves a straight arithmetic calculation of how to get goods from point A to point B as cheaply as possible. The wartime leader faces a more complex problem because the most efficient and direct means of transportation (such as putting large numbers of pieces of critical equipment on a single convoy ship or moving troops directly across a field) simply invites enemy countermeasures—say in the form of enemy submarines or L-shaped ambushes at key points along the trail. In short, doing things in the most efficient way usually leads to vulnerability and disaster. The teaching point: Unless your business finds itself somehow in competition with Tony Soprano, business and war have fundamentally different disciplines and measures of effectiveness.

The distinction may be important for graduate students but it does not quite mean that these two worlds have nothing in common. Probing the walls of separation, one comes up against two basic facts: The business of America really is business—and the military really does prefer its role as a walled-off secular priesthood. As so often happens, history is the main culprit; for if the country was not exactly founded by draft dodgers, then American democracy was profoundly influenced by men who had a working understanding of the need for firm civilian control of the military. Many of them loathed the idea of a standing army, and the Constitutional Convention in Philadelphia grappled endlessly with the practical questions of how the civilians proposed to control such a thing. In characteristic style, the solution was divided control; Congress would raise armies and maintain navies, while the president would be the commander-in-chief. The stage was thus set for what political scientists ever since have called the "invitation to struggle," with the arguments focusing on where to draw the line of control between the generals and the politicians. While having to endure occasional intrusions by civilian Secretaries of Defense like Robert McNamara and Donald Rumsfeld, as well as more routine interventions by congressmen seeking defense welfare for their districts, the military prefers to be left alone. While it is used to being told what to do, it resents being told how to do it.

These separatist tendencies were reinforced in more recent history by the decision at the end of the Vietnam War to end the draft and to set up a voluntary military force. Highly controversial at the time, the subsequent building up of the professional uniformed cadre has since become an article of faith. But, in return for the unquestioned increase in the capabilities of a professional force, there has also been an increased gap between the military and the American people. The reason: fewer and fewer Americans have had any direct experience with—or service in—their military. Although the draft may have made a "people's" army, the growth of the professional army has ever since produced an army's army. Not only are American sons and daughters exempt from U.S. military service, sadly, so are their leaders: senators, congressmen, presidential candidates, and even self-styled media gurus. This persistent and pervasive gap—referred to in some quarters as the "Great Divorce"[2]—has not been bridged even by the advent of the War on Terrorism and is being passed intact to future generations.

One example will suffice: In the spring of 2003, the graduating class at Harvard stood to receive their degrees, proud end products of the most Darwinian weeding-out process the American educational system can manage. Of the tens of thousands of high school hopefuls from across the county, these elite few had been admitted and now 1,586 were on hand to receive the coveted Harvard diploma. But one of the most remarkable moments came when a total of only nine of the new Harvard grads stood to receive their ROTC commissions and to take the oath of office in their country's service. Now in a time of war and national emergency, 9 out of 1,586, or 0.57 percent if my standard Army calculator is working correctly, might not seem like much. But then you would have to appreciate that ROTC at Harvard is a miracle of survival, having endured attacks over the years from peace activists as well as human and animal rights advocacy groups of every conceivable description. Perhaps mindful that a small band of heroes is better than none at all, Harvard President Lawrence Summers spoke movingly of the patriotism and dedication of the new ROTC graduates. But he also lent a note of unintentional irony in recounting how, during a recent Gridiron Dinner in Washington, only a few of that elite group stood to demonstrate personal ties to the nation's military services—and idly wondering what that trend might mean for the country's future leadership.[3]

He is right to wonder. For the present, the parties to the Great Divorce are cordial to one another but show no signs of reconciling. In short, the gap between the military and American society (including the business community) remains broad and deep and is being inexorably projected into the future.

Worlds Apart—But Getting Closer All the Time?

This is not to say that there is not the occasional cross-channel foray, usually when the military wants to learn something from business. Because of the vast administrative, logistical, and technological underpinnings of the Pentagon, the generals and admirals widely assume that businesspeople naturally know how to do things better. In the best cross-disciplinary fashion, Marine generals have been sent on field trips to the floor of the Wall Street Stock Exchange to study decision making under chaotic conditions. And every year, a group of promising young officers is sponsored by the Secretary of Defense for 11 months of high-level "training with industry," the better to get a leg up on the latest innovations in organization and technology—an obvious exercise in *deus ex IBM machina*.

What has not generally been recognized is that the opposite is often true—that military executives have some significant advantages over their civilian counterparts. That realization first occurred to me on the eve of the first Gulf War—when the Army Chief of Staff sent me to look into the latest fad in business leadership: total quality management (TQM). The concept of TQM was the lifework of W. Edwards Deming, an apostle of efficiency who taught the Japanese how to use quality as a competitive tool in the aftermath of World War II—though fortunately not before. So for a week, I attended a business seminar to learn the TQM Fourteen Points, their impact magnified by the miracle of Deming—a man then well into his 90s—being led everywhere on stage by two very attractive 20-something blonds.

After Deming and the blonds had gone away, I returned and told the Chief that there was both good and bad news. The bad news was that the Army did not have a formal TQM program—or anything that remotely looked like one. But the good news was that for years we had instinctively been following most of the Fourteen Points—especially those dealing with strategy, commonsense metrics and, above all, the need to devolve responsibility to the lowest levels of the organization. We already did that: They were called NCOs—the noncommissioned officers who were the backbone of our force. Within months, those sergeants, who had probably never heard of TQM, found themselves in the middle of Desert Storm, demonstrating not only responsibility and their own quality but also the best metric of any strategy: victory.

However separate their worlds may once have been, some pervasive changes are occurring that make the competitive space of the business executive look more and more like the disorderly universe of the warrior. One of those changes affecting every business entity is increased competition. Victory in the Cold War, for example, had a host of unintended geopolitical consequences. Not only was a plethora of new countries born—or born again—out of the bones of the old Soviet empire but the free market economy has also trumped all others in the search for the best model to provide goods and services. By any measure, this is a sea change from the time when most businesspeople studied their economic theories amidst the constant debates about the extent of state control of private industries or the planning and direction of centrally controlled economies. But the bad news (always present in economic theory) is that free market success spawned a new breed of competitors who understand supply, demand, initiative, and the need to go after new markets. But they are not quite as clear on the Marquis of Queensberry Rules that have surrounded capitalism since the late nineteenth century.

Probably the best example is the People's Republic of China, which, after the collapse of the Soviet Union, was left as the only major world state that, at least officially, was an avowed socialist entity. (We can for the moment overlook the anomalous satrapies of Cuba and North Korea, which, aside from tourism and weapons proliferation respectively, can hardly be thought of as economic models of anything.) However, the reality is that the Chinese economy has become a mixed bag that would confuse Mao or Marx, with a gaggle of private and hybrid state-controlled entities operating side-by-side—or even in partnership. Whatever the proper economic description of the post-Mao production machine, the Chinese are nothing if not predatory when it comes to producing goods that quickly find their way onto American shelves. But as trade with the PRC has increased, so has the Chinese propensity either to "make it or fake it." Counterfeiting, copyright infringement, and other forms of product knockoffs have become more common—with fake products that include everything from peanut butter and DVDs to Viagra. By one estimate, the worldwide rip-off of Western goods from China alone may amount to $20 billion a year.[4]

Even when the products are legitimate, American industry now finds itself arrayed globally against competing economies that simply don't have the same notion of acceptable union wage rates. No wonder then that traditional rules like free trade, as incorporated in NAFTA (North American Free Trade Agreement), inevitably mean that jobs flow elsewhere: Given basic economics and the prevailing labor wage rates, how could it be otherwise? Many American corporations also complain about the high cost of regulatory compliance that they must build into their products. Their competitors in the world marketplace are under no obligation to incorporate into their prices the requirements, say, of the Clean Air Act and the Clean Water Act. More serious still are those competitors who, in various forms of collusion with their governments, have become notorious for systematic violations of fair trade practices, including lax enforcement of antitrust rules or outright dumping of products. As the 1997/1998 Asian financial crisis drastically reduced the need for steel there, Asian steel companies—particularly Japanese—dumped vast amounts of steel onto American markets. The result, according to the United Steelworkers of America, was that six American steel companies were forced into bankruptcy, costing thousands of steelworkers their jobs.[5] The bottom line: With more competitors and a highly uneven playing field, the traditional business calculus of competitive advantage has changed.

The second factor is closely related to the first: Globalization is the next wave of economic rationalization, this one closely linked to the technologies of the information age. Pulitzer Prize-winning columnist Thomas Friedman has written perceptively about this trend. He sees it not simply as a homogenizing influence as corporations spread their webs worldwide but instead as the dominant international system of the post–Cold War world: "The world has become an increasingly interwoven place, and, today, whether you are a company or a country your threats and opportunities increasingly derive from whom you are connected to." Just as nineteenth-century networks of roads, railways, and canals enabled industrial age capitalism, twenty-first century information-age technologies—"computerization, miniaturization, digitization, satellite communications, fiber optics and the Internet"—provide the wellspring for pervasive and ever more invasive forms of economic rationalization.[6] Friedman quotes with approval the following *Slate* magazine characterization of globalization: "Innovation replaces tradition. The present—or perhaps the future—replaces the past. Nothing matters so much as what will come next, and what will come next can only arrive if what is here now gets overturned."[7]

A glittering version of the future—but one person who probably worries a lot about being one of those things so unceremoniously overturned is the poor manager who has gotten his MBA, done well in his business, and succeeded—only to find himself unexpectedly adrift in the uncharted seas of global competition. Several years ago, I made a presentation to a large home improvement chain that was idly wondering about the need to enrich their corporate decision making with better business intelligence. The problem was that the company had its origins in a couple of down-home bubbas who had done well in growing a regional lumber business. They were used to thinking about competitive pricing of board feet of lumber, and whether it was better to get it from Alabama or North Carolina. However, with globalization, their market had changed around them, and they now found that to make an intelligent decision, knowing the board foot rate in Taiwan had become a vitally important compass point. They had no real idea about friends, enemies, allies, or competitors in their competitive space, much less about the specific vulnerabilities of the Asian commodities market.

While growing into a new level of opportunity and complexity is a pleasant enough problem, the larger issue is a peculiarly American trait of insularity—often misunderstood by foreigners as simple arrogance. Some people just never leave home—and part of the challenge of global competition is overcoming the assumption that the rest of the world thinks, behaves, and operates as Americans do. One example will suffice: Not too many years ago, my wife went to an investment seminar in Brussels run by a well-known American company. From beginning to end, the course was precisely the same one presented to Americans in the United States—all about the New York Stock Exchange, the Dogs of the Dow, and the peculiarities of investing in the American market. The seminar was a huge waste of time for the largely European audience—a point that was utterly lost on the presenters, all of whom must also have been in the habit of simply shouting more loudly when confronted by non-English speakers.

The third factor that both business and war now have in common is speed. "The speed of business" has rapidly become a cliché mostly because people understand instinctively not only the aggressiveness of new competitors, but also the speed of information. Trillions of dollars move around the globe via electronic transfers every day to settle outstanding balance of payments accounts between large corporations and central banks. World markets are now intrinsically linked from Wall Street to the Nikkei, with the result that capital flows more freely than ever before. Board any airliner, particularly the East Coast shuttles, and you will see firsthand the products that have come forth to help business executives keep up: laptops, PDAs (personal digital assistants), and (most obnoxious of all) cell phones that are only turned off under the threat of direct confrontation by the pilot.

One of the more startling examples both of speed and the importance of staying connected comes from Goodland, Kansas, and wheat farmer Ken Palmgren. With the return of normal rainfall patterns in 2003, he was anticipating a bumper crop of winter wheat. With the market for wheat from the American heartland extending from Europe to Asia and Africa (Nigeria being a particularly big customer for "Kansas hard red winter wheat"), Palmgren points out: "Today our business is so global you have to keep up all the time on your markets and your competition." Helping him and his fellow farmers to do just that are satellite dishes for data networks transmitting 24-hour updates of weather, crop yields, and grain purchases from all over the world. "Some guys have a terminal in the tractor so they're never away from the market news."[8]

We feel compelled to be in touch all the time, and for good reason. Opportunity equals speed. That is a nice way of saying what my drill sergeant screamed at us back in basic training—that there are two kinds of bayonet fighters: the quick and the dead. To be left behind in today's fast-moving world means missing opportunities, losing market share, and probably losing revenues.

The speed of business is another reason it is becoming more and more like war: volatility. More people have entered the economic marketplace because connectivity has been extended to so many of them (and in so many pervasive ways) imparting a new and grim reality to one of the basic laws of economics: that everything depends on everything else. Tom Friedman cites the now-famous example of witnessing the beginnings of the financial crisis in Thailand in early 1998, which seven months later had been transmitted through falling commodity prices to Russia, re-transmitted through hedge funds back to falling Brazilian stock values, retransmitted again through rising demands for U.S. Treasury bills—and finally to a forced bailout of the largest hedge fund, Long-Term Capital Management, to prevent a potential market meltdown.[9]

This action-reaction cycle is due not only to the onrush of information—which most people accept even if they don't understand it—but also to the expanding penumbra of critical information surrounding every core business. Talk to most business executives and they will tell you that they know everything there is to know about their business: soap, cattle futures, pharmaceuticals. But what happens is that events constantly surprise them—that should have been no surprise whatever had they been paying the kind of attention the information age demands. These executives are not unlike the proverbial Army paratrooper whose reserve chute failed while on a training jump. While falling, he struggled to free the ripcord; but while looking down was amazed to see an Army cook rising through the clouds to meet him. As they passed in midair, the paratrooper shouted, "Hey, buddy, know anything about opening a reserve chute?" "Hell no," the cook roared back. "Know anything about lighting a field stove?"

A particularly good example of volatility is the SARS (severe acute respiratory syndrome) outbreak in the spring of 2003, which quickly spread from being a local public health problem in a far-off province in China to having an economic impact not only in Asia, but throughout the rest of the world. David Rothkopf, CEO of Intellibridge, a leading business intelligence firm, points out that anyone paying attention to the Internet and online news resources should have known about the SARS outbreak as early as January 2003—potentially providing an early warning and avoiding the worst excesses of what he sees as an "infodemic." The lesson to be learned: "In the information age, life has changed fundamentally. Increased volatility is routine; events and information about them unfold rapidly; their consequences are amplified. The results are much like a roller coaster ride: exciting, scary, disorienting and all rather different from the view from more solid ground."[10]

Similar problems that take many executives unawares include everything from rumors concerning individual products to currency revaluations to political instability. Unanticipated external events (i.e., disturbances outside the traditional value chain) have a dramatic effect on businesses that thought they were somehow exempt from what Lenin called the hammer blows of history. It is a little like the West Point Officer's Club, which always used to be surprised by lunch. Or, some years back, from her experience in England, my wife recalls an autumn when British Rail trains were delayed and canceled. British Rail, of course, had leaf removal equipment in its inventory—but it explained that the delays were because the "wrong kind of leaves" had fallen on the tracks.

All too often in the post-9/11 world, these unanticipated questions involve matters of security, safety, and survival. And, as we shall see in some detail in Chapter 9, it is in the realm of security that the business leader may have the most to learn from the warrior. Even before 9/11, there was a lively market in corporate security, particularly when it came to executive protection and industrial security. What should have begun to sink in for modern executives, however, is an entirely new category of threats to all types of businesses and from many different directions. Precisely because of globalization, many businesses have become multinationals. Many others have extended supply chains, partnerships, and alliances throughout the world. Economic diversity, so essential for globalization, yields interdependence; and interdependence leads to increased risk. An obvious example: Either an earthquake in Taiwan or a cross-channel attack from the PRC would have parallel and pervasive impacts for chip manufacturers, motherboard installers, and their respective partners in computer manufacturing. In the aftermath of the 7.6 earthquake that hit Taiwan in September 1999, one semiconductor equipment manufacturer pointed out that they were fortunate to have escaped with only $390 million in damages, much of it from power outages. "While power outages may result in several weeks of business interruptions, loss of critical equipment or facilities could result in shutdown of months or years."[11]

To sum it all up, because of increasing competitors, globalization, information, speed, and volatility, the businessperson's environment is quickly coming to resemble the predatory, information-rich, rapidly changing battle space the soldier is so used to coping with. It follows that business and war may not be worlds apart after all—and that basic leadership norms and management techniques (conceptual and analytical) for running the business need to change. Given the scope of all the changes, how could any halfway perceptive business leaders expect to "command" in the same way he learned either in basic MBA programs—or in the school of survivorship needed to ascend the corporate promotion ladder? Some specific tools needed in this new age are discussed throughout this book; but for now just remember this vital linkage: *Information-age tools are useless unless they are wielded by leaders (CEOs or generals) who are fit to command their units in the information age.* All the best intelligence, information-sharing, training, and other techniques laid out here matter very little except to the extent they can be used aggressively by the activist, information-intensive, predatory CEO the times demand.

COMPETITIVE VALUES

There is a final reason the business-as-war relationship is important, which takes us straight back to the point Charles Colson made about embracing a moral code bound by conscience. Much of what the military does in its competitive arena is bounded by a distinct system of ethics and values that allows it to compete and win in the most savage environments imaginable—without losing their moral compass and disgracing themselves or the societies they represent. Think of it as values on steroids.

It is hard for anyone who has not been through it to understand just how important those core values are within the military. Undergoing basic training right at the end of the Vietnam War as a scared, slick-sleeve, whiffle-cut draftee, I was herded together with my fellow captives into a room where a neatly pressed major (practically a celebrity by our standards) in the Army JAG Corps announced that for the next hour he would be our principal instructor in the law of land warfare. Momentarily stunned by the unexpected respite from push-ups, it took a while for the gravity of his words to sink in: words like "war crime" and "illegal order," and new concepts like "duty to disobey" if we were ever ordered to commit a war crime by any superior officer. Most chilling of all was the prospect of court martial and imprisonment at Fort Leavenworth if we were ever convicted of such a thing. After the major was finished with us, our drill sergeants resumed their normal places, all of them recent Vietnam returnees.

Before leading us back for more push-ups, each one gave us the benefit of a personal counterpoint to what we had just been taught. Mostly that we should respect the law because "Uncle" would surely come AFTER yo' ass if you did something stupid like shooting wounded POWs. But remember: Don't ever give the enemy an unnecessary opportunity to kill you—now is that clear, trainee? Actually it wasn't, because there is nothing like the conflict between values in theory and values in action to concentrate the mind. But not to worry—I had similar classes on the Geneva Convention on at least three other occasions throughout my training so that by the time I pinned on second lieutenant bars, I knew exactly what an illegal order was—and that the Army was serious enough about its values to ensure that they were systematically explained, enforced, reinforced, and supported by leaders at every level.

So it is when resuscitating a value system among current and future business leaders. In addition to offering some useful tips for succeeding on dynamic business battlefields, the military also provides a salutary example of how to inject "outside" social values into the cultural bloodstream to affect internal corporate behavior. As the Eagles said in one of their ballads from the 1970s: "Every form of refuge has its price"—and the historical price for being bankrolled by civilians is that the military has had to abide by occasional rules imposed by politicians on behalf of society. However difficult the political struggles may have been, the fact is that these values, though imposed from the outside, have been taken in by the military and have eventually become inseparable from their success. These values begin with an acceptance of the sanctity of civilian control, something that was not seriously questioned even during the difficult period when Bill Clinton served as co-president. He was warmly greeted, but always privately detested by the U.S. military, and I heard senior officers caution more than once: "You guys may not like him, but we're not an 'effing banana republic, so keep your attitude respectful—and your personal comments to yourself." And so we did. Mostly.

Those values-in-action are the essence of the professionalism that Harvard guru Samuel P. Huntington identifies as one of the most enduring "strands of the American military tradition."[12] Decision makers have relied on that professionalism before, as when President Harry Truman issued the Executive Order in 1948 mandating racial integration of the armed forces. Highly controversial at the time, the dividends from that action over more than two generations have included—in addition to Colin Powell—a military that has become the United States' most successfully integrated institution. As our leading military sociologist Charles Moskos puts it, "The Army is the only place in American life where whites are routinely bossed around by blacks."[13]

A similar argument could be made about those decisions affecting the status of women in the military, including their integration into the service academies and into a growing number of combat-related positions. But the lessons here for business are important, beginning with the useful reminder that society occasionally feels the need to impose its values on otherwise reluctant institutions. The military culture in this country—while not always leading the applause—has become used to such external impositions on their internal value systems. Business largely has not. From a strictly laissez-faire tradition, business executives have had to accept an increasingly wider range of legal restrictions throughout the nineteenth and twentieth centuries. But *Fortune*'s Joseph Nocera has it exactly right about the general pattern: "Throughout history, bubbles have been followed by crashes—which in turn have led to new laws and new rules designed to curb the excesses of the era just ended."[14]

These restrictions have been directed mostly at correcting only the worst over-the-line excesses and, as Nocera points out, very much through the rearview mirror. Most of those efforts appear to have been adjustments to the field of play instead of changes to the way the game is played. Professor Scott Snook, who teaches leadership and ethics at the Harvard Business School, explains that organizations are controlled in three ways. Laws provide the basic social definitions of what is—and is not—considered acceptable behavior. Regulations and other administrative restrictions—either from government, professional bodies, or corporate groups—provide a second layer of governance in the form of written guidance further restraining behavior. While basic values are the third way of restraining or rewarding people, it is here, he argues, that business has its largest problem: "Unlike the military, there really is no agreement among business people about what core business values are—and are not."[15]

He reinforces a point made by another prominent scholar, Amitai Etzioni, who has written some alarming things about the difficulties of teaching ethics in the nation's business schools—including some from his own experience at Harvard and other schools. One of the toughest issues: Faculty members at business schools were themselves split over what an ethics curriculum should consist of as well as how to teach it. He quotes one economist—without any apparent intent toward irony—saying, "We are here to teach science" while another wondered whose values should be taught, and a third insisted that ethics were more properly taught at home or at church. The result: "Many business school professors choose to steer clear of teaching morality, pointing out . . . that while it is relatively clear what economics dictate and even what the law dictates, what is 'ethical' is far from obvious." The results were depressing. Etzioni's own students told him that ethics were simply something that the modern corporation could not afford because a company focused on efficiency would drive out of business one focused on ethics. And the future? Etzioni cites an ongoing Aspen Institute survey of the nation's top business schools in arguing, "B-school education not only fails to improve the moral character of students, it weakens it."[16]

There is no set of core business values that can be understood by business scholars, imparted to business students, embraced by business leaders, and enforced by business institutions. Lacking this moral compass, the only thing surprising about the spate of corporate scandals is that the American employee or investor should have been surprised at all. But that is not a bad jumping-off point for our inquiry into the lessons that the CEO can learn from the warrior because a system of values is at the top of the list. Not only is the military an insular world, but it is driven by values that are constantly being evaluated, applied, and reinforced, usually through very public controversies: from the Navy's Tailhook incident in the 1990s, to the decisions about whether to court-martial two Air Force pilots involved in a friendly-fire incident with Canadian troops over Afghanistan in 2002, to the disciplinary regime needed at the Air Force Academy in the aftermath of sexual harassment allegations in early

2003. These incidents underline that the military, like business, is a very human institution, with fallible humans throughout who occasionally transgress the rules and do wrong. But at most of these crossroads, the military value system is visibly and constantly reminded of what is right, what is wrong, and how to tell the difference in a kind of ongoing laboratory for moral reasoning—and for the application of standards.

Which is the final caveat, because this book is hardly the first to suggest a linkage between business and war. Often using military history as their inspiration, other titles range from the 1980s' classic *The Leadership Secrets of Attila the Hun* to the more recent *Leadership Lessons from the Civil War* by Tom Wheeler.[17] Some former military officers have similarly drawn on their service leadership experience to provide advice to business audiences, from Major General Perry Smith in his 1986 *Taking Charge* to former Army Chief of Staff Gordon Sullivan's *Hope Is Not a Method: What Business Leaders Can Learn from America's Army* to the most recent *It's Your Ship: Management Techniques from the Best Damn Ship in the Navy* by former Navy Captain Michael Abrashoff.[18] And other authors have studied the lives of military leaders, past and present, from Oren Harari's *Leadership Secrets of Colin Powell* to Partha Bose's provocative and interesting new study, *Alexander the Great's Art of Strategy*.[19] All are worthy and sometimes thought-provoking contributions to business literature, while some are also "fun reads" into fascinating people or periods of history. But the fact is that most of us are not Alexander, Colin Powell, or even latter-day Huns, nor are we likely to find ourselves in command of ships or armies. Even if we were, many of the lessons those studies suggest do not translate very well across the dividing lines of history, technology, or vastly different value systems. So instead of studying leadership by anecdotes—although we shall encounter a good many—this book tries to shed some light on leadership by systems.

As I write these words, the latest editions of the *Washington Post* bring headlines rising like an upturned middle finger: It seems that CEO compensation grew by 17 percent in 2002, "driven by fatter bonuses and bigger payouts from long-term incentive plans."[20] God be praised, but do you think they're worth it? Neither do I. But read on. For we now turn directly to the business of war and those who lead it—and lately business has been very, very good!

WAR PLAN

MISSION OBJECTIVES

Information-age tools are useless unless they are wielded by leaders (CEOs or generals) who are fit to command their units in the information age.

★ American industry now finds itself arrayed globally against competing economies that simply don't have the same notion of acceptable union wage rates. No wonder traditional rules like free trade inevitably mean that jobs flow elsewhere.

★ Although growing into a new level of opportunity and complexity is a pleasant problem, the larger issue introduced by an increasingly global economy is a peculiarly American trait of insularity—often misunderstood by foreigners as simple arrogance.

★ Opportunity equals speed. That's a nice way of saying that there are two kinds of bayonet fighters: the quick and the dead. To be left behind in today's fast-moving world means missing opportunities, losing market share, and probably losing revenues.

★ The speed of business is another reason it's becoming more like war: volatility. Because more people have entered the economic marketplace (because connectivity has been extended to so many), there is a new and grim reality to one of the basic laws of economics: Everything depends on everything else.

★ Problems that take many executives unawares include everything from rumors concerning individual products to currency revaluations to political instability. Unanticipated external events have a dramatic effect on businesses that thought they were somehow exempt from what Lenin called "the hammer blows of history."

★ Because of increasing competitors, globalization, information, speed, and volatility, the business environment is quickly coming to resemble the predatory, information-rich, rapidly changing battle space the soldier is so used to coping with.

★ All the best intelligence, information sharing, training, and other techniques matter very little, except to the extent they can be used aggressively by activist, information-intensive, predatory CEOs that the times demand.

★ There is no set of core business values that can be understood by business scholars, imparted to business students, embraced by business leaders, and enforced by business institutions. Lacking this moral compass, the only thing surprising about the spate of corporate scandals is that the American employee or investor should have been surprised at all.

3

☆ ☆ War as an Audit ☆ ☆

W hile the corporate world was picking up the pieces from scandals writ large and Martha Stewart was trying to explain away the minor infraction of slipping just a *teensy* bit more caviar onto her cracker, want to know what your military was doing to demonstrate its competitiveness, market dominance, and commitment to shareholder value? Then try thinking of war as a particularly grueling form of audit. And consider what American fighting forces accomplished during their campaign against the Iraqi military in the first months of 2003.

In the face of hostile world opinion that made allies, bases, and comrades-in-arms hard to come by, the United States Army, Navy, Air Force, and Marines deployed a force of over a quarter-million warriors halfway around the world. When all diplomatic alternatives had been exhausted, they unleashed a devastating aerial bombardment as notable for its accuracy as its ferocity. Far from waiting out an extended bombing campaign of the Iraqi capital, American ground forces were on the move even before the dust had cleared. In the face of sandstorms of biblical proportions as well as 300 miles of natural and man-made obstacles meant to delay and deter any foreign invader, armor-heavy forces of Army and Marines attacked in a sweeping advance up the Tigris-Euphrates River Valley. Stunned by the speed of their advancing enemies, some Iraqi irregular forces nevertheless fought surprisingly well, using adaptive tactics, infiltration, deception, and all manner of dirty tricks to inflict casualties on their attackers and to harass their extended supply lines.

Not that it made the slightest difference in the end. Leaving the irregular opposition to be dealt with by follow-on forces, the twin pincer movements of the U.S. 3rd Infantry Division and the 1st Marine Expeditionary Force inexorably closed on Baghdad from the southwest and southeast. Ahead of them, four divisions of the Iraqi Republican Guard lay in wait. It was the only force available to Saddam that might conceivably have been able to inflict large American casualties, delay their victory, and just possibly set the stage for international mediation by Iraq's preferred lawyers—the Russians, the Saudis and, above all, the French—to ensure Saddam's survival yet again.

But in one of the most inept decisions in modern military history, the Iraqi dictator inexplicably kept those armored forces out in the open desert, instead of withdrawing them into Baghdad and turning the city into a Mesopotamian Stalingrad. In what was widely misperceived at the time as an "operational pause," the American armored force massed for the attack, in much the same way that a tiger gathers itself for the final leap at the jugular of its prey. As they did so, the United States Air Force promptly pinpointed the Republican Guard formations and over the course of the next three days simply annihilated their targets from the sky with a barrage of precision-guided munitions.

The American divisions then moved in for the kill, eradicating what was left of their opponents and swiftly driving over the survivors to take Baghdad. In moves that were compared to Jackson at Chancellorsville or the German blitzkrieg through France, the American forces moved farther faster, and suffered fewer casualties than any comparable formation in U.S. military history. But, if anything, the speed, virtuosity, and power of the American advance quickly led some to conclude that the Iraqis had been hopelessly overmatched from the start—and that the U.S. victory had been a walkover against an utterly out-classed opponent. Which it was—but not for the reasons you might think. Such underestimations of American military professionalism have become chronic ever since the end of the first Gulf War. Worse yet, these views are often propounded by the chattering classes of people with more media access than real military insight: So it is perhaps understandable when the public occasionally gets the absurd idea that "you aren't that good, it's just that the other guy was so bad." As I learned shortly after returning home from Bosnia, our success some-times works against us: Despite those operational difficulties, things had gone so smoothly that even friends and colleagues were surprised that American soldiers were still there!

More serious have been the endless questions about the search for weapons of mass destruction; our original motivations for war; the costs of Iraqi reconstruction; and, of course, the de facto guerrilla conflict in which our soldiers find themselves engaged long after the supposed ter-mination of hostilities. With the indefinite prospect of American casual-ties, these questions have become so pronounced and so painful that they have tended to obscure certain underlying realities that soldiers are accustomed to dealing with. The first is that, as soldiers often say in one another's company, war may be hell but peace can be a real pain in the ass, too. Put in slightly more elegant terms: Conflict is eternal so nothing is more normal than to see an enemy defeated by American dominance in high-tech, maneuver warfare seeking to fight on using the messier low-tech methods of classic guerrilla conflict.

The fact that they would do so should chasten those American policy-makers who expected victory in Baghdad to look like victory in Paris in 1944—perhaps forgetting that the French have far more experience in welcoming conquerors. But it should also serve as a sobering reminder to those who expect victories to be permanent. In sports, in business, but above all else in war, history teaches otherwise: Victories are meant to be reversed. Napoleon, who had reason to know, understood this principle quite well, having learned it—if not en route to Moscow then surely on the way back. "From the sublime to the ridiculous is but a single step." But for the record: Despite the second-guessing, American military forces did what good armies are always supposed to do. With their boot prints, they changed the map as well as the geopolitical realities—good and bad—that went along with it.

Although most people had long accustomed themselves to thinking of the U.S. military as invincible, the American victory over Saddam was far from preordained. The American ground force that fought its way into Baghdad was a shadow of its Desert Storm predecessor, relying far more on movement, tight coordination, and devastatingly accurate fire-power than on sheer numbers to overwhelm its opponents. Perhaps best of all, American generalship seemed to have recovered from its Clinton-era aversion to casualties and preference for zero defects.

Again, the Bosnian example: There in 1996, I had learned that those things often went together under the heading of micromanagement. The U.S. contingent was in the habit of having a 6 P.M. briefing called the BUB, for "battle update briefing." While no battles had ever occurred, the BUBs did so with nauseating regularity, usually highlighted by 120 or more PowerPoint slides. They covered every facet of life throughout the Army encampments and included every conceivable statistic—from the numbers of sandbags, morale calls, and lighting fixtures, to the totals of MREs (meals ready to eat) eaten versus MREs digested. The resulting discussions between the commander and his staff could go on for hours, made even worse by the fact that higher headquarters back in Germany were usually doing some electronic kibitzing. Sometimes the sacred BUB evening ritual would even be interrupted by a call from Washington seeking clarification of some press report or other, proving again that all the electrons being thrown at us could not overturn the ancient combat rule that the guy on the ground is often the last to know what's going on.

But the rush to Baghdad made all that seem like just a bad dream. Now there was a noticeable rediscovery of the virtues of audacity, experimentation (often in the face of the enemy), and initiative at the most junior levels. So was the American victory surprising? Not unless you knew what to look for—and that was the truth so often missed in the instant analyses on cable and network television: Victory was certain only to the extent it embodied basic military principles that have always distinguished the winners from the losers in combat.

So it is essential to examine the roots of this latest victory of American arms, which extend much farther back than the three weeks required to overrun Baghdad. Those lessons also have some implications that the American business community needs to understand and take to heart. The story outlined in this chapter is of an American military establishment that, in violation of every ill-informed cliché of the media and educational elites, refused to be seduced by success into preparing for the last war. It is also the story of how basic institutional values sustained that military in the face of what they certainly considered as a hostile takeover: the advent of the Clinton administration. To deal so successfully with the twin stresses of success and duress—all while adapting to a changing competitive environment—is a canonical tale of change that is directly relevant to the challenges faced by every business leader. In this chapter, we highlight the difficulties—and the hidden keys to success that brought about victory in Iraq. So remember these lessons: either in business or war; the fundamentals really matter—and they don't change nearly as quickly as our headlines.

CHALLENGES AND UNCERTAINTIES

The story begins with Bill Clinton's first major misadventure, when in the fall of 1993, he started out with a nation-building mission and found in the end that he had inadvertently committed American troops to a combat mission in Somalia. It was not so much that an American fighting force had been given a dangerous mission in an obscure place or even that they eventually found themselves in some intense combat at a cost of almost 100 casualties. But no one, least of all President Clinton, had bothered to get the attention of the characteristically inattentive American people, to tell them he had seen fit to put the lives of their troops on the line, to justify the risk in terms of some compelling national interest, and to provide some reasonable objective—or "end state" in the policy jargon of the time—toward which the country was now committed. But once awakened, the American people characteristically wanted direct, uncomplicated answers to only two questions: Was the objective worth putting American lives at risk, and did our boys put a serious case of whup-ass on whoever it was they were opposing in the field? The only acceptable answers would have been *Yes* and *Yes.* In Somalia, the answers that came back were *No* and *That sure was a tragedy, wuzn't it?* So the extraordinary courage of the Rangers during the ambush in Mogadishu—and the heavy price they inflicted on their attackers—was obscured by televised coverage of Somali mobs dragging American bodies down the street. And later by a shamefaced President Clinton announcing the hasty withdrawal of U.S. combat forces from the country.

In many ways, Clinton never recovered from that fiasco, because Somalia was just the start of what became a series of foreign policy adventures in which U.S. troops were steadily committed to places that the

American people—already geographically challenged—could barely locate. Indeed, any concept of permanent strategic interests appeared overwhelmed by the seemingly random "Where's Waldo?" game being played by Madeleine Albright and other leading lights of the new administration. Somalia begat Haiti and eventually Bosnia and Kosovo, to say nothing of periodic run-ins with Iraq that resulted only in symbolic bombings—usually by cruise missiles—followed by press conferences. For the American military, these were lean and difficult years. The activist bent of the Clinton foreign policy was oddly coupled with a pervasive set of spending priorities that fully reflected the administration's governing premise: "It's the economy, stupid." The Army saw its strength cut by roughly 30 percent from Gulf War levels—and its deployments increased by as much as 300 percent. All the services had to endure what became known as the "procurement holiday," which, like the depression-era term "bank holiday," effectively meant there was no money for large-scale replacements for aging weapons and infrastructure.

But it is a measure of the tenacity of our military and its institutional values that they endured these privations as well as the temptation to rest on their laurels in the aftermath of victories in both the Cold War and Desert Storm. They hung in there and it was during the 1990s that the seeds of eventual victories in Afghanistan and Operation Iraqi Freedom were planted. We had no serious strategic rivals since the Russians had given up and gone home—a development that provoked a surprising amount of nostalgia and even regret. We were still experiencing the novelty of having Russian military officers attend U.S. policy conferences in Washington during the early 1990s. At one of them, a Russian military officer we all knew as a tough-minded professional responded to an audience question with a painfully diplomatic and careful reply. During the break, one of my Army colleagues—an infantryman—put his arm around the Russian and congratulated him on his performance but concluded: "You know, I liked you guys a whole lot better when we were enemies. Now you're just another bunch of limp-dick allies. Like the Germans. Or even the French."

From both allies and others, there was at first an envious admiration of the American military performance during the 1991 Persian Gulf War. For those of us in uniform, the discreet chest thumping soon gave way to the search for lessons affecting future wars. One notable contributor was Dr. William J. Perry, an authentic technologist and defense intellectual who became Secretary of Defense shortly after the Somalia debacle. Dr. Perry had written one of the earliest and most influential analyses of the first Gulf War, which took on additional significance when he became Pentagon chief. In it, Perry had argued that U.S. forces in the Gulf had enjoyed a thousand-to-one advantage over their Iraqi adversaries because of the superb performance of information-based weapons originally developed to counter the numerically superior armies of the Warsaw Pact. Now, he suggested, the United States had a decisive advantage in three closely related areas: command, control, communications and intelligence, usually abbreviated C3I; air defense suppression, including Stealth aircraft; and the use of precision guided munitions.[1]

What all these capabilities had in common was information: to know one's own position, that of the enemy, and still more data to close that distance with a weapon which would find its target flawlessly. In one form or another, these information-based weapons had come to pervade each of the services. The Navy's Tomahawk cruise missile had been filmed flying down Baghdad streets, executing precisely programmed turns—and then diving into its targets with a satisfying roar from its one-ton warhead. The Army's Abrams tanks, eerily fast and deadly, had efficiently dispatched the legions of the Republican Guard in the largest tank engagement since Kursk, getting first-round hits with their thermal sights and lasers at ranges of over 3,000 meters. Often the first the Iraqis knew of the approach of American armor was when their own tanks exploded into catastrophic fireballs, their gun turrets flipping end-over-end into the sand.

And yet there were problems. The Pentagon is probably the only place in the world where the qualities of patriotism, paranoia, and schizophrenia blend seamlessly together, so it was not long before the euphoria of success over the Iraqis gave way to concern over the vulnerabilities that the new information-based weaponry had created. With computers now more widespread throughout the force than ever before, concern over hacking and intrusion grew apace. In the best Pentagon fashion, committees were duly appointed to study the emerging issue of information warfare and promptly began by trying to come up with a working definition of the term to better clarify what was being discussed.

After much coordination, they eventually did just that, but were then forced to classify the new definition Top Secret, effectively defeating the entire purpose of the exercise. (This flawed procedure was a clear violation of Rule Ten of the Pentagon Action Officer's Basic Rules of Engagement under which many of us had labored so long and hard: "Always attempt the minimum number of coordinations on any action as you will never be able to get everyone to agree on everything. To do otherwise will always result in oatmeal.")

But the new uses of information technology outlined by William Perry carried with them some severe institutional challenges. For if the American military stood on the verge of what was increasingly called a "revolution in military affairs" (RMA), and if that revolution depended on the free flow of information, then seizing this potential meant the defense establishment would have to confront an enduring flaw: a lack of interoperability in the 5–10,000 command and control systems deployed by the four military services. Uniformity is a basic defense requirement; military history contains many examples of the difficulties of imposing standardization on different clothing preferences, railroad gauges, weapons components, and even calibers of ammunition. Because the Army, Navy, Air Force, and Marines have historical roots predating the information age, it was natural for them to procure separate information systems for their own use in much the same way—and using many of the same agencies and procedures—that they used to purchase tanks, ships, fighters, or amphibious vehicles.[2]

The result of this legacy of autonomy was that the services needed no urging from Bill Perry or anyone else to procure the latest information technology to serve their own ends: They did so aggressively and, even when repeatedly told to do so, refused to retire their more costly, older, and obsolete systems. Interoperability was either a worthy but completely voluntary obligation—like attending Sunday church services—or an expensive option—like leather seats or a sunroof—to be instantly discarded when budget reductions loomed. The result was that, just as the potential for integration, coordination, and better teamwork increased with each new generation of microchips, the services inevitably grew farther apart. Consequently, there were problems every time our forces took the field. In Somalia, the common functions of personnel, intelligence, and finance had to be handled by 10 different service-specific data systems, each competing for limited space on the narrow information pipeline supporting the deployment.[3]

Worse yet: Interoperability problems were at the heart of a tragic 1994 incident over northern Iraq in which two U.S. Army Blackhawk helicopters were mistakenly shot down by Air Force fighters, at a cost of 26 lives.[4]

DOING MORE WITH LESS

The military services simultaneously live in three different time dimensions: If history was at the root of the interoperability problem even as the future beckoned so alluringly, then it took considerable effort just to cope with the present. With growing numbers of peacekeeping and humanitarian missions, as well as expanded military-to-military contacts with the reborn nations of the former Soviet empire, it became necessary for the Pentagon to do more and more with less and less. And since the estimable Dr. Perry could not possibly be everywhere, a significant cultural divide occasionally made it a challenge for the uniformed types to deal with lesser political appointees. Early in the administration, I attended a conference at the Army's shiny new war-gaming center in Carlisle Barracks, Pennsylvania, and listened with fascination as a 30-something assistant secretary for environmental this-or-that described the new Army program she was putting together. The program, it seemed, envisioned taking the hulls of old Army tanks, stripping them, and then hauling them out to sea—where they would be dumped overboard to serve as new habitat areas for tropical fish. She finished her presentation and then asked for questions, the first of which quickly came from a visibly upset colonel of armor: "You wanna do *what* with our tanks?" he exploded. "Make 'em into condos for some damn *fish?*" The rest of us eventually restrained and comforted him, but I don't think he hung around for the reception. Yet such was life with the Clintonistas, who often seemed to think of the military as a kind of Sierra Club in uniform.

It is against this backdrop that there is such a stark contrast between the peaceful but troubling times the military went through in the 1990s—and their stunning performance at war in Afghanistan and Iraq almost immediately thereafter. In many ways, business leaders can identify very well with some of the dilemmas their military counterparts had to face during the lean years:

- Increased pressure on operating budgets that made moderniza-
  tion funds scarce;
- Competing strategic priorities from external sources;
- Technological uncertainty—including doubts about which ones
  (1) would actually work and (2) actually constitute an improvement; and finally
- Nagging doubts about how much change was too much—and
  with what effects on the organization's leadership, culture, and
  structure.

It is in the nature of the American political system for Democrats
to argue that America's military was well prepared by President Clinton
for future combat, whereas Republicans will maintain even more strongly
that things improved quickly after 9/11 under the leadership of President
Bush. Both have a point, but so do those noting the constitutional invitation to struggle outlined in Chapter 2 and pointing out that it takes concerted action by both Congress and the president either to streamline the
military or to ruin it altogether.

But three closely related factors may best explain the secrets behind
the military's successful innovation during the 1990s. For now, think of
them as the hidden keys to victory—and as stark reminders of what it
takes when leaders are determined to succeed in either business or war:

1. A strategic vision created an ideal of teamwork that outweighed
   traditional go-it-alone methods and parochial technology choices.
2. Aggressive adaptation built the nuts-and-bolts teamwork to unite
   service actions as well as to explore the use of special forces in
   dealing with new missions.
3. Leadership basically reclaimed the traditional art of command
   from technology-induced micromanagement.

None of these three factors occurred in a vacuum; each owed parts
of its existence to the other two; and none of them were completely
successful the first time they were tried: but the ability to make incre-
mental progress toward a distant objective eventually proved critical.

And, as always, these innovations were decisively shaped by values, foremost among them a driving sense of service to the nation, which eventually came to overrule service loyalty and all lesser considerations.

Strategic Vision

If it is large enough or old enough, each corporation has its own distinct culture—from Ford to Motorola. As venerable institutions, the Army, Navy, Marines, and Air Force are distinctive not only for their uniforms and cultures, but also because of their separate strategic perspectives: landpower, seapower, and airpower respectively. Not only do these mini-paradigms represent what each service is all about, they are also at heart mutually contradictory arguments about the bottom line of national security. As an Army guy, I will tell you that "muddy boots on the ground" are the ultimate form of combat power and that you win the war when you have a beer in the other guy's officers club. Navy-Marine partisans believe instinctively that the United States is essentially a maritime nation, and the Air Force believes—unless forced to be polite when other services are present—that the airplane was the decisive weapon of twentieth-century combat and will be even more so in the twenty-first. If not taken to extremes, these differing worldviews can be helpful in dealing with the global problems of a superpower. But when combined with money shortages, unresolved differences, and competing priorities, then problems like the interoperability nightmare become truly dysfunctional. In fact, the relationship resembles nothing so much as the classic Chinese description of a troubled marriage: "same bed, different dreams."

Because a new, common dream was necessary, the Pentagon debate in the 1990s about the potential revolution in military affairs, or RMA, takes on extraordinary importance. Now you must first understand that an RMA is to the military what the "killer app" is in business. It is a quantum leap in capability that gives you an unbeatable advantage over the enemy: like the blitzkrieg that began World War II or the atomic bomb that ended it. Although theories differed widely, RMA proponents generally shared one idea: Information would forge the wonderfully diverse American military establishment into a new weapon of war that was more than the sum of its parts. At their best, these debates were reminiscent of the tumultuous discussions from earlier generations, when advocates of newfangled weapons like tanks, long-range bombers, aircraft carriers, and submarines argued their positions between World Wars I and II. In influential articles and books, military leaders such as Admiral Bill Owens, former vice chairman of the Joint Chiefs of Staff, argued that the information age had given new meaning to the age-old truism that knowledge is power—and that the considerable military information resources of the United States needed to be rationalized to achieve that objective. "Knowledge is power in military operations only if it can be communicated to combat forces that can use it, a capacity that depends on the network of communications . . . underlying the American Revolution in Military Affairs."[5]

The Navy, traditionally suspicious and downright cranky about anything requiring it to harmonize its operations with other services ("arrogant in victory, surly in defeat, and difficult at all points in between" according to a time-honored Pentagon jibe) now saw a succession of admirals like Owens, Jerry Tuttle, and Arthur Cebrowski taking the lead in exploring the new concepts of joint information sharing. Under Tuttle, "space and electronic warfare" became a major Navy mission while Cebrowski coined the term "Network Centric Warfare" to emphasize the importance of tightly interlocked networks that might include widely divergent and geographically dispersed groups of ships, planes, and tanks.[6]

Like glass shards ground into smoothness against a rocky shore, there is a process in which policy, especially defense policy, gradually results from the winnowing of ideas over time. The RMA debate, the increasing influence of the Joint Chiefs of Staff, and the pervasive effects of the information revolution eventually resulted in a rough consensus of what needed to be done. *Joint Vision 2010,* put out in the mid-1990s over the signature of Clinton's first JCS Chairman, General John Shalikashvili, was written in the usual harumph-heavy Pentagon style as "an operationally based template for the evolution of the Armed Forces." But its message was blunt enough in calling for the development of key joint capabilities in maneuver, precision engagement, force protection, and logistics. And there was some bite to the general's words in stressing that, unlike many other similar pronouncements over the years, this joint vision was to be a "benchmark" for the services and the combatant commands in building toward the future.

The last point is essential because of the repeated attempts over the years to ensure service coordination or cooperation—to say nothing at all of compliance with the many laws and regulations meant to unify military efforts. While those directives had not really been defied, they had often been met with only halfhearted compliance. "The services are insulated from overt disobedience to us through the sheer weight of their own paperwork" one political appointee had complained to me during my initial research into command and control years before. But now things had changed—and not through the imposition of yet more draconian standards or greater centralization of authority. Instead, the seductive vision of the RMA, combined with the increasing authority of our joint military institutions, had been the carrot-and-stick approach that urged the Pentagon forward.

The result was that a lot of little things gradually began to get better as the services became more serious about linking together the building blocks of communications interoperability throughout the late 1990s. Like your worst "Cable Guy" nightmare, interoperability involves lots of nitty-gritty things that must work together: equipment, wave forms, protocols, pathways, standards and even common computer terms, and languages. Obscure—yet as vital as matching the caliber of the bullet to the weapon for which it was designed. But like most unheralded progress, these accomplishments were to assume far greater importance when war unexpectedly loomed half a world away.

Aggressive Adaptation

As significant as it was, there should be no mistaking that pursuing the RMA represented precisely the kind of warfare that the Pentagon most wanted to do: a high-technology pile-on, with all the military services performing their preferred missions in sort of an improved version of Desert Storm. But one of the things that made the 1990s unique was the significant progress in two other areas: improving joint teamwork at the operational level and building up the capabilities of U.S. special operations forces. Both efforts were significant because they involved critical step-by-step improvements at the low end of the technology spectrum, well away from the floodlights of public attention.

The importance of doctrine in the military is another dividing line that walls it off from civilian society. In fact, unless you have been raised in the Roman Catholic Church, it may be bit of a stretch to understand just how deep and pervasive the doctrine goes: It is the source of received wisdom from the past, a reliable guide to acceptable conduct in the present, and an inescapable pointer to the future. But in temporal and secular institutions, there are always human flaws in the formation and application of doctrine. Vice chairman of the Joint Chiefs, Admiral David Jeremiah was fond of telling the story of how, as the great political philosopher Machiavelli lay dying, he was attended by a priest. As church doctrine demanded, the priest repeatedly urged Machiavelli to renounce the Devil and confess his sins—all to no avail. When the priest repeated his demand a third and final time, Machiavelli opened his eyes and said, "Father, I'm dying. This is not the time to make new enemies."

For a long time in American history, there was no doctrine governing interservice relationships—just relatively informal rules of the road governing their incidental contacts when fate decreed the need to work together. For reasons Machiavelli would have understood, the first rule was to make no enemies; the services simply avoided internecine conflict and ducked the really hard choices when actually they had to work together. It was not until after the 1986 Goldwater-Nichols Act reinforced the power of the chairman and made the Joint Staff his responsibility that joint doctrine began to be systematically developed and refined. The need to do so was driven by new geopolitical realities—in short, by how the competitive space had changed. The American military could no longer count on the stabilizing presence of the familiar Soviet enemy; and dealing with unpredictable, global crises in hard-to-reach places with rapidly downsizing forces demanded better teamwork among those that remained. The Persian Gulf War and its aftermath had clearly showed our perpetually crooked seams: everything from friendly fire to logistics and close air support. But suddenly there were new missions that some cynically referred to as "meals on wheels:" humanitarian assistance, support to counter drug operations, noncombatant evacuation. All demanded not only better coordination but also coming to grips with the perpetually vexing question: "Who's in charge?" As one critique from this period noted: "Relationships that exist only in crises have proven to be less and less effective over time . . . It is necessary to pioneer new command structures for peacetime as well as periods of crisis."[7]

Once set in motion, military bureaucracies rarely require much encouragement and by the mid-1990s, the number of joint doctrine publications had ballooned to over a hundred titles, some numbering in the hundreds of pages. Even as these new standard operating procedures were being thrashed out, there were growing requirements for U.S. joint forces. While writing a 1995 study of the U.S. mission in Somalia, for example, I was startled to discover that during those developments in Mogadishu, joint task forces had also been organized for no fewer than 12 other major operations—everything from enforcing no-fly zones over Iraq to flood relief in the American Midwest. Joint training exercises, once a rarity, underwent a similar growth spurt beginning in the mid-1990s. It was certainly possible to survey these developments and to be cynical about many of them—especially the numbers and unreadable language of the new joint publications. Nevertheless, American forces were slowly building a new dimension of teamwork, in which the essential processes of doctrine, training, exercises, and real-world operations were systematically being brought together to enforce and enrich one another. Like interoperability, these processes were obscure and largely hidden from public view. But the effect was the same as comparing a pickup football team, where every play must be improvised, sketched out in the dirt, and discussed—with the disciplined huddle of a Superbowl NFL team, where the quarterback barks out a formation, play, and snap count and can count on every player knowing instantly what to do and when to do it.

Like joint doctrine, the development of American Special Operating Forces (SOF) in the 1990s represents an aggressive and well-hidden adaptation to a changing environment. With a storied pedigree extending from before the American Revolution to the Normandy cliffs at Pointe du Hoc, the United States' special operating forces became a de facto fifth service in the aftermath of the 1986 Goldwater-Nichols Act. With its own unified command, assistant secretary of defense and independent budget authority, SOF was deliberately well positioned to deal with counterterrorist and other sensitive missions outside the traditional roles of conventional forces. In approving these extraordinary arrangements, Congress deliberately set out to redress a long-running antipathy that had made SOF the proverbial "poor relation" of the conventional forces—as well as needlessly dividing its efforts among the Army, Navy, and Air Force. (Organizationally, the Marines are not part of SOF but do have an organic SOF capability.)

From the beginning, the result was, as intended, a force that was a breed apart. Talk to senior SOF officers and they will tell you with quiet confidence that their charges are some of the most dangerous people in the world. While much of what they do necessarily remains invisible, they are some of the United States' best military personnel, customarily given dangerous assignments in surprising places around the globe. During training at Fort Bragg, North Carolina, prior to my 1996 deployment to Bosnia, one of them qualified me with the Beretta .9mm pistol. Whippet-lean, courteous but conspicuously close-mouthed, he would admit only that his most recent assignment had required him to be highly proficient with a pistol. Watching him nonchalantly pull off some prodigies of marksmanship that would have done justice to Buffalo Bill, I casually jingled the change in the pocket of my BDUs and asked innocently, "About how often do you fire?" "Oh, only about a thousand or so rounds a day," he replied modestly. Five-second pause. "More of course on weekends," he added as an afterthought.

Their officers are a similarly unique breed, as one of them told me, "not so much trained how to think but trained in how to be aggressive and creative in solving problems." Some SOF officers describe their culture as far more action-oriented than their conventional counterparts, adding that they are trained in taking risks instead of avoiding them. "If you're looking for a lot of checklists, you don't belong in SOF. And if you somehow get here, you probably won't last very long." Possibly for these reasons, the special operations community found itself becoming a high-growth cottage industry throughout the Clinton administration as new and demanding missions were added to the nation's military repertoire. In his book, *Shadow Warrior,* General Carl Stiner shows how their foreign language fluency and familiarity with foreign cultures made SOF a natural choice for humanitarian demining missions in Afghanistan; crisis response initiatives in Africa; noncombatant evacuations in Sierra Leone, Congo, and Liberia; and military-to-military training missions in many other countries.[8]

But it was the repeated American involvement in the Balkans from 1996 onward that provided SOF with nearly continuous operational experience. Their sophisticated politico-military capabilities were perfectly suited to the confusing environment of former Yugoslavia, where nuance has a power all its own. Used to operating alone behind enemy lines, they were a perfect choice as peacekeepers, serving in small teams in the Bosnian heartland where conventional U.S. formations went about their tasks in four-vehicle armored convoys. Best employed to train indigenous military forces, special forces forged close ties with the armies of the "former warring factions." The result was the SOF contingents operating in the Balkans also forged critical bonds of trust with their conventional military counterparts, with key U.S. intelligence and foreign policy agencies and with allied governments whose support was about to become critical. And all these things happened when budgets were tight, new requirements were coming over the transom every day . . . and no one was thinking that war might be upon us. Or that when it came, the double-edged special forces dagger wielded by a tightly integrated joint force would be one of the decisive weapons.

Leadership

Leadership is the basic stock in trade of any military force if for no other reason than that charging up a hill under intense fire is not a rational act, but requires leadership in its purest form. Think of the military as a kind of leadership laboratory, beginning at the service academies and extending throughout each command slot in an officer's career, and you have some idea of its importance. But because leadership is highly subjective and normally assessed commander by commander, it is sometimes difficult to make meaningful generalizations about it. With that caveat in mind, however, many of us who lived through that era have little doubt about several things: that the military in the mid-to-late 1990s experienced a leadership crisis; that the signs were subtle but unmistakable; and that the crisis was resolved in equally subtle ways that relied heavily on our institutional values.

The pervasiveness of the micromanagement problem in Bosnia has already been mentioned; but there were other indicators of poor leadership as well: One of the most unusual was the numbers of VIPs who regularly descended on us, in what was still best thought of as a combat zone. Often these visits seemed to increase during the first and last days of the month, a mystery until a finance officer pointed out to me that every day served in a combat zone effectively exempted the entire month from the total tax liability of the service member. A couple of well-timed visits each quarter . . . and well, you get the picture.

But perhaps the best example of the micromanagement culture was inadvertently supplied by the commander of one of the allied contingents serving under the American command there in Tuzla. While we were participating together on a patrol with one of his units, he apologized for the limited range of his tactical radios—adding that it was necessary for an American liaison officer equipped with a tactical satellite phone to accompany them so that regular reports of the patrol's progress could be transmitted to Tuzla, presumably for inclusion in that evening's BUB. We chuckled at that—but then he opined that it was a real strain for his officers to become accustomed to such close supervision "since it is our custom to trust junior officer to make right decisions as best way to prepare to become senior officer." I nodded—and tried not to choke, since my companion was a Russian paratroop officer. And we had assumed throughout the Cold War that the best way to paralyze a Soviet unit was to kill the senior officers since everyone knew that their subordinates could not think for themselves.

Instead, through the aggressive application of such seductive technologies as Powerpoints, satellite phones, and ever-increasing bandwidth, we seemed to have inadvertently Sovietized our own officer corps. My uneasiness with this leadership culture deepened after returning home and seeing two of the best brigade commanders I had served with in Bosnia passed over for selection to flag rank—and eventually forced to retire. Both had been superb troop leaders. But one had insisted on telling some inconvenient truths during his tenure on an accident investigation panel, while the other had been equally careless with honesty while within earshot of a reporter. It was sad, everyone agreed.

But how general was the problem? During 1998 to 1999, I participated in a study by the Center for Strategic and International Studies (CSIS) that surveyed more than 12,500 men and women in uniform from all services and primarily examined the issues of command climate and military culture. With many generals and senior officials on the CSIS panel, the language of its findings was carefully chosen. Yet the words were quietly devastating:

> Today, external environmental pressures have complicated the tasks of the . . . officers who train, discipline, and inspire the force. Ever-present organizational imperfections—leadership problems or the tendency to micromanage—thrive under these pressures. For all hands and their families, it is a frustrating time to be in uniform. . . . Although better off today than in the dark days of the Vietnam War . . . the U.S. military is facing potentially serious rifts in its culture, with attending damage to future operational effectiveness.[9]

That sober assessment attracted some attention at the time—and occasioned no small relief on my part because it confirmed much of what I had observed in more limited ways. But none of us on that panel could have imagined that "future operational effectiveness" would be tested in the ultimate crucible of combat just 18 months later. And, however true and disturbing all those dire trend lines may have been prior to September 11, 2001, that somehow thereafter the American military's embedded leadership culture of the military would allow it once again to rise to the challenge of battle. How did this happen?

A number of immediate and facile answers are possible, but current headlines about the aftermath of our invasion of Iraq (difficulties of pacification and the continuing hunt for weapons of mass destruction) are enough to discourage speculation. It is hardly speculative, however, to suggest that the most likely explanation for the survival of the vital leadership culture against long odds may have a lot to do with basic institutional values: loyalty to the nation, loyalty to the institution, a personal commitment to do as good a job as you can, and an abiding faith that somehow, some way that things will be put right. Hopefully in time to make a difference.

A TRIAL BALANCE IN THE AUDIT OF WAR

As these words are written, teams from the Joint Chiefs of Staff and the major American combatant commands are collecting, dissecting, and analyzing the lessons to be learned from their most recent experiences in the war against the regime of Saddam Hussein—even as their comrades-in-arms are still heavily engaged in the nasty business of prosecuting a guerrilla war. As a veteran of some standing in the "lessons learned" process, I know that there are good reasons to be cautious in offering even a tentative assessment. But some of the most salient features of what works in war don't change very much; and those are the factors that may be of the greatest interest to business. And while listed and considered separately, all are intimately and intricately linked.

1. *Revolutions happen.* Those who suggested the advent of a revolution in military affairs were proven right. But how new was it? We have seen many times before in military history that accuracy makes an enormous difference. In this case, the marriage of information to precision-guided munitions enabled devastatingly accurate hits at minimal risk to the attackers while helping to ensure minimal civilian collateral damage. The same thing is true in business: Accurate marketing, accurate business plans, accurate strategies— all of them enabled by the information revolution—can make you smarter than the competition.

2. *Interoperability happens, too—if you make it so.* Information-sharing turned out to be exactly what the RMA prophets had suggested it would be—the lifeblood of competitive effectiveness. Information that took hours or days to share between service components in Gulf War I now took just seconds. In the case of an aerial attack that targeted Saddam Hussein at the end of the war, only 40 minutes elapsed from the initial sensor report to bombs released on target by the shooter. The armored columns knifing so swiftly through the desert were able to communicate with each other, their headquarters, and associated joint forces through tactical Internets that suggested nothing so much as a latter-day version of Rommel's Afrika Korps. Business is not immune from stovepipes either, nor is it uncommon for information to be everywhere it needs to be—*except* in the hands of the operator. But information sharing that leads to action—ah, now that's a strategy that works every time—in either business or war.

3. *Teamwork works!* Multiple examples of improved teamwork abound, the most significant being the closely coordinated pincer movements between the Army and Marine heavy forces that invaded Baghdad from the southwest and southeast. A whole host of lesser triumphs of joint doctrine also were present, from combat search and rescue to theater missile defense. As the mistaken shoot-down by a Patriot missile of a Navy F-18 shows, there is room for improvement, but the dividends of better coordination are equally unmistakable. No argument here from my business colleagues either, of course, because they are paying lots of big bucks to lots of consultants to tell them that teamwork is important. And so it is: It is just that in war, the drawbacks of ineffective teamwork are far more immediate—and final—than in business. Same idea, though.

4. *Use special operations.* Most of what they did remains highly classified, yet what we know of SOF exploits to this point is remarkable. Simply begin with what did *not* happen during Operation Iraqi Freedom: SCUDS were not fired at Israel from the western desert; oil wells were not torched in great numbers; dams did not release their floodwaters downstream. All of these nonhappenings were thought to represent the contributions of SOF. Equally significant were SOF operations in northern Iraq, which together with American Airborne units, led to Kurdish successes against Saddam loyalists with minimal use of American forces. These tentative successes are impressive enough; yet the only thing that is truly certain is the list of SOF successes will eventually be much longer.

5. *Mission-Type Orders.* It is hard to say enough about the contrast in leadership styles between Operation Iraqi Freedom and everything that occurred throughout the 1990s. Not only were speed and audacity the bywords of the American ground advance into Iraq, but commanders were expected to improvise instead of slavishly follow orders. "Fight the enemy, not the plan!" was the constantly repeated battle cry of the ground commander, Army Lieutenant General David McKiernan. With better information at their fingertips, subordinate commanders were able to take

the commander's intent and to carry it out with flexible *Auft-ragstaktik*, mission-type orders that fully reflected rapidly changing battlefield conditions.

Other more specific leadership techniques and information age tools will occupy us in the following chapters. But for now, remember that the hidden keys to victory in Iraq—strategic vision, teamwork, and values-driven leadership—work wonders in the business world as well. Special operations and auftragstaktik are much too highly specialized military functions to have facile business equivalents. But they embody a more classic military principle that holds "the race is to the swift," which is certainly a concept that businesspeople should have no difficulty in understanding. Strategy, teamwork, leadership, and speed distinguish winners from losers in most forms of competition: those things, plus the fact that you want the victory more than the opposition does. So it was in Iraq—and so it is every day in American business.

WAR PLAN

MISSION OBJECTIVES

The hidden keys to victory in the military—strategic vision, teamwork, and values-driven leadership—work wonders in the business world as well:

★ Business leaders can identify very well with some dilemmas their military counterparts faced during the lean years: increased pressure on operating budgets; competing strategic priorities; technological uncertainty; and nagging doubts about how much change was too much.

★ The three hidden keys to victory in either business or war are (1) a strategic vision that creates *an ideal of teamwork* rather than traditional "go-it-alone" methods; (2) aggressive adaptation to build that teamwork *to unite people's actions;* and (3) leadership that really leads instead of relying on technology-induced micromanagement.

★ Leadership is the basic stock in trade of any military force, if for no other reason than that charging up a hill under intense fire is not a rational act, but it requires leadership in its purest form.

★ In Operation Iraq Freedom, the marriage of information to precision-guided munitions enabled devastatingly accurate hits, at minimal risk, to the attackers. The same is true in business: accurate marketing, business plans, and strategies—all of them enabled by the information revolution—can make you smarter than your competition.

★ Business is not immune from stovepipe or bottlenecks, nor is it uncommon for information to be everywhere it needs to be—*except* in the hands of the operator. But information sharing that leads to action is a strategy that works every time, in either business or war.

(continued)

★ With better information at their fingertips, subordinate commanders—in the military and in business—are able to take their commander's intent and carry it out with flexible mission-type orders that fully reflect rapidly changing battlefield—or marketplace—conditions.

★ Strategy, teamwork, leadership, and speed usually distinguish winners from losers in most forms of competition: those things, plus the fact that you want the victory more than the opposition does. So it was in Iraq—and so it is every day in American business.

4

☆ ☆ Building Leaders ☆ ☆ of Character

If leaders are not looking for the truth, if situations are not framed as having moral implications in the first place, then these leaders make decisions based on other criteria, often with disturbing results. Moral sensitivity alone is not enough. Once leaders recognize that a moral problem exists, then they have to decide what is right. This requires moral judgment—discerning which action is most justifiable based on a set of ethical criteria. . . . Without the courage to take action, to DO the right thing . . . all moral awareness and judgment is for naught. . . . True leaders of character demonstrate the moral courage to "choose the harder right over the easier wrong" over and over again.

"Cadet Leader Development System," USMA Circular 1-101 (June 2002), p. 29

This chapter is about leadership, how we do it in the military and what lessons business can learn from that experience. In contrast to the business school orthodoxy that leadership can be studied quite apart from values, our military institutions believe that leadership skills and character go hand in hand. And that those skills must be reinforced and developed—methodically and consistently—throughout a soldier's career. Great leaders, like great athletes, have something special—call it charisma, vision, or presence (think of Eisenhower at D-day or FDR throughout the Depression years). But the task of our military academies, service schools, and war colleges is to take whatever native abilities each officer may have and to develop them, gradually forging that combination of character, management skills, leadership, and courage that the nation expects when committing its sons and daughters to battle.

The preceding extract from the West Point leadership manual states the purpose succinctly and brushes aside the politically correct sophistry that morals are only impediments to be dispensed with on our way to the higher ground of situational ethics. In contrast, the dominant philosophy of our business schools is well summed up by one of my favorite *New Yorker* cartoons depicting an ordinary little man sitting on his ordinary little sofa next to his ordinary little wife. He says, "I wasn't born great, I haven't achieved greatness, but I am still very much hoping to have it thrust upon me." At our military institutions, greatness is not left to chance. Go for a workout at the gymnasium at West Point and you will see the words of a previous superintendent—Douglas MacArthur—carved in stone above the entrance: "Upon these fields of friendly strife are sewn the seeds that upon other fields, on other days, will bear the fruits of victory." Get the point?

Because you can never tell when one of those other fields or other days will pop up, the process has to be rigorous, intense, and continuous. You may not have heard of an Army Major General named Buster Hagenbeck, but he is the commander of the Army's Tenth Mountain Division, and just months after 9/11, he led the assault against Taliban and Al Qaida guerrillas in Afghanistan. Operation Anaconda was fought in the snows and rocks of some of the world's most forbidding terrain against an enemy that simply wanted to engage and kill American troops. During a conversation after his return, we talked for a long time about what his soldiers had done, about their heroism, and about his pride in their efforts. One of those war stories included a harrowing tale of a young sergeant who had voluntarily held his position on the snow—exposed to the cold but in an excellent position to pick off snipers trying to fire on his comrades. When pulled out the next morning, under protest, the soldier's body temperature had dropped to 93 degrees. But when asked to identify the one factor most critical to 10th Mountain's operations there at the top of the world, General Hagenbeck answered without the slightest hesitation, "It was the trust and the integrity that I had in my subordinates and the trust and integrity that they had in me."[1] That is what we mean by values in action.

In contrast, if you spend five minutes examining the god-is-dead, values-don't-matter literature on business leadership, well then you have just wasted five minutes. Here is a time-saving opinion, although admittedly prejudiced: While browsing there, you will find comparatively little that is useful or valuable. It is like analyzing a good joke—the exercise of doing it is tedious and misses the point. But apart from missing completely the importance of values, the most serious drawback of the business literature is that it misses one of the central lessons you can learn from the military model: Leadership skills need to be systematically inculcated, developed, and reinforced over the full extent of a person's career. Without a firm understanding of this basic truth, all the books in the world on the so-called leadership secrets of the great captains of industry are of little use other than to line the pockets of those who write them.

Not surprisingly, in the aftermath of the great corporate ethical meltdowns of 2001 to 2003, there have been several efforts to understand what went wrong. Consider the following five possibilities:

1. **Bad command climates?** Some analysts have looked at Enron and have had the courage to wonder if what happened there could happen elsewhere. The painful answer appears to be: yes it can. The core of the problem? Building organizations in which it is at least theoretically possible to tell the truth.

   If we build a leadership team in organizations that are unfriendly to the usual mistakes—things like operating errors and simple human frailties—we create an environment that breeds deception. People don't generally bury the truth about mistakes because they are dishonest; they bury it because they are smart. Why tell the truth if it will get you killed?[2]

2. **Was it really smart to ignore all that stuff about values?** Adrian Savage, President of PNA Inc., surveyed 200 top executives to identify those leadership values that were prevalent among so-called

natural leaders. He found that the two top values—achievement and success—were also the two most easily distorted by what he calls "the irrational exuberance of the recent past." Success fed on itself, rapidly got out of control, and entirely eclipsed two other widely held values—justice and fairness—normally meant to keep things in some sort of balance. And the prescription?

> Like the public at large, the majority of executives have thoroughly clear standards for appropriate behavior in a corporate setting. It is these inner standards, not rules laid down by the Securities and Exchange Commission (SEC) or Congress, that keep them from falling into excess. Their achievement drive is balanced by their concern to be seen as good corporate citizens.[3]

3. **Will new legislation and regulations solve the problem?** In the year since the Sarbanes-Oxley legislation was passed to improve corporate accounting standards, some analysts have belatedly begun to wonder if we have diagnosed the correct problem:

> Sarbanes-Oxley mandates that companies put in place a new level of auditing and boardroom assurance procedures. The attendant result is to provide great confidence in the validity of the financial reporting that these companies provide and thus protect and reassure investors and the investing public. It's not a bad goal . . . (But) while the legislation is designed to restore trust in accounting, what we really need is an effort to restore trust in leadership. The Sarbanes-Oxley remedy merely addresses the symptoms of . . . trust destruction . . . rather than its causes. *What is required of chief executives is not committee members or codes, but courage.* So where does one start?[4] (emphasis added)

Fair question: How about starting, say, in the nation's business schools? Or by giving a long overdue reexamination to the process of building the business leaders to whom we trust the nation's future treasure and welfare? Think I'm kidding? Just imagine if airline pilots were trained the same as business leaders are prepared for their responsibilities. Would you get on that plane? Nope—neither would I!

4. **I don't care about your Nobel Prize: you don't know jack!** There is no more potent demonstration of the moral and intellectual

confusion in which our nation's biz school faculties find themselves than the following quote by Milton Friedman:

> I don't think there is such a thing as business ethics. A business
> can't have ethics any more than a building can have ethics. Only
> people can have ethics. I don't believe the university is the place
> for that. Family and elementary and secondary schools are. Unfor-
> tunately, in elementary and secondary schools the extent to which
> ethical education is occurring has been very much less.[5]

As it happens, Professor Friedman, a talented and dynamic
speaker, was invited to lecture at West Point while I was there.
The cadets simply loved him. They didn't know very much yet
about either economics or life, so the more he talked about the
wonderful simplicities of the free market, the better it seemed.
Next day in class, I reminded them that they were enrolled in the
most overtly socialist institution in the United States, that every
one of them was on the dole, and that a not so very invisible hand
told them every day what uniform to put on and how far to
roll up their window shades. And that their education was incomplete unless they understood one fundamental rule: When an
economist speaks to you, smile but do not listen. And if it makes
sense to reinforce early religious training with periodic worship
throughout one's life, then why should it seem odd to insist on
basic ethics training and periodic reinforcement throughout
one's business career? Especially when we are insisting on higher
ethical standards among the nation's present and future business
elites? Or did you miss that point in class about character equal-
ing destiny?

5. **This just in from the B-school faculty meeting. . . .** Other than the
pervasive murmuring of the economists, one hears two complaints
about business school faculties in the matter of ethics. The first is
that there is a lack of shelf space for ethics courses—too many
courses chasing too little time, with knuckle-dragging analytics
far outweighing something as inherently subjective as ethics. But
the real crime is even worse: To the extent that there is ethical instruction in our nation's universities and business schools, the entire field has been overtaken by political correctness. In this

formulation, ethics consists of various measures of the "social responsibility" of the corporation instead of any real consideration
of those thorny issues of applying corporate values and ethics.
Saving the environment, protecting the whales, and achieving
the most tasteful possible balance in the makeup of the corporation's racial/ethnic/linguistic/orientation trumps the bejesus
out of making the hard choices of real values-based leadership.
One of the best examples of political correctness eclipsing real
ethics can be found at—you guessed it—Enron, where the Enron
Wind Corporation was one of the world's largest operators of
wind-powered generation. One can take a savage, if uncharitable,
satisfaction in the knowledge that neither the Kyoto Treaty nor all
of Kenneth Lay's machinations saved this subsidiary in the end
from being (ahem) blown away.[6]

The System: An Overview

Having served in every part of the Army's training and education system—from draftee to Dean of the National War College—my view of the
way civilian institutions produce leaders can probably be criticized for
being jaded. But it is difficult for any civilian to appreciate just how
much time the soldier, sailor, airman, or marine spends in training or
how much leadership counts as part of the curriculum at every level. The
basic rule is this: You are either operational and fully engaged in doing
the job the taxpayers sent you to do or else you are in training—and
preparing to do the next job for which the taxpayers (or their surrogates
in the flesh-peddling offices maintained by each of the services) have selected you.

For an officer, the pattern goes something like this:

- Initial entry, service qualification, and first assignment (3 to 4
  years).

- Company-grade career course (4 to 6 months) followed by second
  utilization tour (6 to 8 years).

- Field grade selection, senior service school training, and initial
  utilization tour (9 to 12 years).

- Secondary field grade tour, selection for command position (battalion equivalent), and war college (13 to 18 years).

- Selection and training for senior grade command (brigade equivalent; 18 to 22 years).

- Flag officer selection, special schooling, and utilization (23 to 30 years).

Each of the military services is unique and each can add special qualifications based on an officer's specialty. But simply notice how much time is spent in the schoolhouse, where leadership studies in one form or another constitute the core of the curriculum. Those studies typically can include detailed historical analyses of tactical engagements, especially at the company grade level, where troop level decisions can be pulled apart and dissected in detail. At the more senior schools, the campaigns and battles of the great captains of history are read closely; while at the war colleges, the curriculum is infused with the work of the greatest thinkers of military theory and practice. But the bottom line here is easily summed up in one word: *system.* That means leadership studies are consistently measured, reinforced, and made meaningful in everyday life.

And how does an officer get selected for these educational opportunities? That's how the other part of the system works, creating a progressive leadership laboratory in which selection, advancement, and eventual promotion all depend on how well one performs in progressively more demanding assignments. The best way to prepare for battalion command is to build a solid record commanding at company level, mixed with principal staff positions at the battalion level. And at least once a year, the officer is expected to receive a performance rating that, more than anything else, shows both his or her current performance and potential for future advancement. And the key test of these ratings? How well does this officer lead today? And how well can we expect the officer to lead tomorrow?

Most of us can only envy the rating given to the young George Marshall during an era in which Army ratings did not suffer much from indirection or any failure to "tell it like it is." In answer to the question, "Would you want to have this officer serve under your command in combat?" Marshall's rater had a forthright and arresting answer: "Yes, but I would prefer to serve under HIS command in combat." Turned out to be not only a good rating . . . but a prophetic one.

THE TEN COMMANDMENTS OF MILITARY LEADERSHIP

In pondering the lessons business might wish to learn from the military leadership experience, I naturally want to avoid the schlock of the standard tomes. For example: "Attack wherever your enemy is weakest. And where you are strong." See how easy it is to go too fast for the average reader? Neither is it possible nor desirable to distill the major leadership principles taught in all the war college faculties down to a precious few. But subject to these limitations—and with no suggestion that this list is either comprehensive or timeless—I offer a few of the rules learned over the course of what my MSNBC and military colleagues laughingly refer to as my career.

Lesson 1: Standards Matter

Like so many of us from the draft-induced era, my most memorable example of personal leadership may have been provided by my drill sergeant in basic training. We knew him as Harry (The Devil) Davis, although he encouraged us to address each other by our first names: *Drill Sergeant!* (for him) and Private Shit-head (for us). Think of Louis Gosset in *An Officer and a Gentleman;* then multiply that ferocity 10-fold and that was Sergeant Davis. When I was drafted in 1969, the Army was what we might call "racially diverse." Indeed, my platoon mirrored this—we had tough blacks from the big city, white coal miners' sons, and the odd middle-class, Goody Two-shoes college boy (like me) who plainly had not understood that ROTC was the answer. Harry was like the canonical drill sergeant in every novel ever written about service life. He really could not have cared less what color we were, where we had come from, or the series of misadventures or poor planning that had brought us to him. In the beginning, we simply were all scum. And his mission in life was to save us from ourselves and to turn us into soldiers, which he did with a ferocious determination, from 0400 until whenever he got tired at night. I cannot even recount in decent company what happened when one of the black kids referred to Sergeant Davis to his face as "brother," but it was a mistake that no one ever repeated because Sergeant Davis did *not* believe in equality—far from it. We were at the bottom of the ladder as trainees, while he was at the top—a combat veteran and a noncommissioned officer to boot. And could he ever boot! He was the toughest taskmaster I ever encountered, with painfully high standards that he enforced every day. But gradually an object lesson sank in. Our platoon probably could have turned into a race riot waiting to happen—something that occurred frequently enough in those days. But under Sergeant Davis, we were simply too busy, too tired, and too scared of him to do anything else but become good soldiers.

On graduation day, Sergeant Davis drove me over to the headquarters to pick up some personnel records. It felt odd to be joyriding that way with the drill sergeant, and I may have been sitting at the position of attention the whole way. It must have been eight o'clock in the morning, but Sergeant Davis coolly reached over into the glove compartment, pulled out a flask of some rotgut whiskey or other, pulled off the top with his teeth, and took a long swig. Then, without a word, he handed the bottle to me. That was when I knew I had made it in Harry's estimation. I was a soldier. Nowadays, we would have been besieged by battalions of Alcohol and Drug Abuse counselors tut-tutting reports from every orifice. But at that moment, taking a swig of that horrible stuff meant that I had arrived. Had met the standards. And that meant more to me than any ceremony the Army could offer.

Lesson 2: The Mission Comes First—Then Your People—Then You

Early in my military career, I received a basic lesson in how leaders are developed in the military. Fresh out of college, I was drafted and soon found myself in Officer's Candidate School, which was the Army's way of taking college graduates and turning them into officers capable of leading other people in combat. There was a certain incentive to pay attention because, every couple of weeks, you rated yourself and everyone else in the platoon on leadership performance. The morning after the "bayonet ratings" came out, the bottom 20 percent of the class was gone.

Early in OCS, I was leading a platoon on a training maneuver through the wilds of flood-ridden Virginia. But while leaning over to give one of my guys a hand crossing one of those swollen rivers, I lost my helmet. Now it is always a bad thing to lose the equipment entrusted to you by the Army but in OCS that was simply something you didn't do. The other guys in the platoon understood the seriousness of my predicament, and together we searched for the missing helmet. But after 15 minutes, it was obvious that helmet was gone forever, so I grimly decided to move on and continue the patrol.

When we arrived at the end of the trail and the end of the mission, the tactical officer was waiting for me—hands on his hips and clearly upset. We were late. When I explained what had happened, I was given a valuable if painful lesson in what makes a leader. Losing my helmet was bad; but endangering the mission was unforgivable. In a tactical situation, being late and being distracted from the objective were two things that got people killed. The helmet could be replaced; the men and the mission could not. And if I did not understand that being a leader sometimes involved putting those interests ahead of my own welfare, then perhaps it was time to reconsider my plans for becoming an officer in the United States Army.

Lesson 3: Leaders Have a Clear Vision of What They Want to Achieve, Set a High Standard, Live It—And Expect the Same from Those around Them

That lesson came home to me a few years later while serving as a counterintelligence officer in Germany. Our unit was responsible for enforcing security procedures in Army units scattered across a wide chunk of West Germany. Problem was, our group commander got it into his head that we needed to go the extra mile in setting a good example. To do that, he instituted a series of predawn raids to guard against unlocked safes and similar security weaknesses. As the security officer of our battalion, I was awakened at 2 A.M. one morning and told that we were the subject of one of the dreaded raids—and I should get down to headquarters P.D.Q. I arrived a few minutes later, half dressed in civilian clothes and in something approaching a full flap. A few minutes later, our battalion commander, Lieutenant Colonel Jay Parker, arrived resplendent in a perfectly pressed uniform, medals gleaming, and exuding the kind of calm self-assurance that clearly marked him as the man in charge.

Which he was; only later did I find out that he was a contemporary and close friend of another young Army officer quickly moving up the ladder: Colin Powell.

But Lt. Col. Parker quickly set the right tone—and retrieved a situation that was deteriorating badly. "We welcome the inspection," he said, adding that he and his men were proud of the standard we set. "We will stay out of your way, but do let us know if we can help in any way. By the way, would you like some coffee?" Well, we passed that inspection with flying colors, gaining immediate self-confidence from our battalion commander's coolness and unwillingness to be run off the ranch. But later, the colonel told us privately about the abrupt phone call that, like mine, had awakened him from a sound sleep. When he put the phone down and told his wife what was going on, she with great presence of mind simply said, "Well, Jay, hope you got your shit together." He truly did—in every sense of the word.

Lesson 4: Leaders Keep Their Heads in a Crisis and Are Seen to Lead and Be in Charge—Their Strength and Character Are All-Important

Leadership really counts when push comes to shove. In a book by Lt. Gen. Ret. Hal Moore Jr. and Joseph L. Galloway called *We Were Soldiers Once . . . and Young* (New York: Harper Collins, 1992), there is an unforgettable account of the Ia Drang battlefield in South Vietnam in late 1965. In the movie dramatization, *We Were Soldiers Once*, Mel Gibson plays then-Lieutenant Colonel Moore preparing his troops for their deployment to war. His approximate words, "Look, we are going into a combat zone. I cannot tell you that all of you are going to come back alive. I can tell you, however, that none of you will be left behind and that my boots will be the first ones on that battlefield and the last ones to leave." In the Ia Drang valley, Moore's unit ran into a North Vietnamese unit larger than itself, which was determined to fight the Americans as equals. The movie graphically shows what it took to win that fight and to survive. But more than anything else, it demonstrated just how much Hal Moore's leadership meant to his soldiers. The legacy of that battle had an effect on the Army during and after Vietnam because it showed that leadership meant *U.S.*, not just *me* or *my career*, at a time when the Army was strug-gling as much with ticket-punching careerism as any corporation out there today. Bad as it sometimes was, though, we never believed today's current corporate mantra: every man for himself.

Lesson 5: If Values Aren't Worth Dying for, They Aren't Worth Living For

Hal Moore's example could apply equally well to this principle since his fight involved the ultimate stakes of life-and-death combat on the battle-field. But how do we get ready for such challenges and how do we apply such values in lesser situations? In his new book, *Absolutely American: Four Years at West Point* (Boston: Houghton Mifflin, 2003), David Lipsky writes about the cultural conflicts of a modern West Point class. One of his main characters is Lt. Col. Hank Keirsey, who at the beginning of the book is the Director of Military Training at West Point and is exactly the kind of leader who can inspire the cadets. "We don't know what division will go to the frontier of freedom here. And somewhere in some dis-puted barricade along the frontier, you will meet your destiny. And you will stack this country's enemies like cordwood."[7]

When one of Keirsey's subordinates, an instructor, got into trouble for writing and forwarding a politically incorrect e-mail (with Power-Point slide), there was talk of court-martialing the instructor. Keirsey de-cided that it was his duty to take responsibility for the incident as a matter of loyalty, and with the probability of escaping with just a repri-mand. In fact, he was relieved of his position and dismissed from the Army. But as Lipsky concludes:

> For me what Hank Keirsey did [for that instructor] was one of the clearest examples I have of West Point values. When I tell civilian friends of Keirsey's story I have to go over it twice because they keep asking, "Wait, didn't the other guy make the slide?" A leader takes care of his soldiers; he puts their concerns ahead of his own.[8]

True enough. And on the battlefield and in the boardroom: Leaders have to be consistent and to show what they're made out of.

Lesson 6: Ambition Is Good—Restrained Ambition Is Even Better

Studying the lives and careers of our greatest generals can sometimes bring about not only insights into winning battles but priceless leadership lessons as well. It is interesting to note how Generals Sherman and Grant, two of our greatest Civil War commanders, behaved toward one another and how they restrained their ambition at a time when many other generals did not. By 1865, Grant outranked Sherman, and as the war ended, there was a move in Congress to reward Sherman by passing legislation that would promote him to Grant's level of Lieutenant General. Sherman wrote to his brother, John Sherman, senator from Ohio, to oppose that particular piece of legislation. He said:

> I have all the rank I want and it makes no difference to me whether that be Major General or Field Marshal. I have commanded 100,000 men in battle and on the march successfully and without confusion and that is enough for my reputation. Now I want rest and peace.

And interestingly enough, there is a parallel statement from Grant:

> No one would be more pleased in your advancement than I. If you should be placed in my position and I am put subordinate it should not change our personal relations in the least. I would make the same exertions to do all in my power to make our cause win.[9]

The relationship between the two great commanders was one of friendship, but friendship is often sacrificed when rivalries are allowed to dominate—in either business or war. Grant's reply is revealing: For him and Sherman both, *the cause was everything*. And against that, everything else faded into the background.

Lesson 7: If Restrained Ambition Is Good, Loyalty Is Even Better

Rivalry was no more an issue for Robert E. Lee and Stonewall Jackson than it was for Grant and Sherman. When a colleague privately suggested to Jackson that General Lee was "slow," Jackson took him to task, stating:

General Lee is not slow. No one knows the weight upon his heart and his great responsibilities. He is Commander-in-Chief and he knows that if an Army is lost it cannot be replaced . . . I have known General Lee for five and twenty years. He is cautious; he ought to be, but he is not slow. Lee is a phenomenon. He is the only man whom I would follow blindfolded.[10]

As was the case with Grant and Sherman, it is curious that loyalty ran in two directions, perhaps reminding us of the eternal truth that what goes around comes around. When Lee received word of enemy deployments just prior to the Battle of Fredericksburg, instead of giving explicit orders, he merely said to a staff officer, "Say to General Jackson that he knows just as well what to do with the enemy as I do."[11] That is an idea worth considering in an age in which business loyalty seems curiously out of fashion, or at least most commonly expressed in monetary terms. The examples of Lee and Jackson—or Grant and Sherman—are all the more compelling when contrasted against the conduct of some of their contemporaries—Union and Confederate—who let pure naked ambition rule their every action. But not so these gentlemen, who we admire to this day not only because of their abilities but also because of their character, which was clearly not for sale.

Lesson 8: Command and Control Is Good—Self-Control Is Even Better

Dwight D. Eisenhower and George S. Patton Jr. probably compose the only duo in modern times comparable to either with Lee-Jackson and Sherman-Grant. Ike's son, John S. D. Eisenhower, has written a marvelous book called *General Ike: A Personal Reminiscence,* which provides a unique insight into the problem of self-control. To summarize: Ike had more of it than Patton and either fate or history put him in a position where it was critical in saving Patton from himself. Which was important because Patton was to generalship what Seabiscuit was to horseracing: No one was better in the straightaway when the chips were down, but he gave a whole new meaning to the phrase "hard to handle."

The story that Ambassador Eisenhower recounts came during an inspection trip in England, prior to the Normandy invasion. Patton, always at the limits of self-restraint, lost it entirely while observing a tactical demonstration. We would today describe what happened next as Patton "getting in the face" of a young soldier who was ducking for cover when Patton thought he should have kept running. The high—or low—point came when Patton roared at him: "You have no knowledge of the art of war!" At that moment, the young soldier probably wanted to know no more about war than what he needed to survive—and no more about Patton than how to get as far away from him as possible. The incident ended with Ike remaining curiously and conspicuously quiet about the odd behavior of his talented but erratic comrade-in-arms:

> If Ike spoke to Patton about this bizarre outburst I never heard of it. My guess is that he did not. Certainly he never would have criticized Patton in front of others. I cite the incident simply to illustrate the type of annoyance Ike was willing to undergo in order to save this man for what he was best at: fighting.[12]

And that really says it all about the relationship that existed between those two men because on more than one occasion, such as the famous slapping incident in Italy, Ike saved George Patton from himself and preserved his ability to fight in the Allied cause. The two men were close friends but in this particular instance it was not friendship, but Ike's concept of duty that was absolutely critical to Patton's success, linked as always to his personal ability for self-control. The ability to know when and how to keep his mouth shut made Ike the perfect choice to command the difficult, wrangling, multinational coalition that was Operation Overlord. Then, as now, it is axiomatic that coalitions are ad hoc collections of the willing. Having a boss who knows how to restrain himself helps to make sure that the willing remain so.

Lesson 9: What Can Get Done Today Depends Directly on What Was Done Yesterday

The military has its own unique set of rhythms and procedures and in that respect is not unlike any other large organization or corporation. Simply put, it takes a lot of effort to get anything done. Some liken this fact to the time and space needed for an aircraft carrier to change course. But I prefer to think of institutional change, in the military or anywhere else, as analogous to the problem of making love to the proverbial elephant: It requires a great deal of effort, requires a long time to show any discernible results, and if you don't do it just right, the elephant stomps the hell out of you.

That same thought was put forth with considerably more eloquence by Rick Atkinson, former correspondent of the *Washington Post* and a distinguished military historian. Just after the end of the first Gulf War, he was invited to address the West Point Class of 1991 on the eve of their graduation. But what he said resonated throughout the U.S. military:

> There is a tendency now to believe the victory in the Persian Gulf War was easy and cheap . . . But it wasn't easy. The seeds of this victory were planted more than twenty years ago in the jungles of Vietnam. The officers who were brigade, division and corps commanders in this war commanded platoons, companies, and battalions in Vietnam. They stayed the course after Vietnam when the Army was an institution in anguish, when it was an institution beset with the anarchy of drugs, racial strife, and utter indiscipline. They remained true to the profession of arms and set out to make things right, to develop the doctrine, the training methods, the standards of professionalism that evolved in the outstanding force which you will formally join tomorrow. In this sense, the Persian Gulf War didn't last for forty-two days, it lasted for twenty years. And it was not easy.[13]

No it wasn't but thanks for noticing. And thanks as well to the Sergeant Davises, the Colonel Parkers, and the countless others who stayed and made a difference in the only way that it can truly be made: one day at a time.

Lesson 10: Don't Ever Write a Letter That You Can't Answer

One of the more pleasurable experiences of being a junior Army Congressional Fellow in the mid-1980s was the chance to become personally acquainted with some distinguished military officers who had been asked by Congress to advise them on various matters of defense policy. One of them was Admiral Thomas Moorer, a highly decorated and crusty old sailor who looked and acted the part of a venerable sea dog. Now re-tired and in full possession of his First Amendment rights, the admiral liked nothing better than mixing it up with members of Congress, who knew and valued good copy when they heard it. And so in March 1986, the admiral came before the House Armed Services Committee to testify on defense reorganization.

Because the issues involved weighty considerations of civilian control, the admiral was asked to give his opinion on the especially sensitive issue of reports to Congress. He did so . . . and recounted the memorable tale told here. Back in the Eisenhower administration, then Captain Moorer was serving as an assistant to the chief of naval operations, the legendary World War II Admiral Arleigh Burke. Secretary of Defense Neil McElroy wanted to save money by eliminating torpedoes from the armament of the Navy's first ballistic missile submarine, the *Polaris*. With nuclear missiles, the civilian analysts reasoned, of what conceivable use were torpedoes? Well, the Navy felt differently, and Admiral Burke owed at least nominal obedience to his civilian superiors; but the Navy also had a close personal relationship with another civilian superior, Rep. Carl Vinson, the power-ful chief of the House Armed Services Committee. Hearing about the con-troversy—one naively wonders how—Rep. Vinson sent a letter to Secretary McElroy demanding an explanation and giving it as his opinion that, as with any submarine, the *Polaris* of course needed torpedoes.

In the usual manner of Washington staffing, Secretary McElroy sent the letter from Congressman Vinson over to the Navy to compose a suit-able reply. Moorer recounted what happened next:

> Admiral Burke gave it to me to answer. It went back up. Mr. McElroy signed it and sent it back to Mr. Vinson. Mr. Vinson took Mr. McElroy's letter, sent it directly to Admiral Burke and Admiral Burke gave it to me to answer. So I spent 6 months writing letters to myself. (Laughter) . . . That is hard to do because you have got to be sure you do not write a letter you cannot answer. (Extended laughter)[14]

I now have the advantage of experience on virtually all sides of the Washington conundrum, from Capitol Hill to the Pentagon with various media outposts thrown in, but I never heard it said any better than that.

LIVING THE PRINCIPLES

West Point is a perfect place in which to hold up ideals—usually described as a kind of serene Athens in contrast to everything around it as well as the larger society it helps to defend. That may make it an imperfect reference point for concluding a discussion of values for the hurly-burly world of business. Except that one instinctively turns to such lodestones in applying the certainties of what has worked before to an ambiguous present and uncertain future. One hesitates above all to produce the kind of checklist that virtually every business book provides as a convenient substitute for not thinking at all. But if I were going to invent a checklist for leadership skills, I could hardly improve on the one that West Point uses not only in preparing cadets for careers in the Army but also in reminding faculty and staff about the basics of leadership. Slightly paraphrased here, this code identifies the following functions of leaders and subordinates:

- Abides by the ethical standards of our profession.
- Demonstrates mutual professional loyalty and teamwork.
- Never gains or seeks privilege at the expense of others.
- Respects the dignity and worth of all colleagues.
- Accepts responsibility for one's own actions.
- Establishes clear, obtainable objectives and standards.
- Motivates and inspires subordinates seeking to build a foundation of mutual trust and confidence.
- Enables communication.
- Promotes self-esteem and provides constructive evaluation of duty performance.[15]

A better leadership checklist you are not likely to find anywhere—or a more succinct explanation of what a leader in *any* institution is supposed to do. Most of these qualities are also present to one degree or another in the specific leadership examples throughout this book. But if you look back as well at the USMA extract that headlined this chapter, you have to be impressed at the sophistication informing this philosophy. We assume that there is going to be a moral conflict in doing the job that we are training those cadets to do. And it is terribly important that they get the moral instruction that will allow them to make the right choice at a time when they may be under physical duress and it is not terribly obvious what the right choice is. In many ways, these ambiguities are not all that different from what corporate employees may face—from the mail clerk to the CEO. The difference is that the military understands these answers are not found just in textbooks—but in the knowledge of absolute standards and in practical applications reinforced by long practice. How is this any different from any civilian job? The right answer is not always found in a textbook but in practical leadership values that should be instilled in everyone from the mail clerk to the CEO.

You don't hang around West Point for very long without hearing the Cadet Prayer, which is a similar bedrock of moral certainty in what can be a highly uncertain profession:

> Make us to choose the harder right instead of the easier wrong and never to be content with the half-truth when the whole truth can be won. Endow us with courage that is born of loyalty, all that is noble and worthy, that scorns to compromise with vice and injustice and knows no fear when truth and right are in jeopardy.[16]

In a misguided nod to political correctness, chapel is no longer compulsory at West Point, but the Cadet Prayer remains an intrinsic and inescapable part of the moral upbringing and moral background of everyone who is there. Would that it were taught as well at Harvard Business School. Or better yet, *practiced*.

At the very least, there are certainly lessons here for business managers who seem to be living in a godless world of no fixed values. And for the nation's business school faculties, who try to teach leadership without teaching values. Or indeed for the economists who, as economists will, teach the price of everything, and the value of nothing. As recent history tells us all too clearly, the value of nothing sometimes carries a very high price indeed.

WAR PLAN

MISSION OBJECTIVES

One of the central lessons that can be learned from the military model is that leadership skills need to be systematically inculcated, developed, and reinforced over the full extent of an individual's career.

In contrast to prevailing business school orthodoxy—that leadership can be studied quite apart from values—another central lesson of the military model is that leadership skills and character development go hand in hand.

The military leadership model is one that can also be modified and applied to the nation's business schools: to take the God-given abilities of each officer, to develop them—and to gradually forge that combination of character, management skills, leadership, and courage the nation expects of its future battle captains.

The Ten Basic Commandments put forth in this book are neither original nor comprehensive. They are, however, instructive:

★ **Lesson One: Standards matter.** When building a team of soldiers or coworkers committed to an important task, standards are all-important. Don't leave any room for ambiguity or doubt about what they are.

★ **Lesson Two: The mission comes first. Then your people. Then you.** As a practical leadership standard, these simple priorities are hard to beat but surprisingly difficult to achieve without concerted effort—in either business or war.

★ **Lesson Three: A leader has a clear vision of what he wants to achieve, sets a high standard, and lives it—and expects the same of those around him.** A continuation of the above principle: Vision, values—both are important. Standards: priceless!

★ **Lesson Four: Leaders keep their heads in a crisis and are seen to lead and be in charge. Their strength and character are all-important.** Hal Moore exemplified this in real life: in wartime or a business crisis, leadership is survival.

★ **Lesson Five: If values aren't worth dying for, they aren't worth living for.** Values aren't what you talk about; they are what you do every day. Or they aren't really your values.

★ **Lesson Six: Ambition is good. Restrained ambition is even better.** Among either generals or CEOs, personal ambition needs to be subordinated, if not by self-discipline then by a cause or by values larger than yourself.

★ **Lesson Seven: If restrained ambition is good, loyalty is even better.** One of those values is loyalty, which like character itself is beyond price.

★ **Lesson Eight: Command and control is good. Self-control is even better.** Same as above—but even more important when you remember that corporations, even more than wartime alliances are ad hoc coalitions of the willing.

★ **Lesson Nine: What can get done today depends directly on what was done yesterday.** Most progress that matters is evolutionary rather than revolutionary. And there are no substitutes for committed people who will hang in there over the long haul.

★ **Lesson Ten: Don't ever write a letter that you can't answer.** Admiral Tom Moorer's light-hearted but classic warning expresses this truth: Be careful not to out-smart yourself.

☆☆ Leadership in ☆☆
Business and War

5

☆ ☆ Strategy ☆ ☆

Deliver Us from Process

S trategy is one of the most basic ideas from military history. The most fundamental level represents the all-important relationship between means and ends, the delineation of specific objectives, and the assignment of corresponding resources. It reflects as well, however, an understanding that warfare has a unique and somewhat contradictory logic when confronting a fighting, thinking adversary who learns lessons. While each age in warfare has made its own distinctive contribution to the development of strategy, modern theorists have emphasized two important themes: the function of strategy in bringing rationale into an otherwise chaotic process; and its role in finding the elements of victory required by different operating conditions.

It is here that we rapidly part company from the world of business strategy. Why? Because, with the possible exception of what we observed about leadership, strategy has been studied absolutely to death and with less discernible effects than almost any other business subject. Simply consider the four following approaches to corporate strategy and see where your company fits in:

1. *Hiring a strategy consultant.* There are few if any accounting firms of any discernible size that do not have a strategy consulting

division established as a major part of their practice. There are also lots of stand-alone companies that make their living as strategy consultants, since strategy outsourcing is now a term that is much in vogue in the business world. Best of luck to the companies and people on both ends of that exchange because they are probably worthy folks who pay their taxes and love their children. But to my mind, it suggests nothing so much as that brilliant volume known as *Augustine's Laws*. Norman Augustine was the former head of Lockheed-Martin and a true defense intellectual as well. Augustine's Law 32 is "Hiring consultants to conduct studies can be an excellent means of turning problems into gold. Your problems into their gold."[1]

2. *"If it worked during the last Soviet 5-year plan, it can work here, too."* Some companies build strategies through the operation of a heavily embedded process. A great deal of "evolving" goes on, with an emphasis throughout on building consensus and bureaucratic buy-ins as the price of success. Strategy, such as it is, becomes the incidental by-product of this process, although there is some question whether the effort is worth the costs in time and trouble. (Simply tote up the meeting time in hours, multiply it times the hourly salary rate of everyone present, and come to your own conclusions.) But the real problem is that even if the resulting strategy was right to begin with, how do you change it in response to the inevitable fluctuations in the operating environment without repeating the entire long, painful process? Here again, one of Augustine's Laws provides a helpful perspective: "Law 26: if a sufficient number of management layers are superimposed on top of each other, it can be assured that disaster has not been left to chance."[2]

3. *The strategy du jour.* This approach is the polar opposite of Approach 2 because it assumes that strategy is nothing except a highly fungible and changeable commodity. It follows that strategy is the first thing to be changed whenever anything else changes too. What things, you ask? Oh, say, when a new CEO comes in or whenever anyone in authority has read the latest management fad in

the form of either a hot article in *Forbes* or picked up a trendy bit of management psychobabble. Two analysts from *Fortune* magazine cited the "strategy du jour" approach as one of the 10 deadliest mistakes of corporations—listing former Kmart CEO Chuck Conaway's abortive strategy of trying to beat Wal-Mart at its own game in the late 1990s as "one mistake too many."[3]

4. *Scheduling the corporate strategy session as a weekend retreat.* If you really don't care what your strategy is, then a weekend retreat with the CEO and other top corporate honchos at some pleasant resort or other is a fine way to do it, perhaps punctuated by an inspiring speech from a management guru. There is a variation on this model, and that is simply to schedule the corporate strategy session as the last agenda item before the annual golf game between the board of directors and the top officials of the corporation. One warning, however: Although often used, this approach has somewhat fallen out of favor due to the new Sarbanes-Oxley requirements. Seems as if someone believes corporate strategy is actually a pretty important document—or at least that it *should* be.

Think that's harsh? Or have I been a little too tough—because your company's approach to strategy easily meets the twin tests of relevance and flexibility? That it can be swiftly adapted to market changes while still providing an easily understood baseline everyone can promote, from the guy running the copier to the CEO's secretary? Maybe so, but the track record ain't all that great, even when we turn for guidance to the latest great books by the leading management gurus. Simply opening Jim Collins's book *Good to Great* to page 1 immediately brings one to the following statement:

> Good is the enemy of the great. And that is one of the reasons why we have so little that becomes great. We don't have great schools because we have good schools. We don't have great government because we have good government.[4]

More words inevitably follow, and as humorist Dave Barry might say: I am not making this up! But some 200 pages later, we come to the section dealing with "big, hairy, audacious goals," abbreviated BHAGs, which apparently can be either good or bad. Following the list of BHAGs are some frequently asked questions, one of which is *not,* Why would anyone believe this stuff for more than 5 seconds or waste much time on it? And yet anyone who has attended a strategy meeting recently will tell you that BHAG discussions go on all the time. But the fact that Collins's book has been on the bestseller lists for over a year should tell you all you need to understand about the superficiality and transience of the principal concepts governing strategy in the business world today.

STRATEGIC PLANNING: THE PROCESS

My criticism doesn't mean to suggest that there are not some perceptive thinkers in the world of business strategy. One of them, Tony Manning, writes that two of the problems with corporate strategy are either too much involvement by the employees or not nearly enough:

> . . . in real life the folks at the top might indeed think about the big issues. They might agree on "big, hairy, audacious goals" and they might produce terrific documents and slide shows and make stirring speeches, but then something goes wrong. Things change in the world around them. There's a surprise a minute and not all of them pleasant. Their people don't do what they are told. Their great plans produce mediocre results. Even if by some miracle they manage to do what they intended, it turns out to be wrong.[5]

Results may be so mixed much of the time because so many buzzwords surround—and often obscure—a process that is difficult in some ways, but actually rather simple. In either the military or the business environment, the basic elements are similar. A standard academic treatment suggests that the process consists of the following:

- Setting goals or objectives.
- Assessing and forecasting the external environment.
- Designing and assessing alternative courses of action including analyzing the potential risks and rewards.
- Selecting the best course of action.
- Evaluating the results as the course of action is implemented.

The result of this process hopefully yields a comprehensive plan linking "all of the organization's decisions and activities."[6]

Sounds simple enough, but a parallel strategic assessment—with five similar phases—rapidly becomes more complex:

1. *Strategic intelligence gathering and analysis:* An organization's executives assess the present and likely future trends in markets, competition, technology, regulations and economic conditions. They also examine certain internal variables: the organization's values, capabilities, product and market results and past strategic endeavors.

2. *Strategy formulation:* The top team examines alternative futures and then selects and creates the strategic profile or vision, addressing . . . nine key strategic questions . . .

3. *Strategic master project planning:* Based on the strategic vision, a significant number of projects emerge, often several hundred. These are the tasks that must be completed to ensure successful strategy implementation.

4. *Strategy implementation:* With a well-crafted plan in hand, implementation begins. Several elements affect its success . . . Most strategies flounder because implementation imperatives are poorly conceived and executed. There is a tendency for vision fatigue to set in.

5. *Strategy monitoring, reviewing and updating:* To ensure its continuing efficacy, strategy must be monitored regularly (including) . . . the review of both internal indicators . . . and external indicators that test the continuing validity of basic strategic assumptions.[7]

Like wading into a swamp at night, the departure into the realm of strategy may seem simple enough at first: but one step inexorably leads to the next, the path becomes less distinct, the water gets progressively deeper . . . and why were we doing this again? Small wonder that confining the entire business to the weekend BHAG pep rally at the resort strikes many as by far the best way to go.

Which is a shame because strategy is not only a vital construct but an essential tool in coping with the more volatile competitive environment that businesses find themselves in today. So it is equally important to be straight with ourselves about why we fail at it so conspicuously. I suggest four major reasons:

1. If it is real, then the strategy process is indeed highly complex: and you are usually compelled to engage in it in the company of amateurs—or at least people who have not made it their life's work. Bluntly stated, the strategic education of our executives is uneven at best. And rarely if ever is there agreement on a set of timeless strategic principles in which to ground fundamental assumptions.

2. Beginning with our usual caveat *if it is real,* then strategy equals choice. And precisely because it involves distinguishing winners from losers, and applying resources accordingly, those are hard choices to make. It means choosing one product line over another, one department to have the action and not another—and inevitably taking risks. And if the choices are not hard ones to make, then our caveat applies again with equal force.

3. Business intelligence is fundamental to the strategic planning process. That subject is so important to twenty-first-century business that Chapter 7 of this book is devoted entirely to it. Suffice for now to note in passing that business intelligence is weak, not because the capabilities of producing it do not exist, but because the nation's business leaders are not skilled in using it and are not even sure it is necessary. Not only do they fail to seek out the information, they do not deliberately work into their calculations the countermoves of an intelligent, determined adversary.

4. Today's crop of CEOs are congenitally focused on short-term results, usually expressed in the quarterly balance sheet. That "performance indicator" is itself tied to all sorts of financial expectations, influencing stock prices and, of course, CEO salaries. Even the executives of privately held companies seem tied to the same short-term outlook. While the CEO may say he is concerned about next year, he is more concerned about next quarter and what he has to do to "make his numbers." And unless I have forgotten my "basic definitions for military leaders," that ain't strategy, that's tactics!

STRATEGY: WHAT (SOME) CEOs ACTUALLY DO

Against this backdrop, a zero-based approach makes a lot of sense. Ignore the academics, the strategic consultants with a plan to sell or an axe to grind—and just focus for a moment on what some of the best CEOs actually do. What strategies do they follow and what difference does it make to their companies?

Jeffrey A. Krames, who knows both the practical side of business leadership as well as many CEOs, has written a highly informative book called, *What the Best CEOs Know*. Organized around the personal examples of seven top CEOs, one of the most compelling is Herb Kelleher, former chairman and founder of Southwest Airlines, and a well-known business maverick. Which is a nice way of saying he is an exception to the usual rules of business. Indeed he is, which not only makes him a notable success in an industry where so many others have failed, but also puts him close to the Hal Moore "band of brothers" style of leadership. One has the impression that the people of Southwest would follow him into combat, whereas most corporate employees would do so only if they thought there was a chance of fragging their CEO.

But that distinctive personal philosophy has allowed Herb Kelleher to define his corporate culture as being essential to the competitive niche of Southwest:

> The culture of Southwest is probably its major competitive advantage. The intangibles are more important than the tangibles because you can always imitate the tangibles. You can buy the airplane. You can rent the ticket counter space, but the hardest thing for someone to emulate is the spirit of your people.[8]

Herb goes on to talk esprit de corps, about the enthusiasm that the employees have for the company, about the responsibility of management to involve the people in making sure that everybody understands what is going on and giving them an equal stake in it.

At this point, you may be asking yourself, well what does that have to do with strategy? Well, nothing, unless you think strategy has something to do with coping with changes in your competitive environment. And in early 2000, Southwest faced a crisis that, because of a tripling in the cost of fuel, threatened the company's bottom line. Strategy consultants could have been called in and asked for their opinions—or possibly a corporate retreat could have been organized. Maybe there just wasn't time. Instead, Kelleher asked every one of the employees to find a way to save the company just five dollars a day because if successful, the company would save over 50 million dollars a year. Everybody jumped to answer that call. One group of mechanics found a way to heat the planes for less money. Another department volunteered janitorial services. In fact, in just the first six weeks, Southwest's dedicated employees had saved the company more than $2 million.[9] Kelleher understood something instinctively that so many others miss entirely: Corporate culture—what the organization actually does every day—defines strategy. More than any other factor, it defines the limits—and expands the possibilities—of any strategy.

Another cutting-edge CEO that Krames presents is Louis V. Gerstner Jr., who has also gained considerable notoriety for telling his own story in a best-selling book. Gerstner was named as the CEO of IBM just after his predecessor had drafted a plan to break the company up into the constituent parts that had come to dominate the corporation like so many feudal baronies. As Gerstner himself describes the situation he faced:

> There was a kind of hothouse quality to the place. It was like an isolated tropical ecosystem that had been cut off from the world for too long. As a result, it had spawned some fairly exotic life forms that were to be found nowhere else.[10]

The problem was that each of the baronies understood only its own piece of the IBM technology. But after traveling thousands of air miles and talking to IBM's customers around the world, Gerstner began to realize that what the company needed above all else was integrated business solutions instead of individual IBM technology pieces. In reversing direction, Gerstner inescapably determined IBM's strategy—and its existence:

> So we made the very early decision—the most important decision I'll ever make in my business career—to reverse that direction and keep IBM whole. The alternative (to break-up) was to keep IBM together and to make the

breadth of our products, services and skills, our most potent competitive advantage.[11]

Think about the alternative, and especially by what might have happened in a strategic process that was limited by bureaucratic buy-in and consensus. When he arrived at IBM, Gerstner found the inmates in charge of the asylum, and it was only through diligent, firsthand questioning—probing actually—that he began to grasp the big picture. The baronies—bureaucrats really—wanted their own agendas to the detriment or exclusion of IBM: Only the customers wanted integrated IBM solutions. Gerstner was smart enough to ignore the bureaucrats and to devise a strategy based on integrated corporate capabilities, with the result that IBM survived and prospers to this day.

Another CEO needs to be mentioned in the context of a great practitioner of strategy: Rudolph Giuliani, the former mayor of New York City. Although not a corporate executive in the strictest sense of the term, "Da Mayor" had already established, well before the events of 9/11, an enviable track record for leadership and reform of New York City. As someone who—on the West Point faculty and as an MSNBC employee—has often worked in close proximity to New York City, it has never been clear to me how the place functions at all, let alone in response to something approaching leadership. And no matter what the mayor does, it is always an article of faith that he is in some way to blame for everything that goes wrong, while the things that go right are ascribed to the indomitable spirit of New Yorkers. Giuliani had the temerity to think he could make a difference in one of the most intractable problems of the community: crime. Looking at the unbelievable totals of 9,000 to 10,000 felonies per week and 1,800 to 2,200 murders per year might well have driven even a determined public servant to despair. Instead, Giuliani reasoned, "I didn't want to tinker with the police department, I wanted to revolutionize it."[12]

Well, your Honor, commendable zeal: but how exactly to do that? The chapter heading of Giuliani's book recounting his reform campaign of the police department gives a clue: "Everyone's Accountable: All of the Time." The first step was to open themselves up to a wide-ranging effort that solicited ideas and suggestions about what was

needed in a reformed police department police force "with no precon-
ceptions." But the second step was to track crime statistics every day so
that the police could recognize criminal trends before the criminals
did.[13] Eventually the system was refined to the point that:

> . . . we set 4 parameters that Commissioners had to submit to me. Data had
> to be collected regularly and reliably, preferably on a daily basis, but at
> least once a week. Twenty to 40 performance indicators that got to the core
> missions of the agency had to be established. A regular meeting must be
> convened with a minimum frequency of once a week. Ten or more repre-
> sentative performance indicators that the agency wanted on its page on the
> city's web site had to be submitted.[14]

One does not have the impression that Giuliani believed very much
in outsourcing his strategy. What he did do was get the best ideas that
people had about what needed to be done, give them a stake in the solution, and then give specific measurements to expectations and perform-
ances. The results on that pathway to improvement: Major felonies
dropped dramatically as did the murder and robbery rates: ". . . the evidence was indisputable—New York City's crime reduction far surpassed
that of any other American city. And we not only brought down the crime
rate, we kept it down."[15]

The three examples cited here show the direct effects of strategy
based on three distinctly different approaches: corporate culture
(Kelleher and Southwest Airlines), the reassertion of core system capabilities (Gerstner and IBM), and crime reduction through statistical
monitoring (Giuliani and the New York City Police Department). But
each of those initiatives shared some commonalities:

1. They reflected a strategic response to changes in the operating
   environment, possibly threatening either the life of the company
   or the livelihood of those placed in charge.

2. There was every effort to gather exact operating information,
   but not consensus. The CEO was clearly in charge and seen to be
   so by all concerned.

3. No half-measures or idle slogans were used as a substitute for
   change or to conceal that nothing important had changed very

much. Instead, the signals throughout the organization were un-ambiguous and unmistakable.

In short: When the alternatives are "change or die," there are practi-cally no limits to the adoption of successful strategies.

A PERSPECTIVE OF MILITARY STRATEGY

At least part of the reason a military strategist may be forgiven for look-ing askance at civilian counterparts is just that we have had roughly 3,000 years of recorded history to work our way through some of the basic ideas about what works and what does not. Attend my Georgetown University class in the history of military technology and we will begin our work with the Greeks and the Romans. And the number of potential case studies is truly vast: from the Punic and Peloponnesian Wars, to the Thirty Years War, to the French and Indian Wars, to the War of Jenkins Ear. In the nineteenth century, things get really interesting with the Napoleonic Wars; the American Civil War; the French again, but this time against the Prussians; the Indians again, but this time against the U.S. cavalry. And all of that is in just the *first semester!*

The bottom line is that humankind has been having wars for a very long time, so we have learned many things about strategy and how to em-ploy it. Begin with the word itself: Strategy comes from the Greek word *strategos,* meaning "general." Strategy is quite literally the thing that gen-erals do—and if the Greeks had a word for outsourcing, we haven't dis-covered it yet. But probably the major thing that differentiates military strategy from the strategy they teach in business schools (really a glori-fied form of marketing) is that in our war colleges *strategy is a system of be-liefs.* And in illustrating just how fundamental that system is, especially when the coin of the realm is measured in blood and treasure, it is prob-ably appropriate to do so with reference to Iraq.

One does so with some hesitation, if for no other reason than that the real test of strategy—possibly in business but definitely in war—is not what happens in the initial engagements but rather in how one an-ticipates and accommodates the long-term changes resulting from one's actions. As noted in Chapter 3, the American intervention in Iraq is an ongoing saga, with many questions still outstanding about the original justification for the war as well as the accuracy of estimates by U.S. policy-makers for what would be required to win the peace. And a purist might well object that the initial military tasks facing U.S. forces as they assaulted Baghdad were not so much matters of strategy as "grand tactics"—and that the real test of strategy was how the Iraqis would use other means to confront the overwhelming technological superiority of the U.S. military. No matter, it is sufficient for our purposes here to point out that any strategy invites countermeasures, that the enemy always gets a vote in the outcome of any endeavor, and, consequently, that box scores in either business or war should always be written in pencil.

But for our purposes here, it is also important to note that the basic strategic process is not unlike the five-step solution outlined at the beginning of this chapter, but with considerably more sophisticated intelligence resources forming the basis of the analysis. Thereafter, any resemblance ends. Because the heart of that analysis, even before the delineation of potential courses of action, is a careful consideration of *centers of gravity*. This is a term of art used to focus attention on the specific factors sustaining the opponent in power and, inferentially, what needs to be done to remove those supports. As in bridge demolition, it is often unnecessary to explode the entire structure: It is usually enough to identify the main supporting beams or load-bearing structures—and especially in an age of precision munitions—simply to target them. In the case of Iraq, the principal center of gravity yielded by this analysis appeared not to be Baghdad or any of the other cities of Saddam's domain, but rather the Republican Guard formations that were the key to his entire politico-military structure. If he used them to defend his cities, fine. But wherever he deployed them: Seek them out and destroy them.

This was the latest application of an old lesson, well understood since the Napoleonic Wars: The destruction of the enemy's armed forces is paramount. But the analysis this time was sophisticated enough to include another traditional factor of war—time—that now had acquired a new significance. It was, in fact, the key to two other threats:

1. U.S. troops were at least potential targets for Iraqi weapons of mass destruction whose existence at that time could be neither proved nor discounted.

2. The biggest conventional threat available to the Iraqis was the preparation of urban defenses. If competently planned and executed, they at least offered the potential of turning Baghdad into a Mesopotamian Stalingrad. That possibility in turn suggested a hardened target that would take time to reduce, produce lots of casualties on both sides, and open the window to some form of international mediation.

If time was the major constraint affecting Iraq's ability to target their potential weapons of mass destruction and turn Baghdad into a fortress, then speed was the answer.

Notice that just this part of the planning process had already defined some key variables of the American strategy: the direction of attack, its intended objectives, and the fact that speed had to be a dominant characteristic. This did not mean that there was not still plenty of time for debate, especially about proper courses of action to marry the basic strategy with operational planning.

But whatever the internal disagreements on method, one of the great strengths of the American military establishment is its consensus on strategy as a problem-solving process. For well over half of their careers, our commanders have been extensively trained not only to analyze how to achieve a military objective, but to be innovative and creative in applying the tools of a uniquely American way of war. Those different styles of warfare are what Colin Powell, when he was our top general, used to refer to as his tool kit. And what they are, are a series of ideas about the application of land power, sea power, and air power.

As discussed in Chapter 3, these strategic paradigms have traditionally been the underpinnings of our military services. But today, they provide a matrix of complementary and interlocking capabilities that becomes the first test of any potential military strategy: How do I put together those forces that are best suited toward this objective? With Iraq, these questions were far from theoretical, not only because we would have fewer forces this time than in Desert Storm, but because we had literally bet the ranch on the idea that joint teamwork had been improved to the point that it gave us a competitive edge.

So now the question became, how to ensure those forces would support each other, developing the synergy needed for a decisive combination of speed and combat power? The answer was the combination of Army and Marine ground units chosen to make the daring, high-speed dash to Baghdad, supported at every step by Air Force and Navy tactical air support. On Grenada, these forces had barely been introduced: Now they would fight like brothers.

As shown also in Chapter 3, one of the largest obstacles toward that kind of partnership had been the persistent lack of interoperability between the armed services, which had only grudgingly given way to new concepts of fighting based on information superiority. Now the task of the strategist became, how to distribute that information smoothly and seamlessly throughout the force? The question was not an idle one because Iraq was a highly changeable place, and plans would have to be adapted on the fly. In our war colleges, we had long discussed what the Germans had called *auftragstaktik,* or mission-type orders, usually concluding it was easy for us to talk about but very tough to do. We now had better tools to distribute information: Iraq would be the acid test of whether our strategy had caught up to those capabilities.

Did we succeed? General Tommy Franks expected his subordinate commanders to be flexible. This is the testimony of Major General Buford Blount, commander of the Third Infantry Division that led the attack on Baghdad:

> The ability of our Army to digitally communicate without the constraint of terrain and to track our forces at near-real-time is an awesome ability . . . (The technology provided a current, accurate common operational picture allowing me to command and control the Division across multiple battlefields.) At one point we had three different brigade fights going on simultaneously over a two hundred kilometer area and I was able to control and synchronize them while on the move. This is an incredible capability.[16]

Another of those commanders is Major General Dave Petraeus, commander of the legendary 101st Airborne Division. In an interview from the theater, he reiterated that, throughout the campaign, they always knew what the general wanted them to do. And the combination of understanding the commander's intent and being armed with situational awareness led to an enormously flexible planning procedure. Petraeus describes much of his "planning process" as consisting of hurried conferences with his subordinate commanders over the hood of a Humvee. Nothing new there, of course, because we have watched actor Dale Dye do exactly the same thing while playing a Word War II regimental commander in the 101st in *Band of Brothers*.

What *was* different this time was that Petraeus and his comrades had a detailed understanding of where their own forces were, where the enemy was in relation to them, what the enemy was up to, and what forces were in the best position to attack him. Armed with that information, there was a level of adaptability and immediate planning flexibility that had never been present before. Ultimately, that was what made the difference. As well as not relying on the technology too much, seeing things for themselves, and always leading from the front even when that meant setting an example of indifference to enemy fire. Petraeus recalls telling his men not to shoot an enemy mortar crew that was persistently but unsuccessfully targeting his command group. "For god's sake leave that guy alone. Kill him and they may find somebody who actually knows how to aim that thing."[17]

Amateurs versus Pros: Two Different Strategic Cultures

So how best to summarize what the civilians in the business of strategy can learn from their military counterparts? In a single word: everything. Here are some of the major points that make the military-strategic culture such a powerful tool in dealing with the most competitive environment of all:

1. A common strategic culture provides a core of common beliefs to a force with a strong history of service separatism. As pointed out in Chapter 3, this has not been an easy effort. At a joint services school I attended in the early 1980s, considerable attention was given to the production of a new staff manual that would help its army, navy, air force, and marine students to understand one another better. An unfortunate typo, however, somewhat

compromised this goal, because the stated purpose, "to work together for the common good," came out "work together for the
common *goo*." It was corrected, but only over the objections of
those who argued that the original version was more honest. (I
admit to being one of the ringleaders.) No matter. Out of the
primeval ooze of the common goo, something new and powerful
emerged.

2. The only thing better than having a common strategic culture is
    having a common awareness of that culture. Reinforced by a com-
    prehensive system of military education, the strategic process—
    with all of its embedded disciplines, methods, and objectives—is
    a common reference point for present and future commanders as
    well as the staffs who serve them. No outsourcing, no weekend re-
    treats, no BHAGs, and no BS. Just a solid methodology that gets
    the job done.

3. As a result of patiently working our way through the common
    goo, we have a highly flexible and adaptive war-fighting strategy
    when it comes to mixing and matching our forces—including get-
    ting the most out of limited numbers. Not only was this concept
    helpful in achieving the synergy required by our air and ground
    forces, but it also aided in a smooth transition when the enemy
    reacted to our victory by going over to a guerrilla offensive in the
    weeks after Baghdad fell. When you draw on a body of strategic
    beliefs that actually contemplates enemy countermoves, those ad-
    justments come as less of a shock. The enemy, you see, gets a vote:
    What a concept! The successor to General Tommy Franks, Gen-
    eral John Abizaid, was quick to recognize that challenge for what
    it was—and to insist his commanders adjust their tactics accord-
    ingly. Seems they had all been to the same schools and under-
    stood another basic principle of what is taught there: No military
    victory is ever permanent.

4. Finally, the linkage between a common strategic culture is all the
    more powerful when reinforced by an information regime that pro-
    vides situational awareness from top to bottom of the organization.
    Simply put, enormous flexibility results when the commander has

only to make his objectives and his intent clear. The effect of information in the lowest hands, as well as the highest, means its prompt operational exploitation—whether in a drive for Baghdad or beating a competitor into the marketplace. Which is ultimately a much more satisfying thing than all the PowerPoint presentations in the world.

A distinguished economist named Charles Kindleberger died in July 2003 at the age of 92. Most of us remember Kindleberger because we read his books and remember his clarity in providing us with some basic truths about economics. But one of the more perceptive comments made about his passing was provided by another economist, Robert J. Samuelson:

> History matters. Somehow this common sense has by passed much of modern economics, especially in the universities. The preoccupation with elegant models and mathematical proofs is intellectually narrowing because it excludes almost anything that cannot be reduced to an equation or data set. . . . Some giant economic changes defy equations because they are also political, psychological and cultural. Kindleberger knew that and when today's trendy theorems are forgotten, people will still read (him) for pleasure and profit.[18]

What Kindleberger actually wrote about is strategy at the grand level. It is indeed historical as well as political, psychological, and cultural and it has to be nonquantitative as well as quantitative or else it is nothing. The task of the strategist is not to be surprised by the things that should have been expected. In military strategy, we understand that you are less likely to be surprised when your opponent is a professional, because it's always the amateurs who will get you into trouble. Especially when you read their books or hire them as consultants.

WAR PLAN

MISSION OBJECTIVES

Strategy is not only a vital construct but an essential tool in coping with the more volatile competitive environment that businesses find themselves in today.

★ The strategy process is indeed highly complex, and you are usually compelled to engage in it in the company of amateurs, or at least people who have not made it their life's work. Bluntly stated, the strategic education of our executives is uneven at best.

★ Strategy equals choice: It involves distinguishing winners from losers and applying resources accordingly, and those are hard choices to make. It means choosing one product line over another, one department to have the action and not another, and inevitably taking risks.

★ Business intelligence is fundamental to the strategic planning process. But business intelligence is simply not up to the challenge—not because the capabilities of producing it do not exist, but because the nation's business leaders are not skilled in using it and are not even especially sure it is necessary.

★ Today's crop of CEOs are focused on short-term results, usually expressed in the quarterly balance sheet. That performance indicator is tied to all sorts of financial expectations, influencing stock prices—and CEO salaries. And that ain't strategy, that's tactics!

★ Southwest Airlines' CEO Herb Kelleher understands instinctively what so many others miss entirely: Corporate culture (what the organization actually does every day) defines strategy. More than any other factor, it defines the limits and expands the possibilities of any strategy.

★   One of the great strengths of the American military estab-
    lishment is its consensus on strategy as a problem-solving
    process. Our commanders have been extensively trained
    not only to analyze *how to achieve* a military objective,
    but to *be innovative and creative* in applying the tools of a
    uniquely American way of war.

★   How best to summarize what the civilians in the business
    of strategy can learn from their military counterparts? In a
    single word: *everything*.

★   The only thing better than having a *common* strategic cul-
    ture is having a common *awareness* of that culture. Rein-
    forced by a comprehensive system of military education,
    the strategic process is a common reference point for pres-
    ent and future commanders and their staffs. No outsourc-
    ing, no weekend retreats, no BHAGs, and no BS. Just a
    solid methodology that gets the job done.

6

☆ ☆ Organizing for Victory ☆ ☆

While Shooting as Few Bureaucrats as Possible

T his chapter is about organization, specifically the structural means by which we link leadership, strategy (assuming there is one) and hopefully values. More specifically—the means by which the CEO can figure out what *structure* can do to ease his burdens in actually running things. My standing to address these issues stems from two things: personal involvement in 1986 with a reorganization that reformed the Pentagon command structure; and some responsibility for directing the effort in 1993 that led to the "reinventing government" initiatives that eventually rewrote the entire federal procurement code. The bottom line from these adventures: It is always better to be the reorgani**zer** than the reorgani**zee.**

The latter task was a very significant effort that you may remember because, at the end, President Clinton and Vice President Gore were photographed smashing $200 ashtrays and stacking up front-end loaders with piles of laws and regulations. The procurement reform effort was a real learning experience involving a systematic examination of *the 800 laws* that affected defense procurement. Apparently, Congress had become convinced that DOD officials could barely get out of bed in the mornings without some sort of legislative guidance—which Congress was only too happy to provide by the bagful. Along the way, of course, these laws inevitably added costs, diminished competitiveness, and generally built in all the other knob-dickering tricks that come with federal handouts.

My favorite example of the problem was a case we unearthed during our investigations that had happened during the Gulf War (Desert Storm). Just before the onset of hostilities, it seems the Air Force had an emergency requirement for some 6,000 commercial radio receivers and was willing to waive all military requirements and specifications. Despite the urgency of preparations for war—and because of the likelihood of second-guessing once the urgency had faded—no responsible procurement official could be found who could waive the legal requirement for the company to certify that the government was being offered the lowest available price.

This was the problem: Because the radio was marketed all around the world, there was simply no way to tell if Sam's Direct to You Discount Warehouse in Singapore had it on special that week. Oh . . . and any misstatement, no matter how patriotically well-intended, might constitute a felony. The impasse was complete—until an anonymous Air Force officer with more than a touch of genius found the way out. The Japanese government was persuaded to buy the radios without any price certification, to donate them to the U.S. Air Force—and then to write off the entire cost of the transaction against Japan's financial contribution to Desert Storm.[1] Moral of the story: When your allies have to rescue you from your own self-imposed procurement nightmares, it's probably time to make a change.

Clinton actually introduced that Air Force officer when sending the reform package up to Congress. It was gratifying to play even a small role in such a long overdue change. But in giving speeches about those changes later on, and probably overstating their significance, someone would invariably point out that: (1) We had certainly done an adequate job of changing all those inconvenient old laws but that (2) we had failed to shoot enough of the bureaucrats charged with enforcing them, and that (3) any organizational reforms that changed the law but left the bureaucrats alive was at best incomplete. After awhile, I reluctantly had to concede that they had a point.

A slightly more serious point about organization came about during the 1986 Pentagon reorganization hearings, when Congressman Bill Nichols put the matter in its appropriate context:

> [W]hile we pray for peace, we can never forget that organization, no less than a bayonet or air craft carrier, is a weapon of war. We owe it to our soldiers, our sailors, our airmen, and our marines to ensure that this weapon is lean enough, flexible enough, and tough enough to help them win if God forbid that ever becomes necessary.[2]

In 1986, there was some reason for the Congress to be concerned that winning in combat might become necessary and before it did, that the organizational spear needed to be sharpened. The failure of the Iranian hostage rescue raid in 1980 had been followed in 1983 by the bombing of the U.S. Marine barracks in Lebanon as well as, days later, the invasion of Grenada. All three events had revealed serious underlying organizational flaws whenever the armed forces of the United States were required to work together in combat. So in late 1986, Congress passed the law that became known as the Goldwater Nichols Act. The new law reformed the Pentagon command structure and mandated as its objective the joint integration of American combat power: Army, Navy, Air Force, and Marines. While most Americans had no idea that the legislation had even been passed let alone what it said, four years later, we took that new organizational system to war in Desert Storm.[3]

None of us who worked on that legislation in 1986 had any idea that that the new Pentagon command structure that had been put in place would be put to the ultimate test of combat just four years later.

While technology received most of the publicity, equally important was the organization for victory that set the terms and conditions for success. Well-informed "outside" leadership had been critical on two occasions, beginning with Congress acting as a kind of board of directors with the 1986 legislation. Defense Secretary Donald Rumsfeld, in the role of new "COO," demanded in 2002 to 2003 that the armed forces fight differently in prosecuting a new and different style warfare. Those two examples, the civilian intervention by legislation in 1986 and renewed executive leadership in 2003, should not be lost on today's business leaders be they department managers, CEOs, or members of the board of directors. As anyone in business knows only too well, today's corporations face a wholly different competitive environment than ever before; more chaotic, more difficult to predict, and infinitely more demanding. With globalization has come the necessity to enter new and utterly unfamiliar markets with potentially rich rewards, but also different pitfalls and uncertainties for the unwary. The familiar outline of corporate America with its reliance on hierarchical forms and established ways of doing business confronts its own hurdles in dealing with thoroughly networked international competitors who are only too anxious to engage us with the advantages of lower labor costs and reduced time to market.

It is against this daunting backdrop that corporate ethical meltdowns and the attendant questions about governance and leadership are so troubling. Every time I hear that stock analysts are being prosecuted for defrauding investors, every time I see another chief financial officer taking a "perp" walk, it is hard to suppress the urge to reach out and grab the nearest CEO or board member—and introduce him to Drill Sergeant Davis for some remedial training. Once we had the undivided attention of this corporate giant, it might then be possible to point out that in 1986 the Congress also thought that they had lots of time to straighten things out: *But it was later than they thought.* And that Donald Rumsfeld spent his first eight months in office arguing that maybe Pentagon procedures were not quite up to twenty-first century challenges: *But on September 11, 2001, those challenges came home in a way more painful, more personal than any Cassandra could have dared to imagine.* So, too, for corporate America, which needs to understand that the trendiest measures of corporate effectiveness may not be as valuable as once thought. And that, no less than their military counterparts of a decade earlier, business needs to organize for victory in a slightly different way.

Here again, some candor is in order: My acquaintance with the critical question of organization did not really begin with those stints on Capitol Hill. It really began back in basic training when I began to realize some of the challenges involved in something as simple as organization and as fundamental as the movement of troops at the lowest level. When we weren't being harassed by Drill Sergeant Davis, we were being drilled by his boss, the Field First who was the senior enlisted man in our training company. The Field First was a wiry, thoroughly squared-away Sergeant First Class, named Soto de Morales, who was deeply and profoundly Hispanic, and whose thick accent occasionally led to problems.

There are two critical commands in moving troops, beginning with "forward march," which in our opening days had required additional instruction to be given to the coal miners but by now had essentially been mastered. The second was the command "port arms," in which you smartly brought your rifle parallel to your chest—but did not otherwise move. The problem was that these two commands, as they came off Sergeant Morales' tongue with his Spanish-English accent were linguistically identical. Every time he gave a command, half the company would go to port arms while the other half stepped off and ran smack into them. This was an invitation to anarchy. Sergeant Morales would curse us in Spanish, then in English and then switch back again to Spanish to make sure that he had left nothing out. To make sure our morale wouldn't suffer, he then had us drop for push-ups—a command that he pronounced flawlessly.

PROBLEMS OF ORGANIZATION: MILITARY AND CIVILIAN

It was surely thus all the way back to the Greeks and Romans, whose experiments with the phalanx and the maniple were some of our first attempts to cope with the problem of numbers. The problem is this: How do you add numbers—more spears in the line or archers on the flanks—without sacrificing coherence? Stalin wondered that too when he reportedly said that God was on the side of the bigger battalions. (Actually, this was one of his brighter observations. He also once asked how many divisions the Pope had. As we now know, the answer was: a helluva lot, most of them Polish.) But if you add those battalions, how do you still ensure that your orders are going to be carried out? You need no more military experience than the average parlor game—and no more command experience than the average father passing messages from the eldest to youngest offspring—to understand the operation of Murphy's Law. But unlike matters of strategy and values, there is no definite military advantage here: The fact is that we struggle just as much as our civilian counterparts with the question of organization and fighting bureaucracy. And they really don't let us shoot the bureaucrats, except in the most extreme circumstances.

The seven basic organizational issues every institution faces include:

1. *The numbers/coherence conundrum:* Stalin's "big battalions" conundrum has a direct application to today's business environment in today's corporate terms. As you add new corporate subdivisions, what happens? Every time you add new capabilities, you magnify the problem of commanding and controlling them; in fact, some would say the difficulty is squared. How does the CEO ensure that strategies, policies, corporate communications, and, oh by the way, revenue objectives smoothly transfer into the new organizational lash-up? Especially since he is legally responsible for that continuity? However, numbers are rarely the sole problem.

2. *Unity of command:* This is a variation of the same problem but it actually gets worse when you add diversity: not just additional numbers but different kinds of troops. The military faced this issue whenever we added combinations of arms, classically artillery and cavalry, but in more recent years, naval and air units. All of these represent great additions to our combat capability, but they magnify the problem of command and control because you instantly get into the problem of different organizational cultures in each military service—even though they are on the same side and wear their country's uniform. The parallel in business is what happens as the result of takeovers, buyouts, and other forms of corporate reorganizations: not only are there more units to control, but they may have radically different cultures, expectations, and ways of doing business. The effect on leadership cues and organizational preferences is illustrated in Figure 6.1 showing the difficulty of achieving unity of command across different service cultures. The figure assumes four officers of equal flag rank. But our notional Navy vice admiral on the left side of the chart has between 10 and 100 *movable subordinate entities,* that is, things he has to move around, reflecting the normal assignment of two aircraft carriers to his battle group. The admiral typically has great certainty about their locations, excellent communications with them, and, best of

all, great confidence in his subordinates, usually lieutenant commanders or higher. But now jump over to our army corps commander on the right side of the chart—still a three star—but with two or more *divisions* attached. His command and control problem is an order of magnitude higher, reflecting numbers in the 10,000 to 100,000 range. He typically has lousy field communications, and the subordinate who must get those messages is ultimately a sergeant. Now notice the difference in the organizational and leadership philosophies: *The Navy will typically centralize downward to the level of the ship's quarterdeck, while the Army has no choice but to decentralize everything down to the level of the foxhole.* The teaching point for business: *One size does not fit all.* Different structures demand different leadership styles and organizational solutions.

3. *Centralization versus decentralization:* If there is a weakness to Figure 6.1, it is its implication that these two organizational

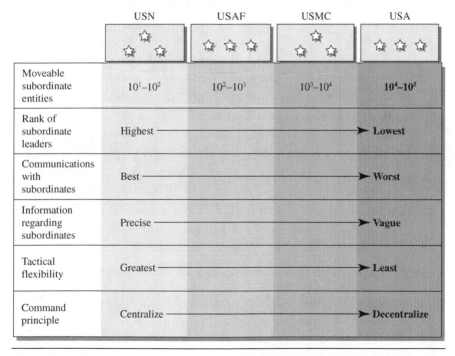

Figure 6.1 Centralized versus decentralized. *Source:* Kenneth Allard, *Command, Control and the Common Defense* (Rev. ed.), Washington, DC: National Defense University Press, 1995, p. 159.

philosophies are poles apart. In fact, there is always a delicate balance to be struck between the uniformity requiring centralized control and the basic autonomy needed for the subordinate units to do their jobs—especially when doing those jobs also requires them to display considerable flexibility and initiative. There is no right or wrong answer on the question of centralization versus decentralization. It is very much in the eye of the beholder—or more properly the CEO or commander, who gets paid to adjust the balance. He or she cannot be too centralized because of the tendency to destroy all independent thought and the ability to be flexible. But neither is decentralization a standard solution because any organization relies on a degree of uniformity. And if you sacrifice that, you sacrifice coherence.

4. *Trusting whoever you left in charge:* We used to call our regionally based combatant commanders CINCs—for commander-in-chief. No more, because in 2003, Donald Rumsfeld decided that this term was solely appropriate for the President, not the generals or admirals, regardless of their mightiness, or how good they might one day look mounted on an equestrian statue. Regardless of whether he is called CINC or a regional manager, there is no more basic organizational problem than aligning responsibility and authority and no more basic temptation than usurping that authority by second guessing the on-scene commander. Usually this is done for what are thought to be good and sufficient reasons or because the technology will allow it. But the temptation to override the guy on the ground, the man on the scene, or the guy you left in charge, is a universal flaw that has only become worse with technology. From Robert MacNamara giving rudder orders to ship commanders during the Cuban Missile Crisis to Bill Clinton approving cruise missile targets, it is a constant fight for military commanders to overcome the tendency of Washington "decision makers" to engage in the practice that is called "skip-echeloning" in which whole sections of the chain of command are bypassed. Some circumstances in either business or war may of course demand it but on either side, trust is a quality that can only be broken once.

5. *Accountability:* Usually expressed as orders given to a general or revenue expectations given to a CEO, and in both instances ambiguity about accountability is to be avoided. At Gettysburg, one of Lee's famous mistakes came on the first day when he ordered General Richard Ewell to take the key Union position on Cemetery Ridge "if practicable." The ever-cautious Ewell decided it was not—and the Union position eventually became the rock against which Pickett's Charge broke itself in vain. The transmission of orders in the American military was gradually streamlined to the point that the directive General Eisenhower received prior to the Normandy Invasion was a model of clarity: "You will enter the continent of Europe and in conjunction with the other United Nations, undertake operations aimed at the heart of Germany and the destruction of her armed forces."[4] That was as clear, simple, direct, and effective as an order could be, leaving no grounds whatever for ambiguity, but considerable room for flexibility. Eisenhower was told what to do; he was not told how to do it. Those same standards are the measures of effectiveness by which orders ought to be judged both in their reception and their execution whether in the form of directives, expectations, strategic plans or measures of effectiveness.

6. *Structure:* From strategy to basic values, the structure of an organization reflects what the unit actually does every day as opposed to what it says it is doing. The real test of leadership is not what the leader says, it is what followers actually do. There is a great deal of military history backing up the idea that if that gap gets too wide, the unit is riding for a fall. This is the reason why we say that organization is the structural component linking the idea of strategy to the most basic values of what the organization is all about. It is also the system by which we distribute the authority of either the commander or the CEO. That means a chain of command linking authority and responsibility at all layers of the organization, from top to bottom. It includes the span of control appropriate to the missions of everyone involved. And finally, the structure reflects the values of the organization, because if the values aren't an intrinsic part of what

the organization actually does—then they aren't values at all, only public relations.

7. *Napoleon's telescope:* Reflect for a moment on everything we have just said about organization: about the careful balances that have to be struck and about ensuring that in the end the structure for distributing authority is sound. This is a tall order for either the general or the CEO. But there is one technique the military has followed over the years as a kind of double-check for the commander, a means of giving him an independent set of eyes and ears while not interfering with his command arrangements. This the concept of Napoleon's telescope and, as the name implies, it is not a new idea in military command and control. In a book by that title some years ago, one of our military historians pointed out how the great commanders have always had a specific group of people responsible to them alone. In this way, the commander's attention—his telescope—could focus on that critical point where his direct intervention was critical. It could be a disputed point where the lines were at risk or a certain critical point in the flow of the battle. Whatever it was, the commander had to use his telescope wisely, not only with a fair amount of operational art but with some judgment and even a fair amount of subtlety. Otherwise, a Napoleon ran the risk of subverting his own chain of command and inadvertently upsetting some of the careful balances outlined earlier. Determining that critical time and place was the work of these trusted agents of a Napoleon, the General-in-Chief or the CINC—and the means chosen were whatever the technology would allow. But the most critical qualities were personal: Basically, these officers were men who possessed great reserves of insight, initiative, and, most of all, tact. That precedent is probably something that deserves to be studied and applied to the CEO's repertoire today. What better way to figure out where and how to intervene at a moment critical to the organization's success than by having one's own set of eyes throughout the organization? And doing so in a way that preserves the chain of command as well as the CEO's ultimate responsibility for all that goes on?[5]

Organizational Perspectives in Business and War

These issues and guidelines may immediately provoke certain skeptical questions, say from business school faculties, strategic consultants, or others criticized in these pages: On what basis has the military gathered these profound insights into organizational matters? The short answer is that the military came of age at a time when, for most societies, it was the biggest organizational entity in sight. As warfare became more mechanized, it also became more highly organized. And you won't get very far in either military history or organizational improvements before coming to the Prussians, who had a talent for such things—just ask the French. With its beginnings in the more precise logistical support needed by mass armies with significant quantities of gunpowder weapons, the organizational abilities of the Prussian General Staff made their highly disciplined armies into a model of military efficiency. In the aftermath of the Napoleonic Wars, the Prussian General Staff system was institutionalized into what one historian aptly called "a genius for war." Its characteristics: an organized method for incorporating wartime lessons into peacetime plans and preparations; thoroughly training future leaders in the preparation of war plans; and finally, testing out those plans in war games that translated concepts into execution.[6]

It is also not coincidental that one of our greatest students of bureaucracy was the nineteenth-century German sociologist Max Weber because in looking at the General Staff, Max Weber saw a model for society. Because the bureaucracy of the late nineteenth-century industrial revolution was the most thoroughly organized and rational way of doing business, Weber proposed a model that suggests nothing so much as a human form of the computer. In true cybernetic fashion, a rational division of labor allowed every task to be organized into subroutines that could be assigned and carried out in ways that were impersonal but highly rational. What is interesting in Weber's universe, was that the rational division of labor and responsibility was the core, not charismatic leadership, but the tightly regulated clockwork of the bureaucratic hierarchical model.[7]

Which is a nice way of doing business, and one that certainly finds its share of adherents even today. When combined with technology, the influence of that model can be like a siren song. So it was in World War I, which in its application of both organizational technique and the technology of destruction, was all that could have been wished. In its aftermath, one of the prophets of the new style of armored warfare was a British Army Major General by the name of J. F. C. Fuller. Fuller's masterpiece, still required reading in our war colleges, is a wonderful book called *Generalship: Its Diseases and Their Cure*. His thesis was that the advent of what he called the hoard army had "... paralyzed Generalship, not so much because it changed tactics, but because it prevented tactics from changing. The one idea being not to improve the quality of fighting, but to add to the quantity of fighters."[8] In short: the traditional tyranny of numbers problem had surfaced yet again.

But in addition to numbers, he was deeply concerned about a new technology that had also paralyzed generalship: the field telephone, which for the first time in World War I, allowed electronic communications to affect the battlefield. Since the Civil War, the telegraph had linked headquarters to their national capital but now the telephone allowed voice control between the most advanced fighting elements and their headquarters. Fuller's opinion?

> In the World War nothing was more dreadful to witness than a chain of men starting with a battalion commander and ending with an army commander sitting in telephone boxes improvised or actual talking, talking, talking in place of leading, leading, leading.[9]

But Fuller's most poignant warning about bureaucratic layering, field telephones, and their effect on leadership comes with words that 75 years later, still leap off the page:

> How do these things affect the personal factor in Generalship? They obliterate it and why? The staff becomes an all-controlling bureaucracy, a paper octopus squirting ink and wriggling its tentacles into every corner. Unless pruned with an ax, it will grow like a Fakir's mango tree. And the more it grows, the more it overshadows the General. It creates work. It creates offices. And above all, it creates the rear spirit. No sooner is war declared than the General in Chief finds himself a Gulliver in Lilliput tied down to his office stool by innumerable threads worn out of the brains of his staff ...[10]

The problem of asserting leadership in the face of entrenched hierarchies in which technology simply seems to reinforce the trenches has more recently attracted the attention of Rudolph Giuliani. As noted earlier, in addressing the issue of police department reform, Giuliani clearly was no novice in his understanding of hierarchies. There is simply no other way to run New York City other than to confront the problem of mass numbers as an army does: with one guy in charge supervising guys who have other guys reporting to them. But it is curious that the mayor seemed to have an instinctive feel for the effectiveness of Napoleon's telescope:

> I certainly relied upon the hierarchy in which the deputy commissioner answered to the commissioner who answered to the deputy mayor who answered to the mayor. You've got to impose a structure to bring together what could easily become chaos. I believe in having both a highly organized system and in subverting it whenever the right idea or situation presents itself. Occasionally one of my deputy mayors would get annoyed if someone (under them) came directly to me. I'd always tell them that anyone, especially someone at the commissioner or deputy commissioner level, should be able to tell me what they're thinking.[11]

The mayor is on that interesting middle ground between coherence and the ability of the commander to intervene at the critical spot. But he is exactly correct in understanding the need of a commander, a CEO, or a mayor to bring his insight to bear in the form of direct intervention when it is absolutely critical. And to be able to do that without subverting the chain of command or compromising your own leadership standards.

Another modern practitioner with worthwhile insights into these organizational questions is Bill George, former CEO of a company called Medtronic. In his new book, George defends his controversial but common sense view that the problems with our businesses result from a failure to focus on the idea of mission. Instead, the interests of the shareholders, boards of directors, and CEOs have been inflated to out-weigh those of the employees and the customers. He specifically asks the following provocative question:

If we select people principally for their charisma and their ability to drive up the stock prices in the short term instead of their character and we shower them with inordinate rewards, why should we be surprised when they turn out to lack integrity.[12]

Why indeed? But if you were wondering about the real effect of all that stuff about missions and values, George is also unequivocal:

Contrary to what the advocates of maximizing short-term shareholder value would have us believe, the best kept secret in business is that mission driven companies create far more shareholder value than do financially driven firms.[13]

It is interesting that these stirring statements about the importance of structure and mission would come from two such highly regarded leaders as Giuliani and George: but there are two others with some important insights into organization that are appropriate to mention here. Not surprisingly, both are included in the portraits provided by Jeffrey Krames in his excellent book, *What The Best CEOs Know.*

Andy Grove of Intel has an approach to organization that can be characterized as a sort of institutionalized paranoia. In fact, paranoia is pretty much what the prevailing organizational dynamic seems to be all about. Groves talks a lot about what he calls strategic inflection points, which sounds like pure strategy-book jargon—but apparently serves a useful purpose at Intel. Basically, they seem to believe that what doesn't kill you makes you stronger.

Strategic infliction points offer promises as well as threats. It is at such times of fundamental change that the cliché adapt or die takes on its true meaning.[14]

And apparently at Intel, fear-induced adaptation is what their corporate culture is all about. They listen to alarmists. They make every effort to encourage rigorous discussion, debating, examining, and being skeptical about the data. So it is a culture of extreme strategic alertness in which everything is geared toward preparing the organization for continuous and dramatic changes. In Intel's business, such is the price of success.[15]

If you paid the slightest attention to my points on leadership, it will come as no surprise that our final good example of a strong organization comes from Herb Kelleher, the former CEO of Southwest. Not only is he a favorite of Jeffrey Krames and myself, but he is routinely cited for breakthrough insights that damned well ought to be common sense:

> If you create an environment where the people truly participate, you don't need control. They know what needs to be done and they do it. And the more that people will devote themselves to your cause on a voluntary basis, a willing basis, the fewer hierarchies and control mechanisms you need.[16]

What makes me want to stand up and cheer when I read these words are two thoughts: Here is a CEO who truly gets it; and Max Weber must be rolling around in his grave! And just about the time you think that you will be publicly and violently ill if you hear one more vice president of human resources talk about "empowerment," the genuine article really is a breath of fresh air:

> We've tried to create an environment at Southwest where people are able to in effect bypass even fairly lean structures we have so that *they don't have to convene a meeting of the sages in order to get something done* [emphasis added]. In many cases they can just go ahead and do it on their own. Our leanness requires people to be comfortable in making their own decisions and undertaking their own efforts ... The bigger you get, the harder you must continuously fight back the bureaucracy and preserve the entrepreneurial spirit. You've got to keep that spirit alive within the company, no matter how big it gets.[17]

Kelleher obviously knows something that should have been well understood not only at Southwest but also at NASA even before the loss of Space Shuttle Columbia: Risk is not well managed by adding more layers of bureaucracy.

The Four Questions

The perspectives of these four highly capable CEOs remind us that an organization is supposed to provide the linkage between four very critical things: mission, strategy, structure, and values. Basically, that is what Giuliani was talking about when he talked about structure; what Andy Grove meant when he talked about strategy; what Jack Kelleher meant about lean organizations; and what George felt had been missed in not focusing on critical mission and values.

These four points are critical and ultimately boil down to four basic questions I once poised a number of years ago in thinking about the basics of command control:

1. Who shall command?
2. With what forces?
3. By what means?
4. To what ends?

Who Shall Command?

There is no more basic question than who shall command, which in essence also involves the closely related question of the mission itself. Who is in charge: Who has the responsibility, the accountability, and the direction for the mission as a whole? Who is that? Is that the chairman of the board or the CEO? Are those two guys one and the same? If so, why? Is that an effective way to organize the entire structure? If it is, there has got to be a reason for that decision—something not to be arrived at lightly. A point that we will cover in more detail in a subsequent chapter but bears mentioning here: What are the leadership qualifications of the one chosen to be in command? Do his qualifications include progressive exposure to positions of increased responsibility? If so, which ones? And does he show any signs that character has been built in—and will not need to added on later in the executive suite?

With What Forces?

The question of forces implies "who is involved" and "what is the strategy for employing them?" Andy Grove is right to be so concerned about strategy and preparing the organization for drastic change because the organization has to be kept lean enough, responsive enough, and flexible enough to move very quickly. What is true in the war on terrorism is also true for today's business warrior: Alertness counts. So does having the right mix of forces that you need to react to any situation. And here is an organizational anomaly: Sometimes teams are not the answer. Sometimes the right individual is the answer; the right individual armed with the right degree of authority. There is a concept here that is worth mentioning because it is an important counterweight to the layering that organizations sometimes do, in the military or in business. Closely associated with a former Air Force fighter pilot, John Boyd, his philosophy was that command essentially consisted of four things: OODA for observe, orient, decide, and act. The resulting *OODA loop* is one way we try to discipline whatever command structure we set in place because whatever structure is set in place has to react more quickly than an adversary. We describe this as getting inside the decision loop of the adversary. And to do that, you've got to react very, very quickly. Andy Grove is exactly right. There is a certain degree of strategic paranoia that does any organization good. And figuring out, when you set up this command structure, the means by which the strategic objective is going to get carried out. How quickly can they react—and how flexible can they be?

By What Means?

What are the procedures and metrics by which the entire leadership structure works together to help shape and implement key decisions? The key metric here is *together* because it is not clear if cultures will have to be meshed. Meshing units is one thing; meshing cultures quite another. There is a tendency in business to think that if organizations can be kept flat, then culture is something we really need don't need to worry about very much. Herb Kelleher would argue quite differently; so would the members of most joint task forces we put in the field. But my favorite "means test" was contained in the best marching orders I ever received after taking command of my company—300 soldiers at Fort Huachuca, Arizona. My battalion commander's orders have always stayed with me. He began by explaining the mission and how my success would be measured. He then went over the resources needed to accomplish the mission and how the battalion was organized to support anything required that I needed in executing my command responsibilities. Then he sat back and asked, "What are your questions? That's the mission and these are the tools for you to accomplish it. If you have any problems come back and see me." Talk about *auftragstaktik!* Those were probably the finest mission type orders I ever received. And the start of a great command tour.

To What Ends?

The question about ends reminds us about objectives. How do we assess the worth and the adequacy of the direction in which those decisions are taking us? This is the linkage between strategy and the organization's basic values. Bill George's point is instructive here: If what is being done is subversive of the organization's basic values, you have expended an awful lot of effort for not very much. If you have chosen those values and that strategy well, then your daily activities will have a way of reminding you about what's important because "drift" is only possible with weak leaders or weak organizations.

There is probably no better way to close this chapter than to tell another story on myself. When I took over as commander of that company at Fort Huachuca, Arizona, I was determined to do what I could to put a stop to the chronic indiscipline that Rick Atkinson (see Chapter 4) talked about all those years later. All of us had had to deal with racial tensions, drugs, and alcohol abuse but this was now *my* command. I was determined to make a difference and routinely made it a point to talk to each incoming group of trainees reporting to my company. The emphasis was on objectives—why they were assigned to the company and what their objectives should be while there. And what we expected from each of them as soldiers. Among the most important rules were the sleeping arrangements: The company was coeducational but the sleeping arrangements were not. I explained that we had separate dormitory floors for male and female soldiers, that that was the way it was and were there any questions. Well, there never were.

Except this one time. A young lady raised her hand, said, "Sir I have a question." This was my first exposure to the soon-to-be ex-PFC Renee D. Watkins. I nodded curtly and she boldly plunged ahead. "Sir, I'm glad to be here. I'm glad to be a soldier. I don't drink, I don't smoke, I certainly don't use drugs, and I don't associate with people who do. But, Sir, I really *do* like to screw and I would like to know where in this particular organization I can go to do that." The silence was absolutely deafening. In my mind's eye, I was transported straight back to OCS and right into the middle of one of those leadership training films they used to show where the camera would suddenly swing and a loud disembodied voice would intone, "Whatcha' gonna' do NOW, Lieutenant?" Well, now I was a captain but didn't have a clue about what I was going to do. But when in doubt, attacking is usually the best policy. I let the silence go for maybe another 20 seconds, leaned over the podium, looked her right in the eye and said "Not on my turf, honey!" And then stalked out to heighten the dramatic effect. There were of course other encounters with ex-PFC Watkins as she made consistent but negative progress down the Army rank structure: We will save them for another time.

Objectives are great things to have, but as I learned that day: If you can't stand the answer then don't ask the question.

WAR PLAN

MISSION OBJECTIVES

CEOs need to figure out what *structure* can do to ease their burdens in actually running things. They need to focus on organization—the structural means of linking leadership, strategy, and values.

★ Corporate America relies too heavily on hierarchical forms and established ways of doing business—which creates hurdles in dealing with thoroughly networked international competitors, which have the advantages of lower labor costs and reduced time to market.

★ The corollary to the above: Risk is not well managed by adding more layers of bureaucracy.

★ There is always a delicate balance to be struck between the uniformity requiring *centralized control* and the basic *autonomy* needed for subordinate units to do their jobs—especially when doing those jobs also requires them to display considerable *flexibility and initiative.*

★ There is no right or wrong answer on the question of centralization versus decentralization. It is very much in the eye of the beholder—or more properly the CEO or commander.

★ There is no more basic organizational problem than aligning responsibility and authority, and there is no more basic temptation than usurping that authority by second guessing the on-scene commander. The temptation to override the guy on the ground, the man on the scene, or the gal you left in charge is a universal flaw that has only become worse in a technological era. Trust is a quality that can only be broken once.

★ From strategy to basic values, the structure of an organization reflects what the unit *actually does* everyday, as opposed to what it *says* it is doing.

★ The *structure* reflects the *values* of the organization, because if the values aren't an intrinsic part of what the organization actually does—then they aren't values at all, only public relations.

★ Napoleon's telescope: A commander or a CEO needs to bring his insight to bear in the form of direct intervention when it is absolutely critical—and to do that without subverting the chain of command or compromising his own leadership standards.

★ Many problems with our businesses result from a failure to focus on the idea of *mission*. Instead, the interests of the shareholders, boards of directors, and CEOs have been inflated to out-weigh those of the employees and the customers.

★ The organization has to be kept lean enough, responsive enough, and flexible enough to move very quickly. What is true in the war on terrorism is also true for today's business warrior: Alertness counts. So does having the right mix of forces that you need to react to any situation.

★ There is a certain degree of strategic paranoia that does any organization good. When you set up this command structure, determine the means by which the strategic objective is going to get carried out. How quickly can they react—and how flexible can they be?

PART
III

★ ★ The Tools ★ ★

7

☆ ☆ Business Intelligence ☆ ☆

Another Damned Thing They Didn't Teach You in B School

Hill 473, National Training Center, Fort Irwin, California, 0600

Yo! Hey, you! Yeah, you there in the business suit! Listen up. Normally, I use the magic of television to talk to you, but sometimes books are better because they force you to use your imagination. Like now. Here we are at Fort Irwin, California, right on the edge of the Mojave Desert. Home of the Army's National Training Center, or NTC, also known as "top gun for tanks." Also occasionally known as the National Trauma Center because of the pucker factor when you come out here for training. Because it's as close to war as the Army can make it—and when you come out here you put it all on the line.

Sunup's in an hour, but there's light enough now to show you the lay of the land. Sure, it looks like the kind of place where you expect to see the Israelis fighting the Syrians, someplace that even Saddam's boys wouldn't defend—or maybe the U.S. Cavalry up against a bunch of Indians without the slightest idea of property values. Anyway, the Whale is that hump over there, then Deadman Pass, the Dust Bowl, and the

*Washboard. That elevation over there is the first glimpse that most peo-
ple have of Fort Irwin as they drive in from Barstow, which passes for the
nearest town: naturally, it's known as Awshit Hill.*

*A tourist attraction it's not, but the reason why the Army's been com-
ing here since World War II are those wide-open spaces—actually about
the size of Rhode Island but without so many Democrats. Back in the late
1970s, the new generation of computers, laser-based engagement systems,
and the necessity of confronting a resurgent Soviet adversary led the Army
to make the NTC into an instrumented range. Without killing anybody,
the computers could tell who lived, who died, who shot whom, with what
weapon, and at what range. Which took most of the guesswork and BS out
of Army maneuvers. Which then led to the OPFOR.*

*Speaking of which: See that little dust trail in that arroyo coming
off those mountains? Here, take my field glasses. Out here dust equals
movement and what's usually moving are a very large and deadly species
of animals, in this case, the OPFOR. That's who that is over there, probably a company moving into their ambush positions. In case you're wondering, OPFOR stands for opposing force and that's what makes the
NTC really special because we have here the world's finest Soviet-style
armored regiment. Sure the Russians are on our side now—sort of. But
the OPFOR is a particularly handy way to generate a convenient stand-
in for the Iraqis, Syrians, Iranians, or the North Koreans.*

*The OPFOR regiment lives out here all the time so they know the ter-
rain like the back of their hands. Not only do they know opposition tactics
and equipment, but being U.S. soldiers they, of course, know our side
pretty well, too. So what does it add up to? Well, basically you have a
group of people who live to kick the asses of the regular U.S. units that
cycle through here—who are up to date on the tactics, the organization,
and the leadership of the ordinary, if that is the word, American units
that we rely on every day. There are stories of how some of these units
came back from Gulf War I, having feasted on Republican Guard units,
but in their next NTC rotations, some of those units got waxed by the
OPFOR. And at the debriefings they were told: Who the hell did you think
you were up against—the Iraqis?*

*When peacetime training is tougher than war, you win. Which is
why we have an OPFOR, as I'm sure you do as well. Oh . . . you don't?
Well, your corporate intelligence officer must have a pretty good war*

game that he prepares for testing out your strategies. I mean for things like product launches, special projects . . . things like that? No? Really? Well, don't you think your company's competition needs to be represented around your own planning table somehow? And that maybe, just maybe your executives would be just a tad more on their toes—if they knew they were going up against people whose idea of a good time was to kick their asses all over your corporate headquarters? Well, please don't get angry but that answer doesn't exactly come as a complete surprise at this point.

B usiness intelligence, also known as competitive intelligence is the next topic of discussion—and we'll see what business can learn from its military counterpart. But first a clarification: It is it is not competitor information, it is not marketing, and it is certainly not about spying. My credentials for telling you all this? Well, actually I *DO* have credentials . . . and a badge, now in Lucite, that they gave me when I retired. As a way of remembering all those times when we mixed it up with Soviet intelligence and West German terrorists during the worst days of the Cold War. But I participated in a small way helping to revolutionize the way we brought combat intelligence to the battlefield. Ever since, I have tried to get business leaders to understand that many of those same technologies and processes are available to them merely for the asking. Because the government now understands very well that they no longer have a monopoly on what used to be some very privileged "sources and methods:" but the really interesting question is—DO YOU?

However, candor suggests that I tell another story on myself. It begins just after I graduated from OCS. While awaiting further training—second lieutenants are always doing that—I was assigned to a unit where the first sergeant was a typically crusty NCO, this one with a background in infantry soldiering that went back to the Korean War. He had two tours in Vietnam under his belt already and was not at all shy about telling second lieutenants where they really stacked up in the Army. (In fact, he kept threatening to call his memoirs, *Women I Have Loved and Second Lieutenants I Have Known* but I doubt he had a publisher.) But he had some authentic war stories, one of which said a lot about tactical intelligence. During his most recent tour, he had been called on the radio by the battalion intelligence officer with an intelligence report to pass along. It seems there was a Vietcong squad a thousand meters to their front that wanted to surrender. They went out—and called their headquarters back several hours later with what the first sergeant called a slight correction. "It wasn't a Vietcong squad, it was a North Vietnamese company. And they didn't want to surrender to us: they wanted US to surrender to them!"

It didn't take long to learn that intelligence was not a career field the Army admired much more than my sergeant. The elusiveness of the enemy in Vietnam had at least revealed the spectacular unwisdom of ignoring one of the classic dimensions of combat—or of populating the intelligence corps with misfits and those who couldn't cut it anywhere else. One Vietnam-era general lamented:

> I knew that finding the enemy would be one of our toughest jobs. It occurred to me that perhaps we might be able to identify the guerrilla, a farmer by night and a fighter by day, by the dark circles under his eyes. As it turns out, our surveillance was just about that sophisticated.[1]

Reporting to my unit in Germany in the early 1970s, I was briefed by a captain every bit as brash as me: "Lieutenant, you will consider every intelligence officer in the rank of major and above as incompetent until proven otherwise." Excellent advice.

If there is one thing I would impress on every corporate official reading these words it is this: *We improved because we had no other choice.* The Yom Kippur War of 1973 scared us badly. Talk about a more challenging operational environment threatening your business? The Russians had always been bigger than we were but the war almost to the death between our respective client states in the Middle East showed us a Soviet adversary that had closed the gap in quality while we had been away on our Southeast Asian adventure. And giving us a watchword for the weaponry of the new information age: "What can be seen can be hit; what can be hit can be killed."

We gradually put together units that combined the technical intelligence disciplines—SIGINT (signals intelligence) and IMINT (imagery intelligence)—with the traditional ones: operational security, interrogation, and ground surveillance. These tools were placed in the hands of tactical commanders, who gradually came to understand that excellent intelligence was not only the key to battlefield success but also a basic responsibility of command. Success bred more success as the ground picture was combined with information gathered by other services. At the end of the Gulf War, airborne radar—in experimental use aboard an Air Force aircraft called JSTARS—was the sensor that directly led to the destruction of the Iraqi forces along the "Highway of Death" outside Kuwait.

Since then, things have routinely improved by quantum leaps. The revolution in military affairs (see Chapter Three) seen in the marriage of information and precision weaponry simply means that war fighting commanders routinely write checks that must be cashed by their intelligence officers. In Operation Iraqi Freedom, both intelligence and the bandwidth to support the new battlefield information flows were fully displayed. In addition to the traditional questions about tracking enemy forces, locating one's own forces and determining the best way to get the one to attack the other, there are now the full range of issues that could only be satisfied by whole suites of sensors, officeware, and matching communications infrastructures:

- Families of unmanned aerial vehicles loitered over the battlefield for hours, providing continuous surveillance and occasionally serving as convenient launch platforms when lucrative targets were spotted.

- Complementary families of aerial surveillance platforms—from aircraft to satellites—were able to pinpoint Iraqi forces in daylight and darkness—and in weather conditions that included sandstorms of biblical proportions.

- Precise navigation allowed controllers to distinguish American troops, vehicles, and logistics from the enemy. Armed with this information, pilots were able to program an array of precision munitions that killed Iraqi targets with devastating accuracy while largely—though never completely—avoiding collateral damage to civilian facilities and minimizing the ever-present problem of "friendly fire."

- Network-centered operations enabled information to be shared quite literally from the foxhole to the Pentagon. Military services whose lack of interoperability had been proverbial ("We have only the same travel agent in common . . .") now found themselves linked to each other and coalition partners with a pervasive connectivity that allowed everything from the exchange of e-mail and graphics to interactive chat room discussions between widely separated command echelons.

The tactical results of this information flow could be glimpsed in several ways. Iraqi artillery batteries could barely fire before their positions were spotted and fixed by American ground and aerial surveillance. The information was immediately passed either to Army ground stations or fighters, setting the stage for devastatingly accurate return fire by rockets or artillery—a "sensor-to-shooter" sequence usually completed within seconds or minutes. Iraqi air defenders quickly learned that to radiate their fire control radars was to invite an immediate audience with the Almighty. Consequently, the Iraqis mostly fired "in the blind" while their American counterparts usually hit their targets with the first round.[2]

It should go without saying that this, the high water mark of the Pentagon's network-centered operations, provided little that a medium-sized commercial company with moderately sophisticated information technology capabilities would not consider somewhat passé. Unless you consider that:

1. The entire network had to be packed up and moved—twice. First from the continental United States to Kuwait—and then from Kuwait to Baghdad. The latter move inevitably took place in stages as units leapfrogged to take their assigned places—and took their signal assets with them.

2. There were other distractions, to wit: heat (upwards of 120 degrees by summer); sand (blown around in sandstorms of biblical proportions); vibration (things on the move getting shaken). Oh and one other thing: Indigenous fanatics of all kinds who were trying to kill you.

3. The information being passed around the network routinely had to be secured—an operational fact of life ever since

World War II—but one that imposed its own legal and practical constraints.

But the real test of an intelligence system is NOT simply the communications backbone on which it rests but on the quality of the information being transmitted. That said, how did we do?

There is reason for considerable caution in attempting final judgments for a war in which only preliminary results are available, in which major engagements still occur every day and when those same judgments are more than slightly susceptible to political coloration. But there is little question that, for a war in which U.S. tactics, weaponry, and overall effectiveness were so devastating, the verdict on intelligence is surprisingly mixed. Two issues have become paramount:

1. Iraqi weapons of mass destruction (WMD) that were not used against U.S. troops, have not turned up in the plethora of other Iraqi weapons, and in retrospect appear highly questionable as a pretext for the American invasion;

2. The use of irregular forces by Saddam and, in the aftermath of his overthrow, the unanticipated emergence of a guerrilla war against American forces in Iraq.

The new commander of American forces there, General John Abizaid, gave this assessment to the Senate Armed Services Committee:

> Intelligence was the most accurate I've ever seen on the tactical level, probably the best I've ever seen on the operational level, and perplexingly incomplete on the strategic level with regard to weapons of mass destruction. It is perplexing to me . . . that we have no found weapons of mass destruction, when the evidence was so pervasive that it would exist . . . I can't offer a reasonable explanation . . .[3]

On both the tactical and operational levels, Abizaid's testimony suggests strongly that U.S. intelligence was not wanting on anything other than WMD, especially since he was the first American official (shortly after succeeding General Tommy Franks) to declare that the

U.S. occupation of Iraq was rapidly becoming a guerrilla war. The kind of intelligence needed to prosecute a guerrilla war has more in common with police work than high-tech god's-eye-views of the battlefield. Interrogations, walk-ins, debriefings, raids, searches, and detentions are very much the order of the day. Although senior U.S. defense officials continue to insist that this transition has been smooth and effective, there is every reason for skepticism. Just as military intelligence in Vietnam had to overcome severe institutional shortcomings, similar challenges must surely await the current generation of American soldiers as they confront a determined guerrilla adversary on his home turf.[4]

Which also leaves that nagging question of Iraqi WMD: did U.S. intelligence fail? Anthony Cordesman, of the Center for Strategic and International Studies, suggests that U.S. reliance on technical intelligence, particularly the intelligence, surveillance and reconnaissance (IS&R) systems of the RMA may have had some unintended consequences:

- The United States did not have enough area experts, technical experts, and analysts with language skills at any level to make optimal use of its sensors and collection.

- The United States had a far greater capability to target buildings than characterize what went on in the building, and the effect of strikes on most sets of structures.

- The IS&R effort mistargeted leadership facilities, exaggerated the importance of C4I strikes, and overtargeted fixed military facilities.

- The IS&R sensor and analytic effort focused more on major combat forces, with heavy weapons, than on infantry or irregular forces. It could do a much better job of locating and characterizing weapons platforms and military emitters than dealing with personnel and forces that relied on light vehicles.

The IS&R effort did much to reduce collateral damage and the risk of civilian casualties. It was neither organized nor capable, however, of assessing either civilian or military casualties.[5]

In short: Our reliance on these systems was the key to our ability to find and to destroy major Iraqi combat forces. However, these enormously capable reconnaissance systems do not solve every military problem and in particular do not lend themselves to resolving the unique acts of subtlety and intrigue that surrounded this one. That specifically includes WMD. No camera, no matter how sophisticated or whether mounted on a satellite, an aircraft, or a drone can see inside a building, a cave or a castle. Nor can they determine the mind of the enemy commander. What they do is remarkable but they cannot substitute for human judgment. My take on Iraq is that the search for WMD was at best a side issue and at worst a distraction from dealing with a problem that should have been solved once and for all at the end of Gulf War I. But that was not a problem of intelligence, but a matter of judgment and political will for which better information is rarely the answer.

Which is not a bad transition point in addressing what intelligence can also do for the business executive. If moving up in life means that you simply get harassed by progressively better classes of people, then intelligence means that you can at least ask more informed questions every step of the way. Business intelligence in isolation will not answer every question or solve every problem: If done correctly, however, it will leave you a helluva lot better off than where you began. And you really *will* have more intelligent conversations every step of the way.

BUSINESS INTELLIGENCE: SOURCES AND METHODS

If you're a CEO and you think intelligence is out of your reach because you don't have the odd billion or two to invest the way the Pentagon does, think again. The world of intelligence reminds me of nothing so much as that classic line: Life's a banquet but most poor bastards are starving to death. In fact, the main sources of corporate intelligence are well within the reach of anyone who knows how and where to look. The reason is simple: digitized information. This is not to say that corporate espionage isn't a threat that CEOs also need to be prepared for (more about that in our next chapter), but the more fundamental fact of life is the quantum increase in digitized information of all types that has altered forever the operating environment of today's corporate leadership.

Mobilized and connected by the Internet, the impact of this digital revolution is often more apparent in our individual rather than our corporate lives. One of the great chroniclers of that revolution, Tom Friedman, who we met in Chapter 2, recounts in his popular work *The Lexus and the Olive Tree* a story that resonates with many travelers. Caught in a bathing suit outside his hotel room with neither room key nor a ready means of identification, Friedman was forced to confirm his identity by reciting the ages of his two daughters, with whom he had previously stayed at that hotel. They might just as well have asked for the last four digits of his Social Security number, mother's maiden name, date of birth, or any of the thousand and one personal details that we routinely divulge to confirm our identities in the electronic age. Friedman is also correct in stating that there is no Big Brother out there, just "a lot of Little Brothers" that routinely collect this information.[6]

For the most part, these Little Brothers seem content to use the Internet—and this information—to get a leg up on the intense competition called forth when individual PCs become tools in the hands of savvy shoppers. One marketing professor at Ohio State University says that, "The twenty-first century should really be called the century of the consumer" because of the wealth of choices empowering them—and the incentives for businesses to compete for sales when control of prices and information has been democratized by a variety of online resources.[7]

While there is evidence that some companies are bright enough to connect the dots of individual consumer preferences into the bigger picture of business intelligence, most do not—another fact of life that is simply astounding given how much information is out there. What kinds of information? Simply visit the web site of the Society of Competitive Intelligence Professionals (www.scip.org) and you can get lots of hints. Actually more than hints: outright declarations of the kinds of competitive information that adds up to intelligence when placed in competent hands. One of SCIP's members is Russell Secker, an executive vice president for marketing of Hoover's, an online database service that tracks some 18,000 public and private companies across 300 industries. "This means we're constantly scouring the news, public filings, and any other sources we can get our hands on to determine what's really going on at the companies our users are following." Some of the most important information resources: local news outlets; 10-Ks and 10Q filings from the SEC; annual reports; press releases; and public information solicited from vendors, partners, and customers.[8]

Another SCIP member, Seena Sharp adds that trade publications are an invaluable source of competitive information:

> The increasing interest in information, especially targeted information, sparks the launch of more than 1,000 new periodicals every year. Virtually every industry is served by 30 to 100 trade publications, yet only the leading two or three are widely read. While there may not be time to check out these other titles, they all contain some substantive, valid information about an industry.[9]

Sure, but aren't all press releases—especially to trade publications—routinely gone over and "scubbed clean" for any competitive information by eagle-eyed public relations officers? Well . . . not exactly.

> Even (tightly) guarded information has a way of sneaking out. Financial details on a very successful private food company were revealed in an industry publication devoted to information technology. The background information (financial and marketing) was included in order to put the information on technology systems into perspective. Bottom line: *A privately owned, very successful, and rapidly growing chain of shoe stores . . . exposed an extraordinary amount of financial, operational, and strategic information in an article devoted to the success of a local retail business.*[10]

If I'm chuckling at this point, it is because intelligence officers routinely deal with their own equivalent of the traditional cop's rule: If all criminals were smart, no crimes would ever be solved. And if all our commanders—or presidents or Cabinet officials—were geniuses, none would ever compromise classified information. Instead, human activity routinely involves screw-ups—and sometimes those screw-ups involve the inadvertent release of some extremely sensitive information.

However, looking at trade publications or other indirect data sources is not the preferred way to sniff out that sensitive data. No, that takes a human—and I'm not talking about spies, merely people who are somewhat skilled at asking good questions—and then listening. As intelligence officers, both Secker and Sharp clearly know the value of such people and their ability to mine the more direct sources of information. Who are those sources? Secker lists salespeople, receptionists, and (in particular):

... human resources personnel (who) are especially helpful when researching private companies. Obtain a list of executive names and then
plug them into news and Web search engines to learn the background of a
company's leadership team.[11]

Maybe it is one of the unique characteristics of our open society, but
it is simply astounding what people will tell you if asked politely to do so.
One of the first times I learned about this astonishing openness was as a
young intelligence officer—when I received derogatory information
during an interview from someone listed by the subject as a character reference! If anything, some companies treat their so-called "low-level administrative personnel" in the front office so poorly (apparently on the
assumption they don't know anything) that almost any form of elicitation
will work—especially if accompanied by a kind, solicitous manner over
the phone.

But there is an additional source of business intelligence—and that is
Internet chat rooms. According to David Rothkopf, CEO of Intellibridge, a
leading open source intelligence firm, these chat rooms are an important
source of local information. If you are doing business, say in Argentina,
you will be interested to know that there are roughly 200 Internet chat
rooms that at any given time provide a wealth of information on events in
that country. Knowing what is being said inside them implies a working
knowledge of Spanish as well as local slang or potentially even dialects.
"Yet the perspectives gained from these local sources can be diametrically
opposed to the supposed mainstream."[12] And that unfiltered information
is where you learn what is really going on—from early warning of the
SARS epidemic to more directly competitive information.

That kind of context information is all too rarely demanded by the
CEO—even some of those in international competition. Rothkopf likens
them to a pilot who might be totally aware of everything going on with
his plane *from the inside*. "But he would be a fool to take off without ob-
taining the latest information from outside his plane: weather information, air traffic patterns, and altimeter data along his intended route of
flight."[13] Although competitive information is a valuable asset in running
any business, one of the major things it can do for the CEO is to stop any
inadvertent violations of the "Doctrine of No Surprises," which was an

article of faith—and a prime directive—for many of the commanders I worked for. No matter what the event, no matter how unexpected the complication, any surprise was unacceptable. It is simply astounding how often businesspeople from the CEO on down the line do not follow that rule. They allow themselves to be surprised by those events outside their immediate responsibilities but—like Rothkopf's canonical pilot—hazards that could easily have been foreseen by simply asking the right questions of the right sources: stock market fluctuations, changes in commodity pricing, and even political upheavals. Well, life is hard, as comedian Redd Foxx classically observed; but it's a lot harder if you're stupid.

APPLICATIONS

Access to industry-specific databases, monitoring trade publications, conducting Internet surveillance in the local language—what else do you need for good business intelligence? Insight and expertise are two additional factors that instantly spring to mind—and it is just those factors that separate the pros from the amateurs among those firms seeking to provide business intelligence products to their clients.[14] The fact is that gathering data is not any great trick in the information age—but making sense of it is. That expertise is also critical in sifting and refining the data, searching for the corroborating piece of evidence that sometimes causes the entire puzzle to fall into place. All intelligence firms have a basic cadre of analysts to draw on; but because these people are expensive to maintain, various arrangements are typically made to "round out the bench" with on-call experts from business or academe. Intellibridge, for example, has an extensive global "expert network" of regional specialists that their analysts can call on for in-depth coverage on issues of interest to their clients.

How valuable are these services? The short answer is that—as with legal advice, tax advice, or military advice—it depends on asking the right questions before the fact—and on timeliness in acting on that advice. Rothkopf, like most other intelligence officers, has stories that illustrate both sides of the question. One client was a Fortune 10 company with extensive interests in Indonesia, whose "local experts" advised ever-closer ties with the Suharto regime as those holdings grew. Intellibridge advised to the contrary: That the Suharto regime was corrupt, intensely disliked, and *when* the regime failed, the company "would be tarred with same brush." The client listened, heeded the advice and, when the regime indeed collapsed, escaped those dire consequences. In contrast, Monsanto gambled on genetically engineered seeds, relying on the assumptions of their own "local experts" that such crops would be well-received in Europe. Intellibridge knew otherwise through their monitoring of the local European press and Internet chat rooms. By the time they realized their mistake, Monsanto had almost gone "belly up."[15]

While understanding and anticipating changes in a local or regional market is basic stuff for the CEO of an international company, there are significant competitive challenges much closer to home. Two *Harvard Business Review* articles that are required readings for my Georgetown students involve understanding the challenges of *disruptive technologies,* that is, those technological changes that can transform an industry or a product line—and also challenge the ability of any CEO to manage them.[16] There is ample evidence that tracking the process of change is an increasingly important function of business intelligence—and also the basis for a "you bet your bars" decision by the CEO.

Such was apparently the case when EMC, a Massachusetts-based information technology company, recognized that Data General, a close competitor in the same industry, had developed a product that constituted a potentially disruptive technology. The Data General product was a highly efficient, more economical solution for an increasingly cost-conscious data storage market, which EMC dominated at the high end. Which led to an interesting problem: What did EMC intend to do about that challenge, which conceivably threatened its own position, which was based on providing more capable but higher cost products. The options (conceivably) included: imitating the Data General product through reverse engineering, leapfrogging the technology or pushing a competing version in an effort to set a de facto standard, leaving the field to Data General and moving on to other product lines, or acquiring Data General.

Fortunately, EMC needed no lessons in appreciating the worth of a competitive intelligence capability, which they had maintained for several years. They were also highly attuned to the whole issue of disruptive technologies—as were their executives. Perhaps for those reasons, the competitive intelligence section at EMC is highly unusual because it has the opportunity to submit its competitive intelligence assessments directly to the board of directors—which not only says a great deal about the company's governance but also about the courage of its day-to-day leadership. In this instance, the competitive intelligence effort was aided by effective Internet surveillance, as well as by a concerted effort to balance that information against the opinions not only of the salesforce but also of leading industry analysts and—what a novel notion!—of EMC's own best customers.[17]

What came out of this effort to gather intelligence through a systematic and broad-based collection campaign was a course of action that was expensive but thoroughly grounded in reality and good business principles: EMC acquired Data General for $1.1 billion—no small stakes. As EMC later said in its corporate report:

> Within three months of acquiring Data General, we fully integrated its CLARiiON storage line—as well as Data General's engineering, development, manufacturing, customer service, sales, and marketing functions—and established Data General's AViiON server business as a separate division of EMC.[18]

Bottom line: As the result of good competitive intelligence, what could have been a company-threatening disruptive technology for EMC had instead been integrated into a new—and highly successful—operating division producing a complementary product line and incidentally ensuring EMC's continued position as an industry leader. And if you think the cost of acquiring Data General was high, just try estimating the price of failure. Want to know how powerful intelligence can be in the hands of someone who knows what they're doing—even if they start out with no special "inside knowledge"? This next story might be more applicable to the chapter on security which follows; but as an insight into what is possible with a determined, incisive intelligence process—aided by readily available information tools and a few determined minds—this one is hard to beat.

The story begins in the aftermath of the Oklahoma City bombing which, together with other studies done by the Clinton administration, had resulted in an Executive Order (Number 13010, July 15, 1996) declaring that *critical infrastructure protection* was an important national goal—and that greater attention needed to be paid to what would later become better known as *homeland defense.* In early 1997, newly released from the Army and determined to remain solvent and out of jail, I was working with a small firm in Northern Virginia that specialized in helping the Defense Department assess its vulnerabilities to cyber attacks.

As part of their effort to "cruise for contracts," this company hatched the novel idea of conducting a vulnerability estimate of "the infrastructure," to identify both cyber and physical vulnerabilities. But some important constraints were built into the demonstration: It would be Internet-based in collecting information; it would proceed using no classified information; and although the analysts would be experienced intelligence officers, they would be privy to no "inside information" in conducting their study. Their potential range of targets potentially included: gas and oil storage; electrical power grids; telecommunications; and even the water supply.

However, the analysts quickly zeroed in on nuclear power plants, even though the conventional wisdom of the time held that they were almost invulnerable. In 1993 Senate testimony, the FBI's Intelligence Division spokesman said that: "The FBI considers nuclear power plants unlikely targets for terrorist attacks because they are relatively well-protected and hard to attack without great risk to the attackers." Yet the analysts kept finding that nuclear power plants offered important potential advantages to an attacker: Reconnaissance was surprisingly easy; there were interesting combinations of cyber and physical attacks; and, after Three Mile Island, the fear factor was in a class by itself. Amazingly, the web sites inviting further scrutiny and exploitation were those maintained by the Nuclear Regulatory Commission, apparently on the assumption that "the public's right to know" and the First Amendment were the twin pillars of some sort of suicide pact underwritten by the NRC on behalf of the American people.

Eventually our analysts found their target: A nuclear power plant somewhere in the United States with sufficient security and safety violations as to suggest deeper problems. Once they had zeroed in, they found that reactor diagrams and other engineering schematics were helpfully linked—assisting them in making reasonable guesses where fissionable nuclear materials were stored. Site diagrams, overlaid atop the engineering schematics, suggested the most vulnerable points for physical attacks against the reactor and key backup systems. A remarkably complete profile of the security force was available, including names, addresses, and even pictures of the key personnel. Finally, there was impressive documentation of the local community's emergency response system, including choke points and radio broadcast frequencies. In short: Were you an Al Qaida member looking to create an American Chernobyl, everything you needed for planning was a modem connection and a mouse click away.

After giving lots of agency briefings, we went public with this information in an op-ed piece on May 14, 1997, that the *Wall Street Journal* ran under the heading, "Internet Insecurity May Prove Deadly."[19] We waited for the inevitable uproar when people realized that the NRC had put them at risk, for Congressional hearings, for appearances on Oprah—or even Phil Donahue! Instead, the bureaucracy simply reacted with a large shrug and life went on as before. And stayed that way—until one month after 9/11, when all those NRC web sites were mysteriously purged—though not unfortunately the people who had originally put them there. We never did get the lucrative government contracts we had been hoping for—but then again, the splash that we made was not a bad investment for only *400 hours of total effort, or 20 percent of a man-year's worth of research.*

REFLECTIONS

The teaching point for the CEO who thinks he can't afford good business intelligence—or the CEO who thinks he is invulnerable to it—is that both of you are only 400 man-hours away from being found out: either having made your foolhardy plans on the basis of nonexistent or faulty intelligence or having your much more well-conceived strategies laid bare to the competition. After all, if discovering nuclear secrets is no big deal for a reasonably talented intelligence officer, just how big an obstacle can your neighbor's strategic plans be? Not, of course, to mention your own!

The fact is that, as the competition intensifies in the business operating environment, the pressure grows to use information as the military does—as a weapon of war. Not every company talks about it, but the good ones do and do it very well. Sam Walton, who built Wal-Mart into the world's largest corporation, was candid about the real reasons for his success: "People think we got big by putting big stores in small towns. Really, we got big by replacing inventory with information"[20] Walk into the Wal-Mart in Bristol, Virginia, in search of a camera battery and, on the way by, you will inevitably find yourself drawn to the display of blue jeans. When you buy a pair, three signals are sent simultaneously by the cashier: one to the store manager, one to Wal-Mart's headquarters, and one to whichever firm supplied the blue jeans.

The supplier's problem is simplest: He has to keep a predetermined number of blue jeans on that shelf at Wal-Mart—that the store, in effect, rents out to him. The store manager has to arrange the displays to lure in unsuspecting customers like me. The stories here are the stuff of legend. Plowing through the data, a Wal-Mart manager supposedly noticed that a correlation existed between the sale of beer and diapers, particularly on Fridays. Further analysis confirmed that men were stopping at the Wal-Mart after work, completing the errands on which their wives had presumably sent them and buying diapers for the baby—but not neglecting to pick up a six-pack for themselves! This led to the decision to place beer and diapers next to each other on the shelf—resulting in increased sales for both![21]

It is at the strategic level that Wal-Mart has built for itself a unique information advantage—its data warehouse. Like the vehicle assembly building at Cape Canaveral which is so big it has its own weather systems, the sheer size of the Wal-Mart data holdings constitute an information advantage all their own. Variously described as over 140 square meters and 100 terabytes,[22] a book containing a terabyte of information would be considerably taller than Mount Everest.[23] What all that amounts to is knowing precisely what sells where, at what times, and having an awfully good idea why. Think of it as the predatory use of information—a point about Wal-Mart's competitive stature that most books on the subject gloss over. But it is close to what Deming meant when he talked about "profound knowledge" of a subject. When that subject is knowing exactly what your customers want to buy, that knowledge is not only profound, it's profitable.

Whether it is the result of solid business intelligence practices—the way EMC did it—or the result of mining your own data warehouse in Wal-Mart fashion, these approaches represent a new way to manage an old problem: risk. The traditional way that businesses managed risk was very simple: They avoided it. Risk "management" was simply an elaborate means of staying as far away from the risk as possible—rather like denizens of Washington, DC, poring over weather reports of an approaching snowstorm and abandoning their cars preemptively. However, when risk avoidance was not entirely possible, businesses "managed" their exposure like actuaries: Essentially drawing a "black box" around the risk and keeping statistics on the survivors. If a predetermined number made it through (sound of computer whirring in the background here) the risk was "manageable"—or as Archie Bunker used to say, "itso-fatso." A crude tool, of course, rather like primitive tribes with numbering systems where the concepts were limited to "one," "two," and "many."

A slightly better idea is to open the black box through the use of either intelligence in the classic sense—or what the military now refers to as "situational awareness." A more precise understanding of what the threat is—and is not—permits a correspondingly more precise appreciation of the risk and the most effective countermeasures that can be applied against it. As in the military, an important corollary is "distributed situational awareness," the idea being that more informed people make better judgments. But in both business and war, the sequence is: Understand the risk, evaluate the opportunity, and take the right risk—but don't take chances.

If there is one consistent theme of these chapters about the application of twenty-first century leadership tools, it is that you should be prepared to connect the dots and to replace fads and anecdotes with bottom-line, baseline business processes. Nowhere is this more important than with competitive intelligence. Can you possibly understand that by instituting a disciplined competitive intelligence process, you can avoid the twin fallacies of the truly desperate?

1. Imagining that all you have to do is collect information on your closest competitor rather than gathering your own intelligence on the marketplace. Have you ever considered that your competitor

may be even dumber than you are? And that he may even have a bumper sticker on his limo that reads, "Don't follow me—I'm lost, too!"

2. Thinking that you even know anything worth knowing about your competition if all you are doing is casually going to conferences, reading annual reports, or perusing competition catalogues.

Finally, if you remember nothing else about this chapter, remember this: if it isn't a system, then it isn't intelligence. And you had better acquire that system before your competition does. All in all, it reminds me of W. C. Fields in a scene from one of his classic films—complete with top hat and cigar, and of course playing poker. An obvious patsy approaches him, takes in the scene, and says, "Ah, is this a game of chance?" The instant and deadpan response from W. C: "Not the way I play it." Exactly. Not the way I play it anymore either—and neither should you!

WAR PLAN

MISSION OBJECTIVES

Business intelligence, also known as competitive intelligence, is not competitor information, it is not marketing, and it is certainly not spying. Think of it as the next step beyond market research.

★ Business intelligence in isolation will not answer every question or solve every problem. If done correctly, however, it will leave you a helluva lot better off than where you began.

★ If you're a CEO and you think intelligence is out of your reach because you don't have the odd billion or two to invest the way the Pentagon does, think again. The main sources of corporate intelligence are well within the reach of anyone who knows how and *where* to look. The reason is simple: The quantum increase in *digitized information* of all types has altered forever the operating environment of today's corporate leadership.

★ Although some companies are bright enough to connect the dots of individual consumer preferences into the bigger picture of business intelligence, most do not—another fact of life that is simply astounding, given how much information is out there.

★ An additional source of business intelligence is Internet chat rooms, an important source of local, unfiltered information, where you learn what is *really* going on, including directly competitive information. This kind of context information is all too rarely demanded by CEOs—even some of those in international competition.

★ It is simply astounding how often business people, from the CEO on down the line, allow themselves to be surprised by

(continued)

events outside their immediate responsibilities—events that could easily have been foreseen by simply asking the right questions of the right sources, stock market fluctuations, changes in commodity pricing, and even political upheavals.

★ For good business intelligence, you also need insight and expertise. Gathering data is not any great trick in the information age—but making sense of it is. That expertise is also critical in sifting and refining the data, searching for the corroborating piece of evidence that sometimes causes the entire puzzle to fall into place.

★ For CEOs who think they can't afford good business intelligence—or that they're invulnerable to it—you should know you're only a step away from being found out: either having made your foolhardy plans on the basis of nonexistent or faulty intelligence or having your much more well-conceived strategies laid bare to your competition.

★ As the competition intensifies in the business-operating environment, the pressure grows to use information as the military does—as a weapon of war. Not every company talks about it, but the good ones do and do it very well.

★ Whether you use solid business intelligence practices or mine your own data warehouse, these approaches are a new way to manage an old problem: risk. The traditional way that businesses managed risk was very simple: They avoided it. A better idea is to have a more precise understanding of what the threat is—and is not—which permits a more precise appreciation of the risk and the most effective countermeasures that can be applied against it.

★ If you don't have a system for collecting intelligence, then it isn't intelligence. And you had better acquire that system before your competition does.

8

☆ ☆ The Other Side ☆ ☆ of the Coin

Enterprise Security

National Training Center, Scenario 2, 0400

As I told you the OPFOR is moving to their attack positions. That was what we talked about yesterday. The OPFOR knows the ground out here very thoroughly. Remember that they live out here all the time—and that playing the opposition to regular American units is what they do for a living. And they are very good at it. They also know that the BLUE force had their scouts out last night. And at 0200 today, OPFOR found and killed those scouts. So now BLUE is blind and OPFOR is rolling in on them. But the OPFOR scouts aren't dead at all. They scouted the BLUE position so they know two things; Number one, it is anchored right there in that hill to the right; and two, BLUE left undefended a back door into their positions from the flank.

Well, that's too bad. It also happened to the Spartans at Thermopylae. Seemed a traitor told the Persian King Xerxes about a little known pathway into the Spartan position and negated one of the most dramatic stands in the history. A couple of hundred Spartans against probably about 130,000 of the Persians according to Herodotus. The battle? Well it was fought in 480 . . . that's 480 B.C. Which is a great lesson, too, then and now, because all it takes is one guy who's willing to betray you. Sit back and watch, because you are going to see what happens to a force that has been compromised and is being attacked by an enemy that knows where they are, what their vulnerable points are and is absolutely determined to roll in on them. Hang in there. We'll be back later.

Much of what I know about the field of security, I initially learned in the Army as a young officer inspecting what used to be called Special Weapons Sites in Germany. The physical and geo-political landscape has changed, but in the early 1970s those Special Weapons Sites used to be at very remote locations scattered across Germany. They were intended to give us an advantage of some kind against the Group of Soviet Forces—if not to deter them—because they outnumbered us by several hundred thousand, not unlike the Persians outnumbered the Spartans back at Thermopylae. Some of these Special Weapons Sites were very remote, so we would always try and go to a neighboring German village and ask for directions. The Germans always seemed to know exactly where those sites were, and they would unfailingly give us good directions. Despite all the security, we thought that the Russians probably knew where those locations were as well.

Make no mistake: The Russians were a thoroughly bad lot—but they weren't stupid. They were extremely professional when it came to employing their intelligence resources to collect on us—and they used them all. Spies are still one of the best means to gather intelligence and the Soviets had lots of them. But they complemented their "take" on us with signals intelligence (SIGINT)—or what the Russians called "electronic reconnaissance." Add to that satellite reconnaissance—which, in another triumph of political correctness, both sides finally acknowledged as "national technical means" to verify arms control agreements and much else. (By the way, those satellites are still up there, but now just the *commercial* imagery is capable of resolving targets of about one meter.)

Recognizing the importance of "all-source" intelligence collection, we engineered a similar approach to defend against it—something called Operations Security (OPSEC). Taking part in one of our early OPSEC projects at a fort in the western United States, it was interesting that the only really secure facility housed the computer. Operated by the major unit on the post, it was a massive main frame the unit was very proud of, and they devoted considerable resources to keeping the unwashed and the unauthorized a considerable distance away. It sat in a secured building that was very well guarded and, most importantly, was electronically connected to nothing. But everywhere else there were problems: The fences had holes, perimeter security was a joke, and the units were sloppy about keeping their safes closed, locked, and initialed in the way they should have.

But worst of all was the fact that if you wanted to collect intelligence on that unit, all you had to do was go ask the troops. In a bar. Off duty. Or in any other social situation where their guard was down and when, like most Americans, they would unhesitatingly accept someone at face value and tell him anything he wanted to know—particularly if the information wasn't "sensitive." So if the thought of commercial satellites peering down makes you paranoid, or if you are a fan of *The X-Files*, just remember that espionage is still alive and well, but that in the corporate world today we call it "social engineering"—and it still works.

But the rest of the world has changed in ways that may make you pine for the days when that stand-alone, well-guarded mainframe was the most secure part of the operation. Our overview begins with a quick lesson from military history: *the development of every new capability carries with it the seeds of an equal or possibly greater vulnerability.* And as we have eagerly made the computer into an ever more efficient slave attending every facet of the modern corporation, the irony is that we have inadvertently built Trojan Horses—in some cases, quite literally. That's the good news: The bad news you don't even want to know about—except that you should. Because nothing in your traditional business background will have prepared you for the challenges of operating in the security environment of the twenty-first century—unless you have either done a stretch in the penitentiary or routinely dealt with people who should have.

THE THREAT: HOMELAND DEFENSES

For a good overview of the problems of corporate security, come visit the offices of Joe Cantamessa, the vice president of corporate security for Dow Jones. Joe is a good friend, a former FBI agent, and an MSNBC colleague, where we often turn to him for authoritative advice on security and terrorism matters. The first thing that will impress you about Joe's office is where it is—right next door to what used to be the World Trade Center. It is impossible to be so close to that site and not to have your mind concentrated on security, how important it is, and how you have to prepare for the unexpected. Dow Jones hired Joe in the immediate aftermath of 9/11, because its executives—their home offices effectively bombed out of existence—had been through a difficult time coming to grips with the new importance of security in the twenty-first century. A global information company, they had real concerns about information assurance, privacy, confidentiality—and many of the baseline security issues outlined in this chapter. They made a smart if obvious choice in making Joe their security honcho—and listened when he gave them some excellent advice about security surveys, information baselines, and a lot of not-so-very technical but very common sense advice about securing the enterprise.

But the key point to remember about the executives at Dow Jones was that they had brought Joe on board long before anyone there knew the name Daniel Pearl as anything other than a talented foreign correspondent for the *Wall Street Journal*. In the hours and days after Pearl's kidnapping by Al Qaida followers in Pakistan, the company's leadership found themselves unexpectedly at the center, not only of an international news story, but of a highly complex international investigation—featuring interagency intrigues, mysterious e-mail exchanges, and other forms of potential ransom demands. All while trying to comfort the victim's family, colleagues, and trying to publish newspapers and news wires. As an FBI investigator, all of Joe's talents clearly aided every step of that process, although the best efforts of everyone involved were tragically unable to save Daniel Pearl's life. This is sobering—but not a bad point to remember in understanding that we live in an age of terror—and will for a long time to come. As George Orwell once put it: "We sleep safe in our beds because rough men stand ready in the night to visit violence on those who would do us harm."

Even if you don't stand as close to its remnants as Joe Cantamessa does every day, the only thing about 9/11 that should have surprised us was the audacity of the attackers—because we received repeated and ample warnings of what was afoot. Any number of books made their appearance in the 1990s that amply documented the threat to corporate America, including the loss of privacy, computer vulnerability, and what businesses needed to do to adjust.[1] That genre continues to this day. As one contemporary review summarizes the problem, "Not long ago cyberterrorists were public enemy number one. Then two planes flew into the World Trade Center and the real physical world became instantly scarier."[2] Those books probably were alarmist. But guess what? They were right. Cyberterrorists weren't our worst nightmare only because of all those other bad guys who were out there. And the bad news for the CEO and for business is that *all those enemies are still out there.* We simply do not enjoy the luxury of having a single enemy we can identify, isolate, and predict. And you know what? That reality ain't gonna change anytime soon.

But the primary point here is that today in corporate America YOU are responsible for your own security because the government cannot and will not protect you, much as it might like to and as hard as it sometimes tries. There is some historical precedent for this state of affairs. Had you been a proverbial merchant of Venice, let us say, during the late renaissance, anything involving the shipping or the exchange of mercantile goods—particularly across borders—had to be funded and secured. That meant weapons and trained manpower, and if the shipment was by sea, that meant cannon and a trained crew. You had to do these things because there were thieves and pirates. Since no government could protect you, the security arrangements—and the tasks of managing or minimizing the risk—were very much the responsibility of the individual merchant. Just as it was then, the need for self-reliance in security is the beginning of wisdom for today's business professional. Even though training in security was not part of a traditional business education, or even something that executives thought about very much. The Soviets we worked against in the 1970s, as well as today's terrorists, drew common inspiration from Leon Trotsky, a revolutionary who knew his trade all too well. "You may not be interested in war," he once said, "but war is interested in you."

The need for self-reliance in security springs from that sobering truth as well as a recognition of three fundamental flaws in our home-land defenses that will continue to exist far into the future—despite de-termined efforts by many governmental and private agencies to correct them. But until that happens, you're back to self-help.

Insecure Borders

There have been numerous occasions in talking about U.S. military oper-ations in places like Afghanistan or elsewhere in the War on Terror that it has been necessary for me to stand in front of a map before a national tel-evision audience and talk with a perfectly straight face about a "porous border" in Iran or Afghanistan or Pakistan. The term simply makes me gag because we have exactly the same situation here—although we are not especially fond of likening ourselves to a third-world country. But we might just as well and get points for candor because the fact is that we own the world's highest-priced real estate—and have "secured it" in only the loosest possible sense of that term. Not only have we failed the most basic test of sovereignty along our common borders with Canada and Mexico but in our airports and seaports as well. Simply stated, there are inadequate forces to observe and secure the borders, where the charac-teristic problems involve aliens and drugs. Now if there are insufficient controls to stop drugs and aliens, there are no grounds whatever for be-lieving that we have any prospect of stopping a determined terrorist. Even more worrisome is the recent assessment of a Coast Guard officer in a po-sition to assess our border defenses: ". . . the existing border-management architecture provides no credible means for denying foreign terrorists and their weapons entry into the United States." The means available to the terrorist are virtually without limits, including the 489 million peo-ple, 127 million passenger vehicles, 11.5 million trucks, and 11.6 million maritime containers entering the United States every year.[3]

IFF

The military uses the acronym IFF—for Identify Friend from Foe—to highlight one of the basic problems of combat: shooting enemies rather than friends. However, the same problem exists in homeland security, one that is exacerbated by the limitations placed on technology by our exaggerated concerns with privacy and civil liberties. Instead, two years into the post-9/11 era, we rely on driver's licenses even though the majority of the hijackers on 9/11 had driver's licenses from my home state of Virginia. Driver's licenses really were not designed to backstop the nation's airline security system—or to serve in lieu of a national identity card. They do say something about minimal proof of residency—and possibly about one's ability to parallel-park a car; but they are unreliable predictors of one's propensity to hijack a plane. Technology is not the culprit here, because facial recognition software, biometrics, and even good old-fashioned fingerprinting offer far more reliable ways of verifying identity rather than the patchwork of half-hearted "solutions" we now settle for in comforting ourselves with an utterly false sense of security. National identity cards are an obvious answer—but are so far removed from the realm of political possibility as to be a pipe dream. Even the most facile attempts to use technology to reinforce security are suspect: A prospective effort by Florida law enforcement officials to link police records with commercially available databases quickly became a lightning rod for criticism about its implications for privacy rights.[4]

Stovepipes

Closely related to the problem of incomplete identification is a recurrence of the same kind of problem we have repeatedly fought in the military: information stovepipes. In fact, you can do a lot worse than to consider the intelligence and security agencies of the United States simply as a succession of stovepipes. As was amply documented by the various Congressional studies and Blue Ribbon commissions empanelled to perform postmortems on 9/11, there were institutional and legal barriers that impaired information sharing between federal agencies ostensibly on the same side. The reasons why the CIA doesn't talk to the FBI which doesn't talk to the local police are virtually identical to the fundamental reasons that once bedeviled our military services: culture, turf, and a resolute belief that information was power. These are also the same reasons why the Immigration and Naturalization Service (INS) sent routine visa extensions to the 9/11 hijackers nine months after the event. And why Attorney General John Ashcroft described the INS as being enough to drive a man to drink—an unusually strong statement for an ordained Baptist minister.

These closely related problems—borders, identification, and stove-pipes—are at the heart of a set of vulnerabilities that Governor Tom Ridge has sworn to overcome as the first Cabinet Secretary charged with defending the security of the American homeland. By any standard, his is a huge undertaking that deserves our applause as well as our taxes.[5] But also understand the fact that this job will not be done overnight. So Mr. or Madam CEO, it's back over to you. This is still your problem because you and only you are responsible for securing your enterprise. How bad is it? Well, the following assessment pinpoints where we stand in corporate America today, according to some of our best security analysts. A preview: The challenges outweigh the responses to this point (sorry if that shocked you!).

CORPORATE RESPONSES: THE STATE OF THE ENTERPRISE

Plans

It was General Eisenhower—himself a former war planner—who said that "Plans are useless, but planning is essential." So it is with security and so it was in the immediate aftermath of 9/11. Unlike the long-anticipated (and largely over-hyped) threat of Y2K disruption, the attacks of 9/11 demonstrate two points about catastrophic events: (1) that they can be widely predicted and (2) still come as a great shock. Not only were all those doomsday books about cyberterror alarming, but networks like MSNBC routinely generated special reports like the "Attack on Manhattan" presentation that I worked on—all of it built around the kinds of future scenarios that the experts said were most likely in the light of current trends. Taking specific actions to balance the trade-off between what is possible and what is likely is what the planner does. According to the widely respected Ernst & Young annual security survey, the best-run companies were those that anticipated worst case scenarios as well as adopted commonsense policies intended to minimize their effects—and bought insurance to mitigate those exposures they couldn't control. Thereafter, the record is somewhat mixed: Although many of the organizations Ernst & Young surveyed stressed their efforts in "business continuity" and "IT disaster recovery," almost 50 percent of U.S. firms still lacked specific plans in these areas. It is apparently easier to spend the money rather than to do the troublesome planning because, since 2001, median spending on insurance and risk management has grown by 33 percent, with insurance costs at least doubling for one fifth of the organizations. And there is no way to survey those plans that are in effect to ensure that they are grounded in reality, rather than simply gathering dust on some shelf.[6]

Other Threats

It is astounding how often, after one of my speeches, someone asks me if U.S. companies are spending enough on security. While it is necessary to manage a polite reply, it is a little like being asked if American farmers are spending enough money on fertilizer. Ernst & Young reports only a 4 percent median increase in security spending since 9/11, which would clearly indicate that those events did not magically open the coffers to corporate chief security officers.[7] That fact probably reflects the commonsense observation that the risk of terrorist attack remains astronomically low for most companies—although the equation gets much more interesting if one calculates the "downstream effects" of such an attack, particularly one directed at infrastructure targets. But if spending to date seems to suggest the continuity of securing the corporation's physical and virtual assets, there is abundant anecdotal evidence underlining the growing difficulty of that fundamental task. Such issues as employee safety, workplace violence, data security (see below), and continuity of operations have clearly grown in importance, the matching resources are thus far not in evidence.

Data Security

For most firms, the greatest security threat stems not from "high-impact, low-probability" terrorist incidents but rather from far more prosaic and everyday irritants of the electronic age: viruses, worms, hackers, crackers, leaks, fraud, theft, and unauthorized access. So well predicted by so many authors, the electronic security threat is alive, well, and seemingly more baffling by the day. Cyberattacks across American businesses have doubled in the past year.[8] According to Ernst and Young, however, only 40 percent of the organizations they surveyed are confident they would detect a systems attack.[9] What is so bad about that? The most successful form of espionage—corporate or otherwise—is when the victim doesn't even know he's been had. More worrying than that for many is the spread and growing virulence of computer viruses. By the summer of 2003, the *Washington Post* reported that the "Sobig.F" virus had become the fastest growing computer virus of all time, even eclipsing the recent "Blaster" worm. The forecast? More of the same as virus writers out-class security software developers—like a "Revenge of the Nerds" competition, but on steroids.[10]

Insider Threats

As alarming as the security situation may be from outside the company, one of the most traditionally overlooked—but most damaging—areas of concern is the potential for loss from the disgruntled insider. Indeed, the most recent statistics show that this problem is, like poison ivy, a perennial as hardy as it is noxious. The U.S. Chamber of Commerce estimates that *as many as one-third of all business closures* result directly from employee theft—although as a solid business group, the Chamber declines to say how many were CEOs. If that estimate seems a little high, then consider the findings by *CSO Magazine,* which surveyed 1,009 executives and found that 53 percent believe that current employees poise the greatest threat to the technology infrastructure because of the challenges they poise to detection and monitoring.[11] If you think those executives sound a little paranoid, then consider the 138 companies that responded to a 2002 survey by *CSO* magazine. "They reported that the loss of proprietary information often in the form of research and development or financial data, cost them at least 53 billion in 2001 alone."[12] All of which suggests that corporate security has to be directed at least as much to the internal threat as anything else.

Regulatory Compliance

What is interesting for the CEO is that, while all these threats have been getting worse and worse, new laws with increased security requirements inevitably raise the stakes for everyone involved in corporate governance. According to one leading analyst:

New privacy and security laws such as the United States Patriot Act of 2001 and the Foreign Intelligence Surveillance Acts will have a direct impact on business specifically privacy issues and sharing of customer information. *The organization's security will be under greater scrutiny than in the past by regulators, legislators, auditors, business partners, and customers.*[13]

In any Army unit in which I ever had any level of responsibility, there was never an inspection of any kind, performed by any higher headquarters, which did not begin with the phrase, "We are here to help you." Similarly, there is just no way that corporate security threats can proliferate in some of the pathways outlined here and *not* attract the attention of "regulators, legislators, and auditors" who are only too eager to help you. You might as well expect blood in the water not to attract the attention of sharks. That degree of outside scrutiny needs to be understood, planned for, and managed by the CEO—before someone else does it for him. Because guess what's coming next?

"Within five years, CEOs will be required to sign as part of their annual audit reports a statement that indicates that an organization's digital assets are secure in the same way they have to attest to the veracity of financial statements. And external auditors will be required to audit the protected measures that a firm has put in place."[14]

Get the picture? There are security threats out there today which may or may not affect you, which may or may not directly impact your bottom line—or the lives and welfare of your employees. But if the terrorists don't get you, the auditors will, and like other forms of shark attack, the only thing they will leave untouched is your smile.

RULES OF THE ROAD

Here are some rules of the road you may want to keep in mind in addressing your security situation, which you obviously are in a far better position to appreciate than me. For those reasons alone, this guidance is absolutely *not* guaranteed to keep you safe from either the auditors or the terrorists. It's like when Geraldo Rivera worked for our network and was going off to some war zone or other. I offered him this totally free and gratuitous advice: "You may or may not come back alive. But it is important that you not get your ass shot off doing something stupid." Same principle here, okay?

1. *The mind of the CEO:* If there is one principle to keep in mind it is that security is not overhead, it is survival. You need to understand that, but more to the point, that thought needs to be communicated throughout the entire organization. I write these words in the immediate aftermath of the largest blackout ever experienced by the people of the Northeastern United States, including New York, Ohio, Michigan, and parts of Eastern Canada. As it was on 9/11, many of those people had to make decisions affecting their lives—quickly and on the basis of incomplete information. Which, God willing, is as close as most of them will ever come to combat, but when you deal with incomplete information, you have to rely solely on what your training tells you to do. And on 9/11, most of the people who successfully evacuated the World Trade Center did one very important, life-saving thing: They got up and did whatever was necessary to evacuate the building despite any instructions or directions to the contrary. When the plane hits your building or the power fails, it is too late for the CEO to try and figure out what he should have done to train his people more effectively. That's what life has a way of bringing to your doorstep: a no-nonsense, no-notice evaluation of how well you have prepared your company for the ultimate survival test. While there are other important rules, everything is secondary to the survival of the company, its key people, its key procedures, its key facilities. While the CEO can delegate many of his responsibilities, nothing is more fundamental than this: That direct, physical survival is no longer guaranteed but needs to be won. And that the test is likely to come, as the Scriptures say, "as a thief in the night."

2. *The strategic plan:* Review Chapter 5 on strategy because your understanding of what it's going to take to secure your enterprise depends first of all on what is in your strategic plan—assuming that there is one. Forget about BHAGs and all that. What is the value of the information that you are trying to protect? What are your competitive secrets? What are those things that you rely on for the competitive edge of your company? To borrow an admittedly military construct: What are those centers of gravity that, if you lost them, would threaten the survival of your business? Government has now been forced to guarantee its continuity in the face of a catastrophic attack on Washington. Bunkers and remote locations are much more elaborate preparations than most companies

need but that mental process is equally important for businesses to understand as well. Among other things, it puts you through the discipline of asking what the company needs to survive? With what information? In what critical facilities? All of which should derive directly from the strategic plan on the theory that if you don't know what you are defending, there's almost no way you can protect it.

3. *The baseline security survey:* There is a straight mental and practical progression here from basic security consciousness through the strategic plan and on to the engineering of a baseline security survey. Unless you are a very unusual company with some unique talent, you don't rely on your own resources for the security survey: Go out and engage the most talented group you can find. The reason is that you're asking these guys to assess your security needs as an organization. The cognitive process is pretty straightforward—not cheap but definitely straightforward. They examine your risks and vulnerabilities—physical, informational, and human—and balance them against the kind of potential solutions that make the most sense, including economic sense. The assessment at its most fundamental level involves asking how much security the enterprise needs and can afford. Traditional enterprise security has largely been based on the fortress mentality: static, undifferentiated, and highly defined by specific locations. It relies on a few traditional mechanisms: strong walls and a locked gate. The second model is the emerging airport model, which is more flexible, more situational, and based on the idea of multiple zones of security. Like a fortress within a fortress, different zones employ multiple overlapping technologies to authenticate and control access. The final model is a point-to-point "dynamic trust model" that is most appropriate for highly networked organizations. Like a military radio network, it requires point-to-point authentication and verification, assuming that all parties to transactions will identify and authenticate themselves on demand.[15] Figuring out which of these models is best suited for your business is what you are hiring these consultants to recommend. Along with locating your weakest links and any single points of failure that may have been highlighted by your strategic plan.

4. *Hire good people:* If your security consultants have done a good job, you should now have a reasonable idea about what your security architecture

should look like, specifically the infrastructure needed to support your enterprise security. The fourth step is hiring good people to run this thing—and, if you are lucky, you will try and replicate what the Dow Jones executives did in hiring Joe Cantamessa. It is important that you hire people to manage the two basic disciplines of the trade—thugs and geeks—meaning its physical and information security aspects. It should be appreciated that these are very different disciplines calling— usually—for very different skill sets that are rarely possessed by a single individual. There is also a lively debate in the security community about whether it makes sense to combine both disciplines in a single organization. There are inevitably some trade-offs but what is vital is ensuring an appropriate balance between physical security and IT security—which can be done by management committees, although you should forgive this contradiction in terms. Remember as well the baseline set by the security survey that should have told you a great deal about what you really need. However, you still need the specific policies—physical and informational—that will flesh out those basic guidelines. How many guards should be hired? In fixed positions or roving? What kind of security software should be the baseline? Should we have anti-virus software, firewalls, or intrusion detection systems? Do we need multiple security zones and biometric IDs? If you're a CEO, then act like one and don't try to make those decisions yourself. When you hire the best people in their respective fields, you should allow them to hammer out solutions to those very practical problems. Figure out if their recommendations make sense for the business as a whole—and if they do then back them up but hold them accountable for the advice they gave you. After all, that's why you hired them. And once they have helped you settle on your basic security policies, give them the long-term project of designing and implementing effective disaster recovery plans and emergency action drills.

5. *Penetration tests:* The fifth major step is one of my favorites: scheduling unannounced penetration inspections, both physical and informational. Why? Well, so far you've done a pretty good job. You've imparted the importance of security to your organization. You have unearthed a strategic plan and figured out what you are trying to defend. You have hired security professionals to do a survey and hired other

security professionals to run the damned thing and put specific policies in place. That's okay, but frankly you're a lot like the coaching staff
of my favorite team the Washington Redskins. Year after year, they
make grandiose plans, trade for incredibly over-paid players—and are
constantly embarrassed when it comes to playing actual games. While
those games may be painful, they are terribly revealing of overlooked
weaknesses, say in the kicking game, the quarterbacks, or the defensive
line. The same principle applies to penetration tests because there is
simply no better way to discipline your security system. Think of it as an
unannounced OPFOR visit. How successfully can your electronic systems be penetrated by hackers, crackers, or by unauthorized access of
any kind? Apply the same methods that those sorts of folks would to
break into your systems: It's cheaper and you will learn a lot. Same
thing applies to your physical plant. What about social engineering?
How well have your people been trained? Do they understand what the
threats are? That kind of periodic penetration inspection does absolute
wonders for an organization because it evaluates what people actually
do as opposed to what they say they do. Above all: Don't forget that the
purpose of the penetration test is emphatically not to serve as a
"gotcha"—or as the camouflage for disciplinary action. Like any test,
however, penetrations are designed to highlight weaknesses and determine if those worthy policies you set in place are actually getting the
job done.

6. *Take care of your people:* If you don't think good personnel policies
have anything to do with security, then you haven't grasped the essence of
the most important component of the system: your people. It is an article
of faith among the human relations crowd that this sort of thing is not
merely good management but good business. But from a security point of
view, the corollary is: The better you take care of your people, the less of
a security risk they will pose to you. Remember the basics we previewed
earlier: More losses are caused from inside the company than anywhere
else—and you can't buy enough surveillance cameras and security software to do more than make a dent in it. So try another approach: basic
decency and trust. What you've also got to realize is that one of the main
threats to any business is having its best people walk out the door—because they will inevitably leave a place that treats them poorly despite all

the debriefing and all the noncompetition agreements you can force them to sign. They walk out with a tremendous amount of the corporate assets between their ears and there's nothing that you can do about that. But fairness goes a long way. So does explicit training so that the workforce understands their responsibilities in carrying out the policies of the organization including what not to say on the phone, what documents not to leave lying around unsecured in the office, what documents are the golden keys to the competition. So take good care of your people, train them, make sure they understand what is expected of them, and make doubly sure that you as a manager do what you do need to do to keep them happy. Security is ever so much easier when you are dealing with well-led, well-trained professionals.

7. *Everyone is accountable—all the time:* This is a direct lift from Rudy Giuliani and his approach to leadership. Whatever he did with the NYPD, whatever he did anywhere in his administration, his leadership style incorporated the idea that everyone is accountable all the time. But if there is no substitute for accountability, then there can be no substitute for measurement. That is not a bad guidepost for the CEO who really understands that security is about survival. If that ideal is to be anything other than lip service, security has to be measured in every way that it can be measured. The geeks and thugs have to be fanatics about looking for physical and electronic penetrations, because what they have to report they will guard against. If we have policies, procedures, and physical safeguards to back those things up, then we have to keep book on the number of times they are effectively penetrated or compromised. Having run security organizations myself, I can tell you that keeping ahead of the opposition (internal and external) is a never-ending battle. Like pressure gauges on a boiler, measurement tells you vital things about the health of your system and what you may need to do to improve it. One leading security analyst puts it this way:

> Many enterprises don't maintain statistics on attacks, responses to attacks, or the effectiveness of defenses. Without metrics, enterprise digital security runs blind. Measures should include types of attacks (both successful and unsuccessful); perpetrators (if known); targets of attacks, effectiveness and per incident cost of defenses and losses attributed to attacks. *Enterprises that*

focus on real risks and pay attention to their program's risk reduction effectiveness will receive the best return on their security investments [emphasis added].[16]

Not to mention that those enterprises may also lose their asses—figuratively or otherwise—unless they appreciate the absolute necessity of making accountability an all-the-time policy.

While there is a certain grimness that tends to accompany the security business, there are some lighter moments too that sometimes teach you a lot about rolling with the punches and being intensely suspicious of elaborate solutions to common problems. Telling one of those stories—on myself, naturally—seems a good way to conclude this chapter, while again illustrating the eternal workings of Murphy's Law.

So there I was, a young intelligence officer working against the Russians in Germany at the height of the Cold War in the early 1970s. It became necessary for me to act as a courier in transporting a highly classified document (probably the forthcoming PX catalogue) down to our group headquarters in Munich. We customarily rode the very efficient German railway system on these junkets and that was the plan this time as well. Except that our group headquarters warned me that, due to the classification of the document under my protection, I would need to be armed. Now that was a hassle, since West Germany was undergoing the same sort of terrorist problem then that we would experience some 30 years later—and carrying a gun on a train simply invited complications at every level, including German police and security forces. The alternative was right out of a James Bond movie—handcuffing the briefcase to my wrist. Except that we had no handcuffs since "Q" was fully occupied at that time outfitting Sean Connery. Fortunately, one of my NCOs was a former military policeman and still had an old set of handcuffs from his previous assignment.

Group headquarters was satisfied, approved the mission, and off I went, accompanied by my pal Joe Ferris, also an intelligence officer and an OCS classmate. From somewhere in the Ozarks, Joe was a bubba before we knew what bubbas were—and his sense of humor had helped make the rigors of OCS more bearable. As soon as he saw the briefcase handcuffed to my wrist, he went into hysterics. Nor did matters improve much when we got to our train compartment, where I secured the whole contraption to the luggage rack. "See how simple this is?" I crowed triumphantly. "Briefcase, handcuffs, luggage rack. Perfectly secure. Now isn't that a WHOLE lot better than one of us having to pack heat?"

All went well until we arrived in Munich and I stood to unlock the handcuffs from the luggage rack. The key entered the lock smoothly enough, but when I turned it, there was a sickening metallic click as it broke off completely, with the handcuffs still locked as tightly as if a perp walk was in progress. I stood there dumbfounded with the broken key in my hand and pondered the options—all of which seemed grim. German luggage racks must be built by the same people who manufacture their tanks because even a cursory tug revealed utterly solid Teutonic construction. Of course, Joe was no help at all. As soon as he realized what had happened, the hysterics resumed. "Perfectly secure," he shouted. "Perr-fick-lee SEEEE-cure. Well whut you gonna do now, boy? Yew done permanently bolted a HAGHLEE SEE-CRET document to a train that's headed over to the commies in Czechoslovakia!"

Actually, he was right. After a brief stop in Munich that was exactly where the train was headed—and at that time Czechoslovakia was still behind the Iron Curtain. The briefcase was an expensive, all-leather model that my parents had given me as a graduation present. Still, there weren't many options. I opened the briefcase—fortunately that lock still worked—and evacuated the classified documents, the other contents, and all identification. "Quit laughing and help me, goddammit," I snapped. "We can hide the documents under our trench coats and get out of here." Trench coats. Wrong choice of words because that sent Joe off into still more hysterics. But presently, with as much dignity as we could muster, two American intelligence officers stepped off the train and made their way out with their trench coats noticeably bulging—one of them cursing quietly but profoundly—and the other demonstrating why the official Arkansas state motto is still "GUFFAW."

So, for whatever it's worth, let that story be a lesson. I still wonder what the border guards and the railway officials must have thought about that empty handcuffed briefcase when it got to Czechoslovakia. But if your guard force insists on being equipped with handcuffs, just make sure they're plastic.

WAR PLAN

MISSION OBJECTIVES

There are two fundamental concepts that must drive the CEO's approach to enterprise security:

1. Security is not just overhead—it is life: the life of the organization and even the lives of the people who work there and the customers who sustain them in business.

2. Security is the fundamental responsibility of the CEO. He can get help in delegating some of his security functions but, like the captain of a ship, the responsibility remains his and his alone.

★ As we have eagerly made the computer into an ever more efficient slave attending every facet of the modern corporation, the irony is that we have inadvertently built Trojan horses—in some cases quite literally.

★ The bad news for CEOs and for business is that they simply do not enjoy the luxury of having a single enemy that we can identify, isolate, and predict. And you know what? That reality ain't gonna change anytime soon.

★ Taking specific actions to balance the trade-off between what is possible and what is likely is what a planner does. The best-run companies are those that anticipate worst-case scenarios as well as adopt commonsense policies intended to minimize their effects—and buy insurance to mitigate those exposures they can't control.

★ The risk of terrorist attack remains astronomically low for most companies—although the equation gets much more interesting if one calculates the "downstream effects" of such an attack, particularly one directed at infrastructure targets.

(continued)

★ Although such issues as employee safety, workplace violence, data security, and continuity of operations have clearly grown in importance, the resources to counteract them are thus far not being spent by corporate America.

★ For most firms, the greatest security threat stems not from "high-impact, low-probability" terrorist incidents but rather from far more prosaic and everyday irritants of the electronic age: viruses, worms, hackers, crackers, leaks, fraud, theft, and unauthorized access. The electronic security threat is alive, well, and seemingly more baffling by the day.

★ As alarming as the security situation may be from outside the company, one of the most traditionally overlooked—but most damaging—areas of concern is the potential for loss from the disgruntled insider.

★ Unless you are a very unusual company with some unique talent, don't rely on your own resources for the security survey: Go out and engage the most talented group you can find.

★ It is important that you hire people to manage the two basic disciplines of the security trade—thugs and geeks—that is, its physical and information security aspects. These are very different disciplines, usually calling for very different skill sets, rarely possessed by a single individual.

★ Schedule unannounced "penetration" inspections, both physical and informational. There is simply no better way to discipline your security system. How successfully can your electronic systems be penetrated by hackers, crackers, or by unauthorized access of any kind? Apply the same methods that those folks would to break into your systems: it's cheaper and you will learn a lot.

★ One of the main threats to any business is having its best people walk out the door—because they will inevitably leave a place that treats them poorly, despite all the debriefing and all the noncompetition agreements you may force them to sign. They walk out with a tremendous amount of the corporate assets between their ears, and there's nothing you can do about that.

★ So take good care of your people, train them, make sure they understand what is expected of them, and make doubly sure that you as a manager do what you do need to do to keep them happy. Security is ever so much easier when you are dealing with well-led, well-trained professionals.

9

☆ ☆ Testing Your METL ☆ ☆

Or What to Do When the Mission Really Is Essential

National Training Center, Fort Irwin, California, 1400: The AAR

Time to take a seat, such as it is. And be careful where you sit down, because you're not back in the CEO conference room now. Also, sidewinders aren't the only worry, because everything else out here bites, stings, or scratches. Sorry about the temperature but it routinely runs about 110 to 115 degrees. That way, Iraq in August isn't exactly a surprise. Not something you ever get used to, of course, but you do learn how to manage it. So make sure that you've got your suntan lotion on. And drink some water, even if you don't feel thirsty.

This gaggle of soldiers that we are looking at here is the BLUE Force battalion that got whacked last night. Remember I told you that, when they lost the RECON war, the rest of the battle was a foregone conclusion. Well, it was because they got whacked—hard. But at the NTC—and elsewhere in the Army—that is not the end of the story. What we are seeing here is a council of war—the day after. The battalion commander, his principle staff, and his subordinate commanders all are engaged in what we call an after action review, *(AAR). You are going to be hearing that acronym throughout this discussion, so get used to it. What you are seeing here is the top of the food chain because the entire battalion—and I mean down to the lowest squad—has been through the same thing. Now that process is very, very direct. What the AAR does is to ask: What happened? Why did it happen? And what do I need to work on to make it better next time? Think of it almost like a Marxist-Leninist, self-criticism class, but on steroids.*

What was that? How obligatory is the AAR? Guess it depends on whether or not you want to stay in command, because if you don't take this stuff seriously then you have a problem: You can't lead and your troops won't follow. And we really are not at all shy about relieving people who don't perform. Let me put this another way: Training is the lifeblood of what we do. There's an old saying that the more you sweat in peace, the less you bleed in war. I'm sorry, what was that? Will they be discussing BHAGs at the AAR? No, I really I don't think so. Although a couple of the majors with this unit went out and got their MBAs between their last assignments, so they might actually have been exposed to BHAGs in B-school. But, hey these are bright guys and with some remedial training, it really shouldn't take too long to get them back to normal.

Now listen up because the commander is giving his assessment of what they need to improve in the next training cycle and how that improvement in turn affects their ability to carry out their war plans. That's the reason why the AAR is so important because war plans are our bottom line. Because there comes a time when you're a superpower that you care enough to send the very best: us and those that fight along side us. I know you have bottom lines in business, too, but you don't have anything similar to the process you're seeing demonstrated here today. If your strategy consultants were here, they would probably nod sagely and say we're aligning our strategy. And that, for another six-figure contract, they can do the same thing for you. But for the time being, this is free—so watch, listen, and try to learn something. By the way, you can have one of these MREs while we're listening. That stands for Meals Ready to Eat or, because we're politically incorrect, Meals Rejected by Ethiopians. You might think of them the next time you have your shareholder lunch at the Four Seasons. I'm sure the food is going to be better. But I'm betting the strategy won't be.

I really do hesitate to tell you what this chapter is really all about. With the greatest respect, dear reader: but you really don't have anything remotely comparable in business today. Unless you routinely sit down after every business engagement, look systematically for "lessons learned" and incorporate them into what you are going to do the next time. And then bring in mission, strategy, training, and corporate leadership, including the grooming of the next generation of CEOs. While I hesitate to use the term, what we are actually doing is aligning the organization. Every since it was coined by Peter Senge, "alignment" has been consistently overused—most often by businesses for whom the term "coordinated" was not grand enough.[1]

But, call it what you will, the lack of alignment is a persistent problem in either business or war. The difference is that the military at least has the means, the methodology, and the will to do something about it—which is what we're talking about here. Adrian Savage, who we introduced during our discussion of strategy, tells a canonical tale inspired by the great Northeast blackout of 2003. It reminded him of when he worked with a London-based company in the 1970s, which was facing disruption from work stoppages in the public transportation system. In England, those things are called "industrial actions" and, before Margaret Thatcher put the fear of God in the trade unions, those sorts of things happened all the time. Savage's company, left with few options but self-help, came up with a brilliant plan to run their own transportation operations with charter buses. Twelve of them, manned by their own people, complete with routes and contingencies to avoid traffic backups. But the next morning, the results were not encouraging because only two buses made it home.

According to Savage, the reason was that no one had focused on the internal elements of the plan, because they fixated instead on external details like the routes. They ignored some key internal elements, like the fact that some of the drivers had never driven a bus before; nor was anyone assigned to double-check the mechanical condition of the buses or whether they had enough gas. And from that example, he asked:

> What ruins implementation? Segments of the organization break down. The systems and procedures they operate are not quite equal to the new strategy they seek to fulfill. Organizations are mostly quite good at collecting and

considering external intelligence about customers, industry, and market trends, the competition and the state of the economy. However, like our poor bus route organizer, they typically fail to collect adequate internal intelligence that will indicate how prepared and how capable their organization is of carrying out the strategies they wish to follow.[2]

What Savage calls "internal intelligence" is what others see as the classic problem of alignment—and what we in the military would deal with by simply court-martialing the poor bus route organizer for a combination of bad attitude and exceptionally inept staff work. The fact is that complex organizations require in-depth planning and execution for anything (1) to happen at all and (2) to happen without making matters worse. As the operating environment becomes more complex, the organization is asked to hit S-curves at 60 mph, and human nature being what it is, someone invariably leans the wrong way at the worst possible moment—and the whole enterprise goes off the tracks. Whether the issues are in security, intelligence, or operations, it probably matters very little in the scheme of things: it is the CEO's job to think about alignment—at precisely the moment when the penalties for nonalignment—or what the consultants would term "incompetent change management"—are growing. And the methodologies offered by some of those same consultants appear suspect—or at least overpriced. So what's a poor executive to do?

Well, let's begin with a word of sympathy. There is a reason why armies have historically been concerned with the problem of alignment—for reasons covered in our discussion of organization in Chapter 6: The greater the number of soldiers, the greater the difficulty of controlling them. Historically, the answers have usually stressed uniformity, inflexibility or both. Until relatively recently, military innovation carried a substantial risk of chaos because of a thousand different factors that all had to be coordinated to make any progress—and seldom ever were. The Soviets understood this as a "permanent factor of war," and to overcome it they primarily relied on mass. While in our defense planning, we asked "how much is enough?" the Soviets simply determined how much was demonstrably *too much*—and then added 10 percent anyway. Their war plans were particularly clumsy—but were meant to work in spite of the chaos of war and the grotesque inefficiencies of their military, economic, and political system. In spite of the disparity in numbers, we looked across the line during the Cold War and took great comfort from that inefficiency—in fact, we counted on it. Armies, you see, fight other armies and we considered ourselves marginally more efficient.

But only just. I remember all too well some of our own problems, so if you think you have problems with inefficiency and "nonalignment," well, we've been there, too. Among my archives, there is a story I have saved for just such an occasion. It occurred over 20 years ago, when the U.S. Army was very different from what it became just a few years later. It occurred at one of our signal units—proverbial at that time for employing the kind of people that even the Army thought were at best a leadership challenge. While in the process of preparing for a field exercise at a radio relay site, a fire occurred. In the cast of characters was one Army specialist, E-4, who shall here be known as Murphy—since this was apparently the only law he knew. In the spare, dry, understated prose of the military police report can be glimpsed those "eternal operating forces" the Soviets worried about, too.

One evening, just after dark, Murphy carried a five-gallon can of gasoline from the cargo trailer to an area near the tailgate of his vehicle where they stored generators to supply power during the exercise. One assumes that the lid on the gasoline might not have been completely tightened because of what happened next. Murphy struck a match "in order to see better," then blew it out and dropped it on the ground. "A trail of fire" immediately sprang up from the location of the dropped match to the five-gallon can. Sensing the onset of disaster, Murphy ran to the now-burning gasoline can and picked it up. But as he sprinted around the vehicle, the can became too hot to hold and he dropped it to the ground next to the left bumper. The front of the vehicle now caught fire. Life in the field is never uncomplicated, as Murphy now noticed his BDUs were on fire too and, at last remembering some semblance of his training, dropped to the ground and rolled to put them out. It was the only tactic he tried that apparently worked but, as he did so, the fire now engulfed the front end of the truck. Seeing that things were not completely normal, Murphy's section chief now entered the fray and, for some unaccountable reason, first left the scene to flag down a passing motorist and, then finally, thought to call the fire department. They duly arrived on the scene, extinguished the flames, and estimated the damages to the U.S. government at approximately $80,000. Murphy got away with only minor burns to his left hand—but probably had to replace his BDUs. Alignment and Murphy's Law—so good together!

THE ARMY LEARNS TO FIGHT—SOME PRACTICAL EXAMPLES FOR CEOs

The old Cold War models began to break down, even as that conflict reached one of its flashpoints during the 1973 Yom Kippur War. That very intense conflict between the Arabs and the Israelis began on a note of strategic surprise—almost shock for the Israelis—and featured desperate battles and levels of destruction that we had not expected to see on anything less than a nuclear battlefield. On the Golan Heights and elsewhere, Israel had come within a whisker of losing. How close they came was brought home to me more than 20 years after those events, when, during a visit by the National War College, I was reunited in Israel with a Harvard classmate who was a hero of that war, Lieutenant General Yossi Ben Hanan. Then a battalion commander of the famed Golani Brigade, Yossi had led his unit in some close-run contests over ground that was a textbook definition of "decisive terrain." "Kenny, it was unbelievable," he said all those years later as we looked across a border that still seemed absurdly close. "We fought tank to tank at point-blank ranges, maybe 30 yards. I still don't know if some of my rounds were armed before they hit." When the battle was over, Yossi was badly wounded and the rest of the Golani Brigade had suffered heavy losses. But as one Israeli account of the battle notes, "Few commanders could credit the magnitude of the 7th (Golani) Brigade victory until they saw with their own eyes the incredible scene of destruction . . . with well over 500 (Syrian) armored vehicles of all types strewn across the valley."[3]

The first war in which precision guided munitions were used in great numbers, we studied those outcomes and concluded that, "what can be seen can be hit and what can be hit can be killed." That was new and different—as was the idea that, although outnumbered, we needed "to win the first battle of the next war," simply because we might not get another chance.[4] In 1976, the Army republished field manual 100-5, its capstone manual on operations, and began a long slow process of fundamental changes intended to catch up to the new realities of war. One of the first things that we began to re-learn was that different leaders had different functions on the battlefield. Generals commanded corps and divisions and concentrated forces, while colonels and lieutenant colonels commanded brigades and battalions respectively, while controlling and directing the battle. As they always had, captains and their companies, troops, and batteries actually fought the battle.

Those divisions of responsibility were hardly new: but the time horizons were. The captain fights a very close battle—up close and personal—often dominated by forces, events, and actual combat no more than 12 hours in the future. Given the speed of modern combat—with the advent of tanks capable of cross-country speeds of 40 to 50 miles per hour—generals concentrated their forces over a time frame between 72 hours out to as many as five days. That basic restatement of responsibilities was significant because it settled the key issue of *who* was responsible for *what:* Captains did not often impinge on the work of generals. But later in my career, I saw many a general who needed reminding that his function as a general was to think about extended time frames, concentrating forces—and to leave the close battles and short-range responses to his subordinates. (Later still, I met CEOs who needed the same sort of reminders. Do you know any?)

The other changes that occurred as the Army went about its doctrinal revolution require a brief mention. The pattern was that we moved by stages from being a conscript force to a volunteer force—but rather more painfully to becoming a professional force. Two key changes made the difference: manpower and money. When Ronald Reagan became president, we began to receive a series of pay raises that enabled the Army to pay its soldiers what they were worth. In 1981, I was a captain on civilian schooling duty in Massachusetts, which was a fairly hard place to spend the winter; but by the end of the year, those pay raises meant we could actually afford to buy our heating oil without scrimping elsewhere in the budget.

More profoundly, Reagan enabled the Army and our sister services to pay enough that we could attract a better quality recruit. General Max

Thurman was at that time the head of the Army Recruiting Command, which for generations had been accustomed to "recruiting" prospective soldiers who were one step ahead of the sheriff. But now with a whole generation of new equipment for the Army on the drawing boards, we were financially able to recruit and retain better soldiers. So why, General Thurman asked in his shy retiring way, were we persisting in the notion that our recruiting efforts should be directed toward the bottom of the barrel? Why not aim higher? "That's the problem," General Max repeatedly told the recruiters, "We need to catch some trout and you guys keep going after carp."

The Army was not sure at first that "quality" was the way to go—but it soon learned that Max Thurman was as determined as he was smart. He amply earned the nickname of "The Maxatollah" and more than lived up to his motto: "When in charge, take charge." He rose to four stars and postponed retirement to command our invasion of Panama. In its aftermath, he finally came to public attention when his troops had Panamanian strongman Manuel Antonio Noriega holed up downtown in the papal nunciatura and bombarded the place not with artillery but with high-volume renditions of the dulcet tunes of Def Leppard and Twisted Sister to make him come out. (Had it been me, I would have preferred the artillery.) Perhaps not sensing that this was the *easy* way, the media demanded a press conference, again perhaps not realizing what they were up against. At the first question about the use of loud music, Max simply pounded the podium and roared: "I AM the officer in charge of selecting the music! Next question!" When in charge. . . .The press quickly gave up and so did Noriega.

Max never did though, not even when, shortly after Panama, the medics told him he had leukemia and would be dead in three months. "Okay, doctor, so much for Battle Plan A. Now tell me about Battle Plan B." Under Battle Plan B, Max fought the leukemia with characteristic courage for almost four years and regularly did things like accepting our invitation to address the National War College while I was there as dean. Before the speech, I briefed him on critical details like the timing of the coffee break—but as a scarred veteran of his staff should have known better than to have wasted my breath. Max spoke uninterrupted for two hours—and had 'em rolling in the aisles. But his real legacy was represented not so much at the war colleges but in those talented young men and women who, as the direct result of his leadership, joined the Army in the 1980s and helped transform it into the professional, quality force that endures today. As he was being carried out of the chapel at Fort Myer to nearby Arlington National Cemetery, the band struck up a tune much too lively to make a convincing funeral dirge. But the song was the best of all memorials because it represented the ideal that Max had given to the Army and to our soldiers: *Be All That You Can Be.*

I tell you about these things so that you can better appreciate that generals like Max Thurman, Norman Schwarzkopf, and Colin Powell were something more than just distinguished public servants who accomplished much for their country—as significant as those achievements are. But, together with all of us who wore the uniform in those days, they also participated in one of the greatest turn-around management chapters of any institution in our history. Beginning in the 1980s, we re-engineered, transformed, turned around, and otherwise transmogrified the entire United States Army: its people, its equipment, its training, its doctrines, and, most significantly, its leadership. All because we were trying to become a professional force who fought the nation's wars and was determined never to lose another one. And that whole process was encapsulated when two critical elements were brought together and became a critical mass: the way we planned for war and the way we trained in peace.

Those are concepts that we learned to test at places like the National Training Center. The heart of that process—the basis for the maneuvers, the live fires and the after-action reviews—is something called the Mission Essential Task List (METL). Derived directly from the unit's war plans, those tasks are fundamental to the real-world combat mission it has been given. Those operational plans constitute the core of what that unit is expected to do if push comes to shove in places like Afghanistan, Iraq, or Korea. Figures 9.1 and 9.2 are taken from the current Army manual on training and illustrate how real-world war plans are translated into specific unit training requirements.

Figure 9.1 (METL Development Process) shows where we get those critical wartime tasks: from the unit's war plans, from its understanding of the operational environment, and from specific guidance by higher commanders. The METL is not developed in isolation by some commander

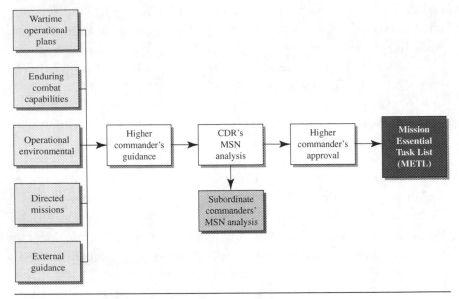

Figure 9.1   METL development process. *Source:* Army FM 7-0, "Training the Force," Washington, DC, October 22, 2002.

"doing his own thing," but rather in close coordination with higher and lower units: we are after all a *team*.

The second half of this process is illustrated by Figure 9.2 (Integration of Collective and Individual Training) and shows how the METL determines what the unit actually does in its day-to-day training. The process begins with a basic assessment by the commander, typically at the battalion level, which is the Army's basic fighting unit. As shown by this illustration, *the differences between the standards mandated by the METL and the battalion commander's assessment of its current capabilities are what drives the training.* If the unit is expected by its war plans to be proficient in crossing rivers, the commander makes the all-important assessment of how well it can perform those jobs today—and then plans any remedial training accordingly. At each step, he is supported by his unit's noncommissioned officers, who are responsible for ensuring that the training is relevant to the individual soldier. Also at each step, the assessment of how well the training conforms to expectations is what drives the after-action reviews—at every level, involving every soldier all the way up to the battalion commander.

Figure 9.2   Integration of collective and individual training. *Source:* Army FM 7-0, "Training the Force," Washington, DC, October 22, 2002.

Now go back to our NTC scenario at the start of this chapter. What are those guys doing? They were using the AARs to evaluate what they just did in the training exercise because that tells them something about their ability to perform as they would in war. In our scenario, BLUE FORCE had left an undefended flank that OPFOR used as a convenient attack point into their position. What you do in training you are likely to repeat in war. The BLUE FORCE battalion commander has learned a valuable lesson about deploying his own reconnaissance forces—valuable because what he learned was a lesson that improved the competence of his unit but didn't cost the lives of his men—which is what effective training is all about.

The AAR is so deeply embedded in the Army culture that it not only governs training—but also provides a ready frame of reference for what goes on even when units are deployed to a war zone. One of the most memorable AARs I ever witnessed took place in Bosnia, when I accompanied a U.S. cavalry patrol that was conducting joint reconnaissance exercises with their Russian counterparts in one of the hotter (in every sense) and more remote parts of our area of operations. Prior to setting out, the patrol leader—an Army captain—discussed not training tasks but real-world responsibilities of the unit: exactly how the patrol would be organized, order of the vehicles on the road march, who sat where, with what weapons, preplanned fire support (if needed), and rules of engagement. And most critically: What the objectives were for the patrol and the standards he expected from his men. Turning to me, he asked if I had anything to add. Actually, no I didn't because I had never seen a patrol so well planned—including the ones I had organized.

The patrol went off without a hitch, including our joint exercise with the Russians—who were good soldiers but not nearly as well organized. After we returned to the base camp, the first thing the captain did was to get everybody rested, check that weapons were unloaded—and then conducted the AAR. To do that, he simply reviewed the original objectives and demanded feedback from his lieutenants, sergeants, and corporals. What transpired was not a bitch session—which it easily could have been. Instead, I had the unmistakable sense that these soldiers were taking ownership and responsibility for what went on. One soldier had noticed a problem with radio frequencies, another commented on the fact that his soldiers had been too distracted by the children in one of the villages— and weren't paying enough attention to covering their assigned fields of fire. Not a round had been fired, of course, but the process was as deadly serious as if it had. The captain concluded with a short evaluation of his own—and the AAR was over. Were they doing it because I was there? No— this was what they did every time they took the field—and it showed in large ways and small. Relaxing later over dinner with the captain, I asked him about his Russian partners in the peacekeeping mission—and how good they were. "Sir, they're real good," he replied, "in fact they're a lot like us. But you know, if we ever had to get into it with them, we'd kick their ass." That might sound like bravado—but then you didn't witness the AAR either.

Like that captain in Bosnia, the ultimate point of training is ensuring that each soldier knows precisely what is expected. The figures shown here indicate how a unit takes its Mission Essential Task List and breaks it down to individual responsibilities, much like a play in football. But the same process applies to every activity supporting the battalion: maneuver units, fire support, air defense artillery, combat service support, combat intelligence—all have specific responsibilities under the METL. And, like a football team honing its plays, once you have the backs understanding their assignments, you bring in the offensive linemen and finally the quarterback to run the plays. The process is systematic, circular, and thorough, always driven by the basics: METL, commander's assessment of what training is needed and AARs to assess how effectively it was.

Don't forget that our battalion is part of a brigade that is part of a division that is part of a corps. So training is an exercise in alignment in which each one of those constituent elements is given a specific responsibility. It understands exactly what it is supposed to do and how it is supposed to train in order to carry out its combat readiness responsibilities. It does so using what the Army refers to as Task, Conditions, and Standards. Those specifications are nothing less than an alignment effort in which everybody understands exactly what they are supposed to do under the operating conditions and to the standards required by the METL. It is a baseline that unifies the entire Army in the way it trains and prepares for war.

But the larger principle here is also important to understand. It is the idea that the lessons you learn from current operations should be captured for the organization and its future. Taking the best of what has been learned from the present and recycling it into the future is a powerful tool for any organization. The most topical application of that idea came during the writing of this book, when I was invited to attend a Pentagon briefing on the lessons learned from the latest analysis of Operation Iraqi Freedom. Those lessons, fascinating in themselves, were all the more remarkable for the obvious care that had gone into collecting and verifying their content—essentially a souped-up version of the AAR process. In contrast, I had personally seen how the "lessons learned" process after Somalia had been an effort in fault-finding and spin control—not so much "lessons learned" as "lessons identified."[5]

But simply consider what the military gets out of its applied process of alignment:

- How to synchronize strategic operational plans with training plans.
- How to link training plans with day to day activities.
- How to get lessons learned out of that process.
- How to apply those lessons learned into daily activities.

When you think about it, this is a wonderful alignment process, one that ensures that the taxpayer is getting maximum payoff from the money invested in us. But in addition to honing our warfighting skills and aligning the organization, what we also found was that this same process identified, honed, and assisted in evaluating leader development skills—particularly at the higher command levels. The reason is that all of our training does not just occur at the National Training Center. We use a number of different forms of simulation to work out problems at the higher levels of warfare—in command postexercises, crisis scenario development, and what we call "map exercises without troops." All of these activities—like the METL itself—are driven by our war plans and the need to test them out conceptually to see if they pass the "common-sense" test. But what is also interesting is that this process becomes an extraordinarily valuable way to test future commanders, not only on their command and war fighting skills but also their future leadership. At some level, these exercises may seem theoretical. They aren't. Remember that quote from MacArthur when we were discussing leadership? "Upon these fields are sown the seeds that on other fields and on other days will bear the fruits of victory." So it is here. As useful as exercises are in preparing to fight wars, they are even more useful in preparing leaders. Which is also a key point for business that we shall return to over these last two chapters. While everybody talks about alignment and learning organizations, very few people do them, and even fewer think about how they are training future leaders for future responsibilities.

THE SEVEN CEO RESPONSIBILITIES WHILE TESTING YOUR METL

1. *Balancing the present against the future:* Your organization and you in particular need to balance the needs of the present against the needs of the future. This is probably one of the most difficult challenges for any business manager because of the relentless pressures of the quarterly bottom line or the last bump in your stock price, which affects bonuses and so many other things. This is not to understate the pressures that are a part of your current operating environment, but there has got to be a balance between the immediate and the essential. Okay, so your board chairman tells you that, your vice president of strategy tells you that, and for all I know your wife tells you that—so why listen to me? How about this nasty dose of reality: corporations focused on the short-term are effectively betting on instant replays and setting themselves up for failure. You presumably remember that the nation's business schools are still teaching the regular operation of that phenomenon known as the "business cycle:" that thing that routinely goes up and down? And that none of our vaunted economists know very much about fixing? If that is the case, then both bad and good times are not permanent. So the good times, when they are here, have to be used to get ready for a much more demanding environment. Even if you read nothing more profound in the business literature than basic economic history, you know that the bad times will surely be present sooner rather than later. And you simply need to get ready for that in the same way that the Army in peacetime has to get ready for war. In almost every one of our training manuals, we repeat the nostrum that the more you sweat in peace, the less you bleed in war. The business equivalent: The more that you think and prepare for the future, the less you will have to worry when the tough times arrive—and they will. The only question is whether your organization will be ready when they do.

2. *The relationship between strategy, lessons learned, and implementation:* As we have seen, the world of defense is always trying to recycle lessons learned from current operations and make them work for our future plans—from individual Army units on up to the Secretary of Defense mining the insights from the War on Iraq for insights into Pentagon

transformation. Yet business conducts operations all the time and seldom if ever seems to learn much from the experience. How should we collect those lessons? How should we evaluate them? Did we do a good job or a bad job—and how do we tell the difference? It is startling to recall Deming saying very much the same thing in offering his 14 points of quality, because quality improvements of the kind he was talking about were impossible in the absence of a disciplined effort to evaluate performance and use it to build for the future. Consider that a leadership challenge because the CEO needs to be in charge of that process. If he does not demand these things, if he does not require them of his subordinates, then they simply will not get done. There is no better teacher than experience, but only if you are attentive to the lessons that experience can teach you.

3. *Understand the past, understand the future:* There needs to be a systematic effort to understand the nature of the future operating environment. If you have a competitive intelligence section, this had better be one of their main missions—the same way that EMC looked out at their competitive environment to try and understand it a little bit better. What are those disruptive technologies out there, and how will we react to them? We have a nasty habit in business, or for that matter in war, of always being able to find the time to react to a crisis. Why not use the same amount of time to prevent one? Have you noticed how few of the really serious problems in the world are bolts from the blue? From power failures to the Columbia shuttle disaster, predictable consequences have a way of coming true! So do disruptive technologies, so why not try to spend some reasonable amount of time preparing for them? If you are the CEO, have your subordinates ever once heard you express a concern for understanding your operational environment to the point that you are shaping it rather than having it shape you? That preparing for future opportunities involves understanding the operating environment, anticipating its requirements and learning the lessons, core competencies and new skills needed to stay competitive. And producing the kind of leaders who can be in charge of business combat in the twenty-first century? In short: Demings or lemmings?

4. *Aligning your organization for the future:* If you are really serious about preparing your organization for future business combat, then

you should investigate how to apply some of our methods. Things like war games, commercial equivalents of which are available from a variety of firms, including those specializing in commercial intelligence. There are also exercises called staff rides that have similar potential for communicating useful lessons for business competition. We are constantly studying battlefields like Gettysburg, and at the National War College we took our students to the very spot where Lee ordered his troops forward so that our students could appreciate what that order meant to the men who made up Pickett's Charge. There is something wonderfully instructive about learning those kinds of lessons on precisely the same ground where they took place, but—aside from the odd forays for sheer entertainment value—business hasn't begun to exploit the competitive potential for war gaming, simulation, exercises, staff rides, and other practical exercises that can be directly applied to a business. Another innovative leadership tool that remains largely unexplored: setting up regular exercises with the business equivalent of the world class OPFOR, the opposing force, the same kind of thing that we see out at the National Training Center. If you are Pepsi, that force might well resemble Coca-Cola. If you are Wal-Mart, that opposing force might look like Target. Whoever you are, a direct competitor exists in your organizational battle space, so why not try and replicate them? We call that process "giving the enemy a seat at your counsel table" and it can work at least as well for business as it does for war. The major functions: evaluating sales plans, analyzing strategic plans, and determining whether your operational plans have a prayer of succeeding when they are attacked by somebody who knows you as well as you know yourself That's how we got as good as we are out of the National Training Center in all those exercises that we have briefly reviewed here. And wouldn't you rather be defeated in a theoretical board exercise than in real life? That's the whole point: The more you sweat in peace, the less you bleed in war.

   5. *Managing to the level of your pay grade:* This is a continuation of point one, but it bears restating here. But you have to put your money—or your time—where your mouth is. Where do you put the major thrust of your leadership? Managing the generals or micromanaging the captains? Coordinating forces for the distant engagements or fighting the close battle?

Remember what we learned as far back as the 1970s: Captains are supposed to be fighting the close battle, but generals are supposed to be fighting that distant battle three to five days out. If you are in the current fiscal year and you are not two years ahead in your thinking, you are probably wrong. No matter what the pressures are, you've got to be the one, you and no one else, to extend that planning horizon out to where it needs to be. During the Gulf War, I enraged a church audience by suggesting that Bette Midler's anti-war song, "From a Distance," was in reality a subtle tribute to stand-off weapons. Because I believe in reaching out and touching someone before he even knows we are in range. And so should you. If all you want to do is to fight the close battles then you simply are ignoring your responsibility for coordinating future forces. And one of those close battles will get a lot closer than you ever imagined. It will be the thing that suddenly jumps out and bites you on the ass. I guarantee it.

6. *Identify and train your successors:* Maybe you want to think about this responsibility at the more general level of your industry or your economic peer group. I give speeches before such business audiences all the time and there is a great influence that those groups can bring to bear in the marketplace. But whatever the level, there are four major responsibilities in training future business leaders:

(1) What are the leadership qualities needed at the senior levels, what it takes to succeed and the specific tasks that have to be accomplished by those senior leaders?

(2) What are the ethical values and the character traits those senior leaders are expected to portray?

(3) What are the standards of performance they should be expected to exemplify?

(4) How should they be expected to lead?

I will admit to a bias here and that is that none of these leadership qualities is something that an outside recruiter has any business determining—except perhaps at the most basic level. The reason is that the grooming of future leaders is one of the primary responsibilities of business leaders, particularly the CEO. From the day he steps into the chair, he has that responsibility to the future of his organization. While that task is normally thought of in the platitudes of the human relations crowd, let me suggest here and now that the entire process would get much more interesting if the higher level business simulations recommended here also had the parallel purpose of vetting the leadership pool to succeed the CEO. Resumes are nice: Showing how well you can project yourself in simulated business combat is even better.

7. *Set the example:* There is no more basic principle I am aware of in leadership than that to be a leader people must be willing to follow you—but before you can lead them, you must lead yourself. "Be technically and tactically proficient" is another way of saying it. But whether the leadership principles are taken from Officer Candidate School or Plebe Year at West Point, they all come down to the same thing: Personal leadership comes mostly by personal example. For a CEO, that means putting priorities out there that show that you are in charge of your schedule and your calendar rather then them being in charge of you—fighting all the things that, as J. F. C. Fuller said, tie the general-in-chief down like Gulliver in Lilliput. While assigned to West Point, a group of us used to go fishing on Long Island Sound with a commercial fisherman who customarily talked to us as we hadn't been talked to since we were second lieutenants. When we hooked into a big one, he had a standard line: "Hey, are you in charge of that fish—or is he in charge of you?" With fish like giant bluefin tuna, that wasn't a bad question. But it's also not a bad leadership question. Are you in charge of your business or your organization—or is it in charge of you? Are you applying leadership or is it being applied to you? Or is it pretty much a tie game? Think about those answers in the chapter that follows, because there WILL be a test. It's called reality—and I'm about to show you how you can get a jump on it. And be in charge of it rather than it being in charge of you!

WAR PLAN

MISSION OBJECTIVES

Complex organizations require in-depth planning and execution for anything to happen—and for it to happen without making matters worse. As the operating environment becomes more complex, the organization needs to move faster—warp-speed faster—and someone invariably leans the wrong way at the worst possible moment, and the whole enterprise can go off the tracks. It's the CEO's job to prevent this—which means focusing on alignment.

★ The lessons you learn from current operations should be captured for the organization and its future. Taking the best of what has been learned from the present and recycling it into the future is a powerful tool for any organization.

★ Consider what the military gets out of its applied process of alignment: how to synchronize strategic operational plans with training plans, how to link training plans with day-to-day activities, how to get lessons learned out of that process, and how to apply those lessons learned into daily activities.

★ Your organization—and you in particular—need to balance the needs of the present against the needs of the future. This is probably one of the most difficult challenges for any business manager, because of the relentless pressures of the quarterly bottom line or the last bump in your stock price. This is not to understate the pressures that are a part of your current operating environment, but *there needs to be a balance between the immediate and the essential.*

★ Today, corporations that are focused on the short-term are effectively betting on instant replays and setting themselves up for failure. Both bad and good times are not permanent. So the good times have to be used to get ready for a much more demanding environment, because bad times will surely be present sooner rather than later. You simply need to get ready for that, in the same way that the army in peacetime has to get ready for war.

★ A direct competitor exists in your organizational battle space, so why not try and replicate it? We call that process "giving the enemy a seat at your counsel table," and it can work at least as well for business as it does for war. That is how you should evaluate your sales plans, analyze your strategic plans, and determine whether your operational plans have a prayer of succeeding when they are attacked by somebody who knows you as well as you know yourself.

★ If you are in the current fiscal year, and are not two years ahead in your thinking, you are probably wrong. No matter what the pressures are, you've got to be the one—you and no one else—to extend that planning horizon out to where it needs to be.

★ The grooming of future leaders is one of the primary responsibilities of business leaders, particularly the CEO. From the day he steps into the chair, he has that responsibility to the future of his organization.

★ Personal leadership comes mostly by personal example. For a CEO, that means putting priorities out there that show that you are in charge of your schedule and your calendar rather then them being in charge of you.

10

☆ ☆ Putting It All Together ☆ ☆

In these chapters that we've covered together, if you have paid the slightest attention to what has been said, then you must be wondering whether any of this is possible in the real world—or if it's all just theoretical. In fact, you must be saying something like: "Sure, it's fine for the military to have all these elaborate planning and training mechanisms you have written about, but they are tax-supported institutions and don't face quarterly earnings statements and many of the other short-term pressures that business leaders face. But business is business and there is no taxpayer support—well, okay, but not all that much. But if what goes on here cannot be supported by the bottom line, then we don't do it, awright?" Understood—but read on because what we are dealing with in this chapter is the hands-on challenge for the CEO, the CFO, the CIO, the VPs, and the board: how can the whole damned bunch of you people put all these things together in a way that builds competitive advantage for *you, your company, and your industry?* The suggestions for you in this chapter are more than theoretical and are intended to show you that good planning, good strategy, and good leadership can actually succeed in the real world. No leaps of faith, no BHAGs, no hornswoggling of the stockholders, just a clear focus on the most essential business processes—and how to weld them into an interlocking series of actions that can put you ahead of the competition.

The larger dynamic at work in this evolution is one that is common to many different types of organizations. Stated most simply, it holds that policy is a function of ideas over time—business policy, defense policy, legislative policy—indeed any policy where leadership is required to bring about choices that decisively influence the outcome of events. The operation of this dynamic first became apparent during my time on the Army staff when I was asked to use my newly minted doctorate to help reconnect the Army with the national security community, which at that time customarily confused the terms *strategic, nuclear,* and *significant.* One of my professors at MIT had spent the entire semester explaining to us as members of the great unwashed the major elements of nuclear weapons strategy: launchers, warheads, effective mega-tonnage, and overall probabilities of kill. The final exam required us to multiply all these variables together in a pleasing way so as to depict the U.S.-Soviet nuclear balance. The second semester was precisely the same methodology but now unthinkingly and uncritically applied to conventional forces—and at this point my disbelief soon made me into a classroom discipline problem. That same flat-headed thinking about our general purpose forces still afflicted our strategic thinkers—even as the Pentagon in the mid-1980s was forced to deal with real-world conventional arms control issues as Gorbachev began to restructure Soviet forces—and eventually the face of Europe.

Even today, there is a gap between the traditional orientation of the Army, with its preference for large, heavy, armored forces, and the civilian leadership of the Defense Department under Donald Rumsfeld, which is equally intent on a lighter, more flexible and more easily deployed force more appropriate to fighting the War on Terror. But in either setting, the point is unmistakable: You first need to fight the war of ideas if you want to shape events. That is doubly true if out of that war of ideas you also expect to generate the strategic concepts needed to translate ideas into action. Remember the basic idea: *With time, you have at least the potential to shape events; without it, you do not.*

For almost all business leaders today, but particularly the CEO, that concept has a special significance because so much of contemporary corporate culture assumes that time is the one luxury that no one has. We have seemingly come to accept the idea that the day is best broken down into micrometer-sized chunks—and that the ultimate time horizon is whatever reporting period is driving the price of the company's stock.

So I need to get your attention and then begin changing your outlook. Fortunately, I learned how to do this while working with Army interrogators back in Germany in the 1970s. One of the best was a German national who worked for us—"Otto"—a trim, clipped, and correct professional. Though too young to have been one of those textbook SS officers forever interrogating downed American pilots in the World War II movies, he looked the part and apparently had strong genetic predispositions. We used him for our toughest cases, one of which was a notoriously dissident GI (we had many in the draftee Army of those days) who had resisted every attempt to break him. One day we informed the GI that "a German representative" would soon be arriving to inform him of his "rights under their laws." In walked Otto, immaculate in a severely tailored black suit. He halted directly in front of the GI and—I am not making this up—clicked his heels. "Unter ze CHER-man law . . . you have ze RIGHT . . . to . . . CONFESS!" he shouted. Which the GI promptly did.

So let that be a lesson to you. I really don't care about the usual view of corporate America's time. Instead, I assume that, first, as a business leader, you are in charge of your calendar and not the other way around; and, second, that you know enough to spend your time the same way you spend your money—where there is the greatest payoff for success. Which is what we are talking about here: How to have time working for you rather than against you—and how to use that advantage to achieve better strategic planning and better synchronization of what the business actually does.

DISCIPLINED INNOVATION: THE CONCEPT

Think back to all the activities we have discussed thus far in this book: value-centered leadership, better organization, more effective strategy, corporate intelligence, and enterprise security. Remember also that we have examined those issues because all are different facets of the new and incomparably more challenging business environment of the twenty-first century—and in one way or another all must be dealt with. Now ask yourself the following question: How do I do any or all of these things and ensure that they are (1) not mutually contradictory and (2) not beyond the capabilities of the organization? All are constituent parts of the classic problem of alignment: The answer suggested here is what we call disciplined innovation. Figure 10.1 depicts a very tightly interlocked process composed of four basic planning steps: vision, mission, strategy, and business plans. At least on paper, this process is, if not identical, then at least is similar to *what nearly every major corporation in America says it already does.* But do they—or do you? Read on—and then decide for yourself.

We need to be clear on the basic purposes of this process. As indicated by the chart, they are:

- Synchronization—otherwise known as alignment—of multiple activities across the corporation.
- Balancing anticipated changes in the business operating environment with corporate response.
- Linkage of CEO leadership perspective with accountable implementation actions by individuals.
- Extending the planning horizon.

In short, this methodology implicitly picks up the idea that the more time available to the leadership of an organization, the greater their potential choices; *but only if they use the time wisely to take the planning steps outlined here.*

Vision

The entire planning process is initiated by the CEO's vision. The "vision thing" contemplated here is most emphatically *not* the usual corporate drivel dreamed up over a corporate retreat or between the ritual contemplation of BHAGS. Far from it! I also admit to having been exposed to more than my fair share of the military equivalent of "visioning." It is an article of faith that two of the most dangerous things in the world are a large-fingered general standing in front of a small-scale map: if you see him making broad gestures and then hear him say, "I envision"— then run! In business and war, visions have consequences, and the basic purpose here is to kick off the entire series of corresponding actions

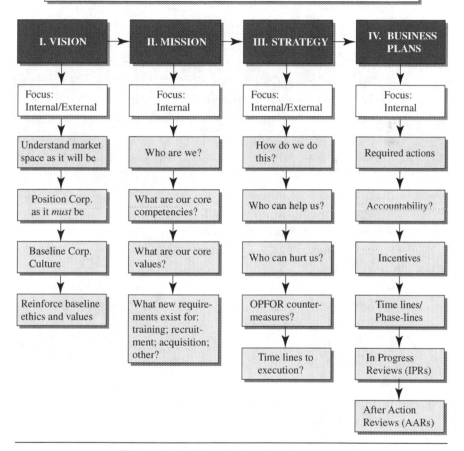

Figure 10.1 Four basic planning steps.

discussed next. CEOs often get far too hung up over the wording, rather than the content of their vision statements, and the basic rule is what Admiral Tom Moorer stated back in Chapter 4 while convulsing the Congress with his wonderful statement that, "You don't ever want to write a letter that you can't answer." Similarly, you don't want to say anything in the vision statement that you do not mean to go out and actually *do*. If you don't mean it, then don't say it! It is just that fundamental!

Equally fundamental is a clear understanding of what the vision statement attempts to do: It is both an internal and an external view of reality *because it must balance the business environment as the CEO thinks it is most likely to be with the position and capabilities of the company as they must be to succeed in that environment*. Notice that this critical balance does not result from stargazing or examining the entrails of birds. Instead, it is an important by-product of the war of ideas. Rather than having his time monopolized by relatively small and insignificant tasks, the CEO needs to be a full-time, high-level sensor of what is happening in his competitive battle-space: How viable is the industry? What new products or services are coming to market? What labor-saving or money-saving technologies have now matured to the point they are viable? And, most importantly, what potentially disruptive technologies are out there on the horizon?

You will recognize from what I have said earlier about military command and control that, to execute his "vision" functions, the CEO is also responsible for being his company's Number One consumer of *situational awareness*. Where does he get it? From everything he does—the books he reads (including this one); the conferences he attends; the people he talks to; and, above all, his experience and judgment that led to his selection as a CEO in the first place. Like a good driver, his first responsibility is ensuring that he doesn't outrun his headlights. But he is constantly looking for landmarks, maps, and anything else that will give him clues about the way ahead. It is difficult to conceive of a CEO active in the way he should be active who does not fully engage both his competitive intelligence section and his market researchers: What do our customers think of us? What do they think of our competition? What products do they want from us? Do we deliver on our products, services, and promises? Talk about the war of ideas!

By asking such no-nonsense questions, the CEO is also getting an in-depth perspective of the organization's real capabilities—as distinct from what he thinks they may be. That is important because he has to strike a balance between what the environment requires—and what the organization can respond with. Several of the major constraints in achieving that balance are corporate culture, ethics, and values. Those things represent the organization as it really is—and its people as they really function. Why is that important as you approach the critical issue of change? Because change can be disruptive, before you ask people to accommodate those stresses, you have to know how much they can stand, how fast they can stand it, and what's in it for them. In some sense, the CEO here is not unlike a pilot understanding the capabilities of his aircraft to execute a turn: wing loading, engine capacity, and control surface parameters. The best idea: Operate within those parameters—and make sure that "taking care of your people" is an intrinsic part of the planning process.

There are many CEOs out there who will simply be seduced by the present banalities and superficialities—because writing vision statements occupies a familiar place in the typical fare of typical business gatherings. But what makes our approach different is that it represents a realistic way to push the traditional planning horizon out by three to as much as five years. In today's business world, where "now-ism" has attained sacramental status, *three to five years* must seem like stargazing. But consider the alternative: Keep the planning horizon much closer than that, and you are invariably allowing yourself to go back to fighting what we refer to as the close battle, the business equivalent of guerrilla war, which, as we are now finding out in Iraq, is a particularly nasty way of being forced to fight (although occasionally necessary).

It also means you aren't so much determining the future as having it determined for you. That in effect means accepting not only the fluctuations of the business cycle but all those other "not our fault" limitations on growth and market share that better planning would help you avoid. My travel agent has grown weary of telling me that I need to make travel plans longer than five minutes before planning to leave for the airport: It not only limits seat availability, it's expensive. Clearly, I should be a CEO with such habits because CEOs unthinkingly accept business combat under similar conditions, which always means entering a contest where the only real choices are between the rocks and the hard places. Like any tactical commander, you have to choose your ground more wisely—and if you can't come up with a methodology for fleshing out your vision statement, you're better off recognizing it for the useless document it is.

Now it is possible that you may already be waving your hand in the air—and trying to get my attention to point out that you already have meetings there in your organization—pretty long damned meetings, some of them. Their purpose is advertised as "strategy" but you mostly just put up budget numbers and then maybe talk in general terms about "growing the business." Sorry, pal—but you are repeating the classic mistake that too many American businesses make today: putting the cart well before the horse. Just imagine if an architectural firm started out having meetings on the number of square feet of steel they needed for a project and how much it would cost—but without having settled on the purpose of the building, illustrated with at least a few artists' drawings of what it might look like in the end. Sound far-fetched? That nobody would do anything that dumb? Well, I hope not, but if you are beginning your planning process without a clear vision then you are in effect constructing a building without blueprints. And if you think the meetings are long *now,* just wait until later when things start to go wrong! Or to put it in military terms: Dig the latrines not upstream but *downstream* from where you get your water—and start your strategic planning process with a vision of where you want to be at the end of it! Understand?

Mission

I have never had the concept of *mission* explained to me so clearly as by our battalion executive officer (XO) when I was a lieutenant serving in Germany. A major, he had been involuntarily transferred to intelligence duties primarily because German was his native tongue: There was no other conceivable explanation. Even Otto found him tedious. He was consequently placed in charge of the logistical (meaning "nonoperational") side of things. Prior to our annual general inspection—in which our group headquarters kindly sent the usual teams to "help" us—the major explained how an obscure piece of communications gear was something we were responsible for maintaining. At this point, one of our last serving draftees interrupted. He hated the XO even more than he did the Army, and now demanded, with all due snideness, "Is that really our mission?" "Hey, I tell you vut ist our mission," the XO shouted back, his accent noticeably thickening. "Ve do vut ve're DAMP SHURE TOLD to do! Und DET'S vut our mission is!" The XO left the Army shortly thereafter to seek his fortune in tire recapping.

As Figure 10.1 illustrates, there must always be an intimate connection between the vision and mission statements—not unlike Russian dolls nested tightly one within the other. Not that this is any guarantee, because as with vision statements, ringing declarations of "the mission" are a dime a dozen around the business world—unless you really mean it by providing linkages on both ends. At the most basic level, the mission statement says: This is our mission, this is who we are, and these are our core competencies. You cannot hope to figure that out without looking back at the vision and seeing how it determines the parameters of the mission, beginning with the core competencies it requires.

The theme of the last chapter comes into play here, because, naturally, the mission should generate a Mission Essential Task List (METL). The same thought process that they apply everyday at the NTC works here as well: If I have to perform missions A, B, and C—then METLs X, Y, and Z are absolutely critical. (Here is a passing hint for your company: If you have more than a dozen of them, go back to the drawing board because you have inadvertently created a Useful Functions Task List—NOT the same thing!) Two other useful steps at this stage:

1. Make it a point of asking about adjustments to a potential change in our mission, ideally by building into the planning process a series of "what if" drills. (Remember Eisenhower's point again about plans being useless but planning being essential?)

2. Based on your prior consideration of culture, values, and ethics, begin the preliminary estimate of what potential changes are needed by the organization as it adjusts to new or changing missions or METLs. Will the changes entail new recruitment or training programs—or even new acquisition strategies? If so, this is the stage to begin planning for them.

Strategy

Once the mission is fixed, then comes the strategy—and again, notice the inherent linkage of things that are too often considered in splendid isolation from one another. Like the visioning step, strategy involves both an internal and an external view of the worlds, that is, both inside and outside the company. For reasons we already have talked about at length elsewhere in this book, strategy also answers the most basic "how do we do it" question after the mission has determined specifically *what* we are to do. But it is here that there are lots of opportunities to evaluate the full range of potential strategies to execute the mission: How do we do this? Who can help us? Who can hurt us? And what are the basic time lines to mission execution? Is this a long-term or a short-term undertaking? If you do it right—and only if—researching, building, and deciding on a strategy is an intensely collaborative process. If you don't, to echo the points made earlier, save yourself the trouble: Determine your strategy in magnificent isolation during the annual convention, ideally at a place like the Homestead—or off in Palm Springs somewhere. However, if you insist on doing strategy the right way, then it is very much a joint process. Here is where you bring in your competitive intelligence people to work with your market researchers and your futures team to build a scenario that makes sense. Have you been clever enough to have some of your intelligence/futures people represent the "enemy in counsel?" Hurray! Turn 'em loose on the prospective strategy like the opposition would! Those are all essential steps in the fundamental requirement of coming up with a corporate strategy that goes across all facets of the business, rather than just some of them. Remember as well what we said in the last chapter about the great fallacy of conceiving a strategy that the company cannot possibly execute. If you do it right at this stage, you're specifically testing a potential strategy out against known, proven capabilities: yours and the opposition, which puts you at least 50 percent ahead of most companies practicing today! But the basic idea is that the strategy you arrive at should be informed by the best advice you can get from your intelligence and your R&D people about the way the world is going to look—and how you intend to extend the planning horizon out as far forward as you can. Because: the farther out you extend that planning horizon, the more your choices. The closer in it comes, the closer your competition comes to engaging you in that close battle—and determining your choices for you.

Business Plans

The final steps of implementing the strategy are the business plans—and again, please take note of the internal consistency in the planning process. A very general but still focused vision statement generates a more specific mission for the company and its core competencies. From that—and enriched by a collaborative planning effort—comes the strategy, the "how to do it" part of the equation. And out of that comes the business plans. All of these things must be internally consistent, because they share the common purpose of generating an interlocking series of accountable actions by specific individuals. The consistency, cross-corporate coordination, and individual accountability are what makes this approach to business—as in war—so terribly effective. Many companies can certainly point to similar planning steps, but the question is how effectively the planning is reinforced by procedures, by what the company actually *does* on a day-in, day-out basis.

The business plans are also intended to answer all the potentially loose ends left by the strategy: What are the required action plans? With what phase lines and time lines? What are the measures of merit and accountability that may be required? What incentives are attached to these indicators of performance? It is these detailed plans with well-defined deadlines for action and execution that give effect to the hard conceptual work done earlier in the process by the CEO. Without them, it is exactly like having wall jacks and power outlets in a house where the power has been turned off. But with detailed planning mechanisms, the stage can be set for other actions by the leadership team: weekly management meetings with the vice presidents, for example, including the chief of strategy in which these documents are the score with the CEO as the conductor. Other possibilities include the use of the use of in-progress reviews (IPRs) to assess current progress as well as well as AARs to review completed actions.

All these tools are intended to guide actions, not just to provide a convenient pretext for organizing meetings. More to the point: They can also provide a way to extend the CEO's grasp by aligning processes that are normally disparate and occasionally dysfunctional. But possibly the greatest incentive of this model comes from its ability to guide disciplined growth over the long haul. In any commercial setting, potential choices are at hand every day. What contracts to pursue, which ones to let go, and how to tell the difference? All of them call for the constant re-evaluation of strategy—while staying focused on more permanent goals. It is difficult to do that in the absence of a strategic baseline but, as we have also seen, establishing a baseline is often something accompanied by a heavily embedded and highly bureaucratized process. The methodology outlined here, in contrast, hits all the essential bases without being so encumbered. Yet, it can provide a yardstick for evaluating where the company needs to go—and where on that continuum it is located.

THE IMPLICATIONS

1. *Aligning the organization:* Let us return again to the challenges with which we opened this chapter. The key business areas outlined throughout this book will be a part of the corporate landscape for some time to come. So assuming you make the changes suggested here, how are you aligning these things? How do you define success? Which way is up? Which way is down? Because you see, Senge and all the others who worry about alignment basically are correct: They and their consultant devotees simply haven't a clue about how to achieve it! In fact, this is not a process that makes any sense at all unless you have a methodology equal to or better than what is suggested here, not because it was initially explored by the Army or even because it has been suggested in the context of this book, but simply because *it cuts across so many diverse business processes and provides a commonsense way for the CEO to coordinate them with his leadership at the center of the process.* I have my own ways of staying inspired and on the wall of my office are the thoughts of a truly great American who had something important to say about all this: Vince Lombardi. In *What It Takes to be No. 1* he said, "Winning is not a sometime thing; it's an all-the-time thing. You don't win once in a while, you don't do things right once in a while, you do them all the time. Winning is a habit. Unfortunately, so is losing."

A good business wins the same way a good football team does: Because it practices fundamentally sound business practices and does so every day. Figuring out how those practices fit together in concert with a strategy, business plans, and related activities is what is so terribly important here. It is all about consistency, accountability, and, yes, even alignment—and making measurable progress toward those goals. This is not an academic exercise, which is why you may not find it mentioned very prominently in business schools. But it does have the considerable advantage of being grounded in reality. And what has been proven in war—the harshest of all realms of competition—should work in business as well.

2. *Not rocket science:* The model outlined here is one that inherently envisions alternative futures—including success and failure. But it really is not a very difficult process, nor is it one that will strike anybody who has looked at it for more than several seconds as being very odd—or even very original. In fact, it seems so oddly intuitive that you can't help wondering if you haven't somehow missed something that common sense might not have suggested on its own. In fact, there's the rub: What is really unusual about this approach to applied strategy is that so many businesses talk about it and simply don't do it or apply any of its four core processes—vision, mission, strategy, and business plans—in a way that produces consistent, accountable actions by specific individuals. Anything else is simply a waste of time, because what you are "visioning," creating, or aligning must be grounded in these fundamental business processes. Businesses do not suffer from an absence of creative inspiration in determining their futures, but rather a failure of disciplined methodology in carrying them out. Often these are simple things—like testing prospective strategies against known opposition capabilities or having a mission specific enough to generate an METL. What is missing and needed even more desperately are the connections and linkages that enable all these worthy activities to occur in coordination with one another rather than utterly random events. Anything else is stargazing. So consider this a Lombardi-esque appeal. Get back to renewing basic business processes in this structured, disciplined way: relatively cheap, terribly effective, yet honored mostly in the breach by business. To its shame.

3. *Selection and training of future CEOs:* As we pointed out in the last chapter, by focusing on the essential war fighting process, we also created

the next generation as a by-product. The reason: The resolute focus on understanding the present and projecting it into the future is a kind of natural selection process for identifying leaders best able to cope with that environment. In contrast: The way we select our leaders in corporate America today often resembles what happens in a third-world country. Much of it involves who's who in the corporate pecking order and the sterile comparison of resumes, but almost all of it reflects a resolute view of life through the rearview mirror. To illustrate: Several years ago, a number of my friends—retired military officers—worked for Company X. Company Y had invited them to evaluate their leader development process and suggest how it might be made more effective. In doing so, various rising stars of Company Y were called in and my friends had the opportunity to interview them. The interview subjects were all potential candidates for the CEO position and were all at that point regional vice presidents. The other thing they had in common was that they were themselves all former chief financial officers (CFOs). As you might expect of accountants, the reason why they had been selected for these regional vice presidencies from their former position of being CFOs, was because all had "made their numbers." Now two things must impress you about this tale: First if an accountant does not know how to make his numbers, he probably doesn't know very much. But the second thing is the utter banality of apparently confusing financial competence with executive leadership, because that and that alone was what constituted the potential leadership pool. If these putative CEOs were being groomed—and one of them eventually selected—like the survivor of one of those insipid reality TV shows, the process might have made more sense—but then again, almost anything would.

The contrast with the Army's senior leader development and selection process could not be more startling, because, while imperfect, it rested on the assumption—not of an earned reward—but of a clearly demonstrated potential for further national service. The leaders it produces are often imperfect. My MSNBC colleague and former Air Force Lieutenant Colonel Rick Francona remembers one of his bosses telling a group of subordinates that, "Around here, the absence of punishment is reward enough."

But the military does an excellent job of testing future leaders for their ability to conceive and execute a strategic vision. We test them in simulations such as the Battle Command Training Program in which they have the opportunity to show how they perform in these alternative futures. The corporate world right now simply does not do that. It doesn't select its future leaders by putting them into a "futures" situation and seeing how well they do. It essentially makes the selection the same way it chooses its strategy: By contracting out. And the outside firms who perform that service compare resumes the same way they might compare BHAGs. Think about my earlier point that CEO selection today resembles succession arrangements in the third world: dominated by strong individuals chosen in a random way—and assisted by headhunters. Sound familiar?

4. *Prevailing civilian practices:* Think that's an exaggeration? Then let me give you an overview of prevailing practices in the civilian world. As evidence, I rely on a book by two distinguished authors, Robert M. Fulmer and Marshall Goldsmith, *Leadership Investment—How the World's Best Organizations Gain Strategic Advantage Through Leadership Development.* Fulmer and Goldsmith surveyed a number of leading companies and came up with what those companies apparently viewed as the critical issues of leader development. On leader development:

> Best practice leadership development processes are internally focused and externally aware. New business demand dictated the need for change, within each of the best practice organizations, but certainly did not create a framework for how to create the change.[1]

Or on leadership:

> A majority of the best-practice organizations have identified leadership competencies or at least tried to define characteristics and qualities of successful leaders.[2]

What is especially interesting about these insights is not just the fact that they are exceedingly vague but also that the "best practice organizations" represent a corporate Who's Who: Hewlett Packard, General Electric, Johnson & Johnson, and Royal Dutch Shell. These are companies with strong reputations for excellence and which might be expected to have strong leader development programs. But what is more startling is not only that even "the best of the best" seem pretty vague on some basic leader development ideas—but that these concepts are so vaguely disconnected from the business processes outlined in these chapters. A look at the authors' key findings briefly illustrates the point:

- Distinguish between executive education and other training.
- Recognize that the process (of executive education) and the content are equally important.
- Focus programs on creating a shared view of the company's programs and opportunities.
- Give top managers a role as teachers.
- Require participants to make tangible on the job commitments.
- Reinforce the lessons of the program and the company's day-to-day operations.[3]

Now it makes sense to survey leading corporations and see what they are up to—and the authors present some worthy and worthwhile findings. But the point to consider here is that this process seems curiously disconnected from the real-world evaluations that should help in selecting and honing the company's next generation of leaders. How well do you link "executive education" to the company's strategic development? Or its business development? Or its organization development? In the Army and presumably at some top corporations as well, they have acquired the useful habit of producing leaders as a by-product of a system of excellence—a system of excellence in leadership.

It is that critical aspect alone that really distinguishes what we're really looking for in business, where we perpetually search for competitive advantage. Because it always comes down to the question of leadership: You either have it or you don't. It is either embedded throughout your organization or it isn't. And if business still has a few lessons left to learn, then hopefully this book and the examples we have covered together will help to make a difference to those twenty-first century corporate leaders who will search for the better way. And may you not owe your elevation to headhunters.

Coda: The Case of BIZWAR, Inc.

Before we leave this chapter, I cannot resist the urge to do what we so often do in the Army: Check student understanding, ideally through a practical exercise that insures the key ideas have gotten thru. So . . .

Congratulations! You have just been elected to the board of directors of BIZWAR, Incorporated, a small (but mythical) private holding company formed just under five years ago and named after a fabulously successful book by the same name. The company's total holdings are approaching $100M with the firm being active in the energy field, providing an increasingly rich array of products (energy transmission hardware, including gas pipelines), services (information and research), and raw materials (mostly natural gas). While as a private company, you are not subject to the requirements of Sarbanes-Oxley, you are well aware of the need for any company that hopes to attract investor capital to operate with greater degrees of transparency than ever before. Naturally, as a new board member, you are also acutely aware that—liability insurance notwithstanding—there are also strong incentives for you to ask hard-hitting and maybe even probing questions of the BIZWAR leadership team. Sure, they are very nice guys but, how else to ensure you can personally achieve the independent judgment required by today's corporate governance environment—and your own responsibilities?

Fortunately, you have come across a new book that promises a baseline methodology that may be useful here in provoking some probing questions. With that book open beside you, and your yellow legal pad next to it, you begin jotting some notes prior to your first board meeting.

Vision

Apparently the author of your business text believes there ought to be something more to vision statements than you have typically seen at most points throughout your career, so let's give him the benefit of the doubt and take this one more seriously than usual. What is the company's vision for how the energy market will develop over the next three to five years? In particular, how will public policies and the regulatory environment affect companies—will those policies be more or less volatile than in the recent past and with what effects on the industry? There is a movement afoot to focus on the national energy infrastructure: will government spending be made available to cover these costs? Considering those changes, how is BIZWAR positioned to exploit these public and private dimensions of the energy market?

Mission

Having checked with a number of colleagues in the energy industry, you are well aware that missions tend to change less frequently than strategies. But you are particularly interested in how the often fine line between public-private energy policy will affect BIZWAR's development of core competencies. How smoothly can it make the transition between one market sector and the other? And what recruitment and training programs may be required to speed these transitions in the future?

Strategy

What specifically are the strategies of the BIZWAR leadership team? How have they been derived? How reliable is our market research in this area? Do they reflect our vision of the way the energy market is developing? Have any of our strategic plans been subjected to a penetrating "red hat/blue hat analysis" that would show the effects of potential competitors? Is so, what were the outcomes—and have we adjusted our plans accordingly?

Business Plans

Sorry—but just as you were getting warmed up to write some more penetrating questions, this time about business plans . . . the board meeting began. But it actually looks like you are pretty well prepared for it, and somehow it seems unlikely that the discussion is destined for many lapses.

Teaching point: Although I have some friends in the energy industry and have had the distinct pleasure of addressing a number of their industry groups, the fact is that I am far from being an expert in this field.[4] But note what the methodology does: By stressing the fundamental purposes of underlying business processes—and knowing how they ought to be connected—it is possible to pose some fairly accurate questions about a company's leadership activities. Not final questions, to be sure. But good starting points that, combined with more specific backgrounds and information about individual industries and corporations, provide a reasonable start for oversight. And an even better perspective on where and how to begin CEO insight.

☆☆ Epilogue ☆☆

The After Action Review (AAR)

National Training Center, Hill 473, 1900

So, what did you think? That you were going to get out of this without an AAR? Don't think so—wouldn't really be in character, would it? Plus this is a nice place from which to wrap up our subject. This time of day, it's easy to see why people come out to places like Palm Springs—about 50 miles southwest of here—because the desert and the mountains are so beautiful—especially now at twilight, when the shadows begin to lengthen and the heat is more bearable. Actually, it gets a little cold out here at night. But every bit as arid, of course—so take another drink of your water while we talk. Your transportation will be here soon: one of the OPFOR Blackhawks—that's a helicopter—to take you back to Barstow in style. They usually fly with the side doors open, because it's more interesting that way. Just make sure they strap you into the seat. You won't be that far above the ground, of course, but like they say in airborne school, it isn't the fall that kills you, it's the sudden stop.

Let's go back over what an AAR is supposed to do, even though it should be old hat to you by now. You focus on three things: what happened, why it happened, and how you are going to plan improvements. As that process applies here, think back to what I told you at the beginning. The traditional view of the relationship between business and war was that they were utterly different activities that had little or nothing to say to each other. What changed—and is changing as we speak—are the characteristics of the business operating environment, which is coming to look a lot like the one the warrior is used to: chaotic but not unpredictable, information-intensive, and terribly unforgiving of inattention or incompetence. It is against this backdrop—not only promising more intense competition for basic business success but even for basic survival—that we made the case for applying some of the traditional tools of the military to the domain of business—as well as some of the more modern ones.

The reason why we chose military tools—as distinct from traditional business "solutions"—was not only because the military had been first to experience the new disciplines of twenty-first century competition (and with some considerable success in the post-9/11 environment) but also because it brings to bear the terribly great advantages of a system *of applied leadership. So much of business literature—and teaching—is episodic and anecdotal; in fact, only the field of elementary school education may be more inclined toward the values-free inculcation of fads and "latest theories" sprung whole from the foreheads of educators. And only motivational speakers or self-improvement gurus may have a commendably clearer view of their own motivations: simply to sell more books, motivational speeches, or courses.*

We also talked a lot about values-based leadership—*also a contradiction in terms if you listen to the people being paid to instruct us on such things who buy the argument of the Milton Friedmans of the world that values have as much place in corporations as they do in buildings. Or those who may agree with him in principle but offer the "social responsibility" of the corporation as a politically correct alternative in place of hard choices about right and wrong. Eventually such people run up against the simple fact that all the legislation in the world is no substitute for character—and those who have become accustomed to applying it in often ambiguous circumstances. When you are facing complex, confusing and even dangerous times ahead, what kind of leader do you want to follow? One with a clear set of values and a track record of applying them when the chips are down—or somebody chosen by headhunters because he has a track record of making his numbers?*

We also talked about strategy *and that you ought* not *to do to what the b-school faculties customarily do and confuse it with marketing. Because it isn't: It's about* winning *and how to do it. Nor should you be deceived by those who think strategy is so unimportant that it can be left as a purely symbolic function of a company's leadership. Or give aid and comfort to those who think they can simply read the odd business strategy book, come up with a BHAG or two—and call it a day. Nope—strategy is a deadly serious business, derived from a company's unique vision and mission statements, enriched by intelligence-based examination, disciplined by competitive analysis, and implemented and executed by business plans. In short: It is a central function of how the leadership actually runs a company—or it is nothing at all.*

The best way to summarize our discussion on organization *is to remember what General J. F. C. Fuller said about pruning the bureaucracy with an axe. No better time to do that either than during a merger or acquisition. Our local bank just went through one of those all-too-familiar escapades in which they merged with a larger, better-known bank. There was much hoo-hah with painting, redecorating, and new signs—and even new and more obscure deposit forms were designed and distributed. Only one thing had been left to chance—actually getting anything done when you called the new, convenient toll-free number and were first connected with a call center somewhere in the third world. ("Thank you fuh callink. To vote faw new CEO, prease to dial one. Faw all uthuh entry, prease to press two now.") To get out of voicemail hell, you were required to know or to guess the new organization tree of the merged bank—which was fully replicated in the new voicemail tree. A wrong guess and you were back in the third world. Teaching point: Somewhere in the rush to automate call centers and cut costs with ever more specific divisions of labor, we lost sight of the concept of seamless service. And apparently accepted the idea that the only person capable of integrating corporate functions should not be the CEO—but rather the poor bastard customer trying to do business with us. If you don't immediately apply Fuller's Axe to the necks of the entire corporate board, then every one of them should receive an indefinite sentence to penal servitude in whatever call center in whatever hell hole was chosen by the CFO to handle its fictional commitment to "customer service."*

Okay, sorry about that but I will admit that at certain points while writing this, I have had to suppress the urge to grab the nearest business executive by the lapels and start shaking. Why? Because the points are so important and they need to understand the effects of their actions—usually inadvertent effects. And those inadvertent effects are a helluva lot more serious than risking the annoyance of the author. Why do you organize your business so that it seems that you are hell-bent on selecting that course of action best able to irritate the customer the most—to make him or her do almost anything but return to your store, to buy your product, to renew that contract with you. In her prize-winning book about World War I, The Guns of August, *historian Barbara Tuchman wrote about the "unwisdom" that gripped European political and military elites on the verge of war—and made their descent into the abyss inevitable. Today, unwisdom is not just the purview of generals, admirals, and prime ministers: It is an epidemic among corporate leaders. Many of whom have not learned the most basic lesson that Deming and others tried to teach: That it is the worst kind of folly to use your customers as the primary way to root out corporate errors and shortcomings. Nope—that's your job, so get to it without any further discussion, okay?*

Which also brings us to that insignificant item called corporate intelligence. *Remember this: If you don't have it and aren't taking steps to get it, you are in exactly the same position as a pilot taking off minus a flight plan and a radio. The FAA doesn't allow that and neither should you or your corporate board. In short: You could have your own OPFOR and your own intelligence section to keep tabs on the opposition and enrich your own strategic plans. So why don't you? To repeat Redd Foxx again: "Life is hard, but it's harder if you're stupid." We live in an information age and if you're stupid, it's your own fault because you are deliberately choosing to be that way.*

On security, *basically two concepts: Security is life, not just overhead, and you, the CEO, are ultimately responsible. You can delegate that authority and you probably should: The responsibility is yours and yours alone. That is especially true until we straighten out this whole homeland security nightmare. Please remember that you are facing one of*

*two challenges, either of which is a certainty—and maybe both. You face
either an actual threat from terrorists, hackers, crackers, virus junkies—
or old-fashioned criminals using new electronic means to do their dirty
work. Or else you face the threat of auditors who understand twenty-first
century security threats and your responsibility for ensuring the virtual
integrity of the enterprise—and that's tomorrow's corporate scandal just
waiting to happen. But I cannot overstate the importance of your responsibility for training your workforce ahead of time so that they can deal
with these potentially job-threatening and life-threatening situations. As
this book goes to press, there is another stark reminder in the release of
emergency transcripts from 9/11. There are heartbreaking stories of those
who called for instructions and were told repeatedly to "Stay near the
stairwells and wait for the police to come up." In one such case, a group
of about 20 people led by a New York Port Authority official followed that
advice—until it was too late. Finally, told to evacuate the World Trade
Center, they heard the upper floors collapsing even as they belatedly tried
to descend the stairwell. A New York Port Authority spokesman says that
evacuation orders had been given almost immediately and that any instructions to the contrary were due to "the confusion and uncertainty of
the moment."[1] Actually that concept is called* friction, *it is an intrinsic
part of war and the first time it happened to us we had a right to be surprised: No more.*

*Security, intelligence, organization, and strategy are just four of the
major areas in which leadership performance is being tested by the new
realities and complexities of the business environment. This is a lot to
manage, let alone synchronize or align; which is why we introduced the
concept of the Army's training system—and showed how the METLs and
AARs represent a methodology that has been proven in war and is ready
to be applied to business. Finally, there is the translation of that system
into an aggressive and effective plan for capturing market share and
achieving disciplined growth. And what we have just done here is a
mini version of that AAR process, so I hope you took careful notes.*

*There is, of course, a missing element here—and that is how what
we have done is going to influence the future of the organization—but
that frankly depends on you, not me. That whole situation is well
summed up in a story Dick Cheney regularly used to tell when he was*

still a congressman—even before he became secretary of defense, let alone vice president. In fact, it was even before our invasion of Iraq, when he reacted to any criticism by referring to Barry McCaffrey, Wes Clark, and me as "retired military officers embedded in TV studios." (As I pointed out to several reporters who called for a comment: Barry and Wes had four Silver Stars between them to none at all for Cheney— or me—so I thought they had earned the right to second-guess Cheney or damned near anybody else.)

Anyway, when Cheney still had a sense of humility, he used to talk about running for re-election to his second term as Wyoming's sole congressman. Driving along a back highway out there in God's country, he spotted a farmer plowing his field and pulled his car over for a little impromptu electioneering. When the farmer came over to the fence, Cheney introduced himself: "Hi, I'm Dick Cheney and I'm here to ask for your vote because I'm running for Congress." "Well," replied the farmer, "you got it because that fool that's in there now is no damned good."

Obviously, the farmer had one view of Cheney's leadership—and Cheney had quite another but it's hard to know how these moments of epiphany come about. We usually make the mistake of thinking we have more time than we actually do. That certainly was the case with the Goldwater-Nichols Act when none of the players had any inkling they were re-aligning the nation's war-fighting machine barely four years before it would be tested in combat. Or Donald Rumsfeld, who argued so vigorously for defense transformation—right up to the day before the 9/11 hijackers flew into his building. Or Colonel Ken Allard, who knew better but thought he had forever to bring his weight and blood pressure under control—but that's another story. Suffice for the moment to say that those moments are guaranteed to no one—so use the time as if it were your last chance. Because it just might be.

But that black dot on the horizon is your Blackhawk—should be here in about two minutes and, yep, looks like they have the side doors open. But it's been a pleasure to have you along with me to show you how we train—and hopefully to have you learn some lessons from it. It's also been a pleasure to introduce you to some great people: Drill Sergeant Davis, Lieutenant Colonel Parker (later Major General Parker, by the

*way), and General Max Thurman. I owe them all a lot one way or an-
other—and so do you, although you didn't know it until now.*

*Anyway, hope we get to see each other again, either on TV, the radio,
or in one of my speeches to business groups just like yours. Be sure to
come up and introduce yourself because we have been through a lot together and it's always a pleasure to shake hands. But most of all I want
you to leave here with a warning: The Good Book says that to whom
much is given, much will also be required. Take that seriously as a business leader because you have an enormous responsibility to those who
look up to you. Don't let them down, okay? We'll keep on taking care of
the troops but you take care of your people—or I WILL be there to kick
yurass, understand? Hooahh and good luck!*

WAR PLAN

MISSION OBJECTIVES

The characteristics of the business operating environment are starting to look a lot like the one the warrior is used to: chaotic but not unpredictable, information-intensive, and terribly unforgiving of inattention or incompetence.

★ Strategy is *not* what the b-school faculties customarily confuse with marketing; it's about *winning* and how to do it. Strategy is a deadly serious business, derived from a company's unique vision and mission statements, enriched by intelligence-based examination, disciplined by competitive analysis, and implemented and executed by business plans.

★ Don't organize your business so that it seems like you've *tried* to irritate your customer the most—to make him or her do almost anything but return to your store, buy your product, or renew that contract with you. It is the worst kind of folly to use your customers as the primary way to root out your corporate errors and shortcomings.

★ If you don't have corporate intelligence and aren't taking steps to get it, you are in exactly the same position as a pilot taking off minus a flight plan and a radio. The FAA doesn't allow that, and neither should you or your corporate board.

★ Security is life, not just overhead, and the CEO, is ultimately responsible. You face one of two challenges, either an actual threat from terrorists, hackers, crackers, virus junkies, or old-fashioned criminals using new electronic means to do their dirty work. Or you face the threat of auditors who understand your responsibility for ensuring the virtual integrity of your enterprise—and you're tomorrow's corporate scandal just waiting to happen.

★ Security, intelligence, organization, and strategy are the major areas in which leadership performance is being tested by the new realities and complexities of the business environment. This is a lot to manage, let alone synchronize or align, which is why business borrows a page from the military training system.

Notes

Chapter 1 Introduction

1. Lee Kopp, Speech to Client Reception, Minneapolis, MN, June 24, 2002. Reprinted as "Malignant Greed," *Minneapolis Star Tribune,* July 14, 2002.

2. Robert J. Samuelson, "CEO Welfare," *Washington Post,* April 30, 2003, p. A23.

3. Jerry Useem, "Have They No Shame," *Fortune,* April 28, 2003, pp. 56–64.

4. Jed Babbin, "The American Mood," *National Review Online,* June 13, 2003.

5. Major Leibner's personal story was first reported by David M. Shribman, "One Year After: Plunging Into the Fire," *Boston Globe,* September 8, 2002.

6. John A. Byrne, "Restoring Trust in Corporate America," *BusinessWeek Online,* June 24, 2002.

7. Joseph Nocera, "System Failure," *Fortune,* June 24, 2002.

8. Charles Colson, "Law Isn't Enough," *Washington Post,* July 30, 2002.

Chapter 2 Worlds Apart?

1. Edward N. Luttwak, *Strategy, The Logic of War and Peace* (Cambridge, MA: Harvard University Press, 1987), especially chapters 1–3.

2. See, for example, Arthur T. Hadley, *The Straw Giant* (New York: Random House, 1986).

3. Office of the President, Harvard University, Statement at ROTC Commissioning Ceremony, June 4, 2003.

4. Mark Litke, "Faking It," ABC News.com, April 21, 2002.

5. See the USWA web site, available from http://www.fairtradewatch.org /steelcrisishistory091400.htm.

6. Thomas L. Friedman, *The Lexus and the Olive Tree* (New York: Anchor Books, 2000), pp. 8–9.

7. Ibid., p. 11 (quoting James Surowiecki in *Slate* magazine).

8. T. R. Reid, "High Plains Relief," *Washington Post,* June 21, 2003.

9. Friedman, op. cit., pp. xi–xv.

10. David Rothkopf, "When the Buzz Bites Back," *Washington Post Outlook,* May 11, 2003.

11. Stanley T. Myers, president, Semiconductor Equipment and Materials International, November 1, 1999. Available from http:/www .insite.net/semiconductor/index.asp.

12. Samuel P. Huntington, *The Soldier and the State,* 7th ed. (Cambridge, MA: Harvard University Press, 1981), p. 193.

13. Charles Moskos and John Butler, *All That We Can Be: Black Leadership and Integration the Army Way* (New York: Basic Books, 1998), p. 2.

14. Joseph Nocera, "System Failure," *Fortune,* June 24, 2002, p. 2.

15. Telephone interview with Professor Scott Snook, June 1, 2003. See also his book on organizational dynamics, *Friendly Fire* (Princeton, NJ: Princeton University Press, 2000).

16. Amitai Etzioni, "When It Comes to Ethics, B-Schools Get an F," *Washington Post,* August 4, 2002, p. B4. The study referred to is by the Aspen Institute, New York, New York, "Where Will They Lead? MBA Student Attitudes About Business and Society." Where indeed?

17. Wess Roberts, *Leadership Secrets of Attila the Hun* (New York: Warner, 1989); and Tom Wheeler, *Leadership Lessons from the Civil War* (New York: Doubleday, 1999).

18. Perry M. Smith, *Taking Charge* (Washington, DC: National Defense University Press, 1986); Gordon R. Sullivan and Michael V. Harper, *Hope Is Not a Method* (New York: Random House, 1996); and D. Michael Abrashoff, *It's Your Ship: Management Techniques from the Best Damn Ship in the Navy* (New York: Warner, 2002).

19. Oren Harari, *Leadership Secrets of Colin Powell* (New York: McGraw-Hill, 2002); and Partha Bose, *Alexander the Great's Art of Strategy* (New York: Penguin, 2003).

20. Ben White, "Excellent Year for Executives," *Washington Post*, June 19, 2002.

Chapter 3   War as an Audit

1. William J. Perry, "Desert Storm and Deterrence," *Foreign Affairs*, vol. 70, no. 4 (1991), p. 76.

2. Here the reader is respectfully asked to excuse my long obsession with this issue. For example: see my excruciatingly in-depth historical study of the U.S. armed services and the interoperability problem, *Command, Control and the Common Defense*, rev. ed. (Washington, DC: National Defense University Press, 1996). But only if you must.

3. Kenneth Allard, *Somalia Operations: Lessons Learned* (Washington, DC: National Defense University Press, 1995), pp. 77–82. Suggests that we don't need the UN to help us screw up military operations, but that we are more than capable of doing that on our own.

4. Scott Snook, *Friendly Fire* (Princeton, NJ: Princeton University Press, 2000).

5. See, for example: William A. Owens and Joseph S. Nye Jr., "America's Information Edge," *Foreign Affairs* (March/April, 1996); the citation is from William A. Owens, *Lifting the Fog of War* (New York: Farrar, Straus and Giroux, 2000), p. 138.

6. For example, Arthur K. Cebrowski and John Garstka, "Network Centric Warfare: Its Origin and Future," U.S. Naval Institute *Proceedings*, January 1998, pp. 28–38.

7. Frederick R. Strain, "The New Joint Warfare," *Joint Forces Quarterly*, Autumn 1993, p. 23.

8. Tom Clancy with General Carl Stiner, *Shadow Warriors* (New York: G. P. Putnam's Sons, 2002), pp. 498–499.

9. Edwin Dorn and Howard Graves, co-chairs, "American Military Culture in the Twenty-First Century" (Washington, DC: Center for Strategic and International Studies, February 2000), p. xvi.

Chapter 4   Building Leaders of Character

1. Interview with MG Buster Hallenbeck, June 24, 2003.

2. James R. Lucas, "You Could Grow up to Be Like Enron," essay for *M.Q. Journal*, February 1, 2002.

3. Adrian Savage, *M World* (New York: American Management Association, Summer 2002).

4. Robert Galford and Anne S. Drapeau, "It Will Take Courage to Restore Investors' Faith," *Boston Globe,* March 2, 2003.

5. Milton Friedman, quoted by John Verlau, "Is Big Business Ethically Bankrupt?" *Insight on the News,* vol. 18, no. 10 (March 18, 2002).

6. Ibid.

7. Quoted by David Brooks, "'Absolutely American:' Culture Wars at West Point," *New York Times,* book review, July 13, 2003.

8. Ibid.

9. Quoted by Edgar F. Puryear, *American Generalship: Character Is Everything* (Novato, CA: Presidio Press, 2000), pp. 303–304.

10. Ibid., p. 307.

11. Ibid.

12. John S. D. Eisenhower, *General Ike, a Personal Reminiscence* (New York: Free Press, 2003), p. 61.

13. Rick Atkinson, remarks to the USMA Class of 1991, West Point, New York. Reprinted in *Prologue, Conduct of the Persian Gulf Conflict: Interim Report to the Congress,* July 1991.

14. Testimony of Admiral Thomas Moorer, USN (ret.), March 4, 1986, *Hearings before the Investigations Subcommittee, Committee on Armed Services,* 99th Cong., Second Session, p. 369.

15. USMA Circular 1-101, the Cadet Leader Development System, June 2002, p. 32.

16. Ibid, p. 31.

Chapter 5   Strategy: Deliver Us from Process

1. Norman R. Augustine, *Augustine's Laws* (New York: Penguin Books, 1986), p. 282.

2. Ibid., p. 232.

3. Ram Charan and Jerry Useem, "Why Companies Fail," *Fortune,* May 27, 2002.

4. Jim Collins, *Good to Great* (New York: Harper Business, 2001), p. 1.

5. Tony Manning, *Making Sense of Strategy* (New York: American Management Association, 2002), p. 3.

6. Phillip Boyle, "From Strategic Planning to Visioning—Tools for Navigating the Future," *PUBLIC MANAGEMENT,* vol. 83, no. 4 (May 2001), p. 23.

7. Mike Freedman and William Shine, "Strategy in Uncertain Times," *Journal of the American Management Association,* Fall 2003.

8. Quoted by Jeffrey A. Krames, *What the Best CEOs Know* (New York: McGraw-Hill, 2003), p. 143.

9. Ibid.

10. Louis V. Gerstner Jr., *Who Says Elephants Can't Dance* (New York: Harper Business, 2002).

11. Louis V. Gerstner Jr., quoted by Jeffrey A. Krames, op. cit., pp. 112–113.

12. Rudolph W. Giuliani, *Leadership* (New York: Hyperion, 2002), p. 71.

13. Idid., p. 72.

14. Ibid., p. 88.

15. Ibid., p. 77.

16. Major General Buford Blount, personal communication, July 2003.

17. Major General David Petraeus, telephonic interview, June 2003.

18. Robert J. Samuelson, "Wisdom of a Renegade," *Washington Post,* July 24, 2003.

Chapter 6   Organizing for Victory: While Shooting as Few Bureaucrats as Possible

1. *Streamlining Defense Acquisition Laws: Executive Summary Report of the DOD Acquisition Law Advisory Panel* (Washington: U.S. Government Printing Office, March 1993), p. 4. If the wording here seems a little too close to the Panel's report without benefit of quotation marks, just remember who wrote it!

2. Opening Statement of Hon. Bill Nichols, Chairman Investigations Subcommittee, *Reorganization of the Department of Defense, Hearings Before the Investigations Sub Committee, Committee on Armed Services,* 99th Cong., 2nd Sess. (February 19, 1986), p. 3.

3. See the standard history of this legislation from the perspective of one of its key participants. James R. Locher, *Victory on the Potomac: The Goldwater-Nichols Act Unifies the Pentagon* (College Station, TX: Texas A&M University Press, 2002).

4. Cited by Forrest C. Pogue, *The Supreme Command: Official History of the U.S. Army in World War II* (Washington: U.S. Army, Office of the Chief of Military History, 1954), p. 53.

5. Lieutenant Colonel Gary B. Griffin, *The Directed Telescope: A Traditional Element of Effective Command* (Ft. Leavenworth, KS: U.S. Army Command and General Staff College, July 1991).

6. Col. Trevor N. Dupuy, *A Genius for War: The German Army and General Staff, 1807–1945* (London: MacDonald and Jane's, 1971).

7. Max Weber's definitive work is *The Theory of Social and Economic Organization* (New York: Free Press, 1947).

8. J. F. C. Fuller, *Generalship: Its Diseases and Their Cure* (Harrisburg, PA: Military Services Publishing Company, March 1936), p. 60.

9. Ibid., p. 61.

10. Ibid., pp. 66–67.

11. Rudolph W. Giuliani, *Leadership* (New York: Hyperion, 2002), p. 311.

12. Bill George, *Authentic Leadership: Rediscovering the Secrets to Creating Lasting Value* (Hoboken, NJ: Wiley, 2003). Quoted by William J. Holstein, *New York Times*, book review, July 27, 2003, business section, p. 5.

13. Ibid.

14. Andy Grove, quoted in Jeffrey A. Krames, *What the Best CEOs Know* (New York: McGraw Hill, 2003), p. 178.

15. Ibid., pp. 142–152.

16. Herb Kelleher, quoted by Jeffrey A. Krames, op.cit., p. 182.

17. Ibid., p. 185.

Chapter 7   Business Intelligence: Another Damned Thing They Didn't Teach You in B School

1. Lieutenant General Harry W. O. Kinnard, *Army*, vol. 19, no. 8 (August 1969), p. 23; cited by M. B. Powe and E. E. Wilson, *The Evolution of*

American Military Intelligence (Ft. Huachuca, AZ: U.S. Army Intelligence Center and School, 1973), p. 120.

2. Portions of the preceding section were published in an article written for *CIO Magazine;* "The Information Advantage in the Iraq War," *CIO Magazine,* September 2003.

3. Quoted by John Hendren, "Weapons Reports Called Lacking," *Los Angeles Times,* June 26, 2003. Cited by Anthony Cordesman, *Sufficiency of Intelligence on Iraq: Emerging Issues and Lessons Learned* (Washington, DC: CSIS, September 2003), p. 37. Hereafter CSIS Report.

4. I am relying here on a series of personal interviews throughout July and August, 2003 which, under existing rules of engagement, can only be attributed to those elusive and quasi-anonymous "senior defense officials," including one on August 3, 2003. However, by late October, sharply contradictory information had arisen from internal Army investigations which, by press time, could not be independently confirmed. (See Thomas Ricks, "Intelligence problems in Iraq are detailed," *Washington Post,* October 25, 2003.) Best advice: stay tuned . . . and of course stay skeptical.

5. Cordesman, op. cit., CSIS Report, pp. 3–4.

6. Thomas L. Friedman, *The Lexus and the Olive Tree* (New York: Anchor Books, 2000), p. 426.

7. Cited by Margaret Webb Pressler, "We're Empowered by the Internet and Intense Competition," *Washington Post,* August 10, 2003, p. F1.

8. Russell Secker, "Ten Key Sources of Competitive Data," *SCIP Online,* vol. 1, no. 14 (August 22, 2002).

9. Seena Sharp, "Truth or Consequences: Ten Myths That Cripple Competitive Intelligence," *SCIP Online,* vol. 3, no. 3 (January/February 2000).

10. Ibid. (emphasis added).

11. Secker, op. cit.

12. David Rothkopf, personal interview in Washington, DC, on August 1, 2003.

13. Ibid.

14. Ibid. Rothkopf notes as well that "competitive intelligence equals information plus insight."

15. Ibid.

16. See Joseph L. Bower and Clayton M. Christensen, "Disruptive Technologies: Catching the Wave," *Harvard Business Review,* January/February 1995, pp. 43–53; and Clayton M. Christensen and Michael Overdorf, "Meeting the Challenge of Disruptive Change," *Harvard Business Review,* March/April 2000, pp. 67–76.

17. Telephonic interview, Bob Madaio, Manager EMC Competitive Intelligence, August 12, 2003; and Greg Eden, Manager, EMC Public Relations, August 12, 2003.

18. EMC Annual Report, 1999; available from http://www.emc.com/ir/annual/annual99/layers/letter3.htm.

19. Howard Whetzel and Kenneth Allard, "Internet Insecurity May Prove Deadly," *Wall Street Journal,* May 14, 1997.

20. Sam Walton, quoted in Richard Tomkins, "The Formula to Beat," *London Financial Times,* May 5, 1999, p. 25.

21. Claire Gooding, "Boosting Sales with the Information Warehouse—The Use of Historical Data to Plan Corporate Strategy Is an Idea Whose Time Has Come," *London Financial Times,* March 1, 1995, p. 15.

22. R. G. Edmonson, "Hi-ho! Hi-ho! It's Data Mining We'll Go," *Journal of Commerce,* June 13, 2002; Bertrand Marotte, "Powerful Eye Mines the Depths of Consumer Spending," *The Ottowa Citizen,* January 14, 1998, p. C3.

23. "Key Role for Business Intelligence," *London Financial Times,* April 1, 1998, p. 1.

Chapter 8   The Other Side of the Coin: Enterprise Security

1. Among the many examples: James Adams, *The Next World War* (New York: Simon & Schuster, 1998); Ira Winkler, *Corporate Espionage* (Rocklin, CA: Prima Publishing, 1997); Winn Schwartau, *Information Warfare* (New York: Thunders Mouth Press, 1994); and Whitfield Duffy and Susan Landau, *Privacy on the Line—The Politics of Wiretapping and Encryption* (Cambridge, MA: MIT Press, 1998).

2. Clive Thompson, "Digital Doomsday" review of *Black Ice—The Invisible Threat of Cyberterrorism* by Dan Verton, *Washington Post,* August 10, 2003.

3. Stephen E. Flynn, "America the Vulnerable," *Foreign Affairs,* vol. 81, no. 1 (January/February 2002), p. 64.

4. Robert O'Harrow Jr., "Florida Data-Sharing Network Raises Privacy Concerns," *Washington Post,* August 6, 2003.

5. According to *USA Today,* it would draw from the budgets or activities of eight current Cabinet agencies, have more than 169,000 employees, and supervise a budget of $37.4 billion. Mimi Hall and John Diamond, "Flaws in Security Structure Are Well Known," *USA Today,* June 7, 2002.

6. Courtesy, Ernst & Young Technology Risk Services, "Global Information Security Survey, 2002."

7. "A Corporate Security Management," report issued by the Conference Board, July 9, 2002.

8. Simson Garfinkle, "You Can Catch More Spies with Honey," *CSO Magazine,* May 2003.

9. Ernst & Young Technology and Security Risk Services, "Global Information Security Survey 2002."

10. Charles Duhigg, "Weak Software," *Washington Post,* August 21, 2003.

11. Lorraine Cosgrove Ware, "The Evolution of the Chief Security Officer," *CSO Magazine,* August 2002.

12. Syradi Scalet, "Snooping by Hook or by Crook," *CSO Magazine,* May 2003.

13. Ware, op. cit. (emphasis added).

14. Malcolm MacTaggart, president and CEO of Crypto Card Corp. in "Sidebar: More Security Predictions," Mitch Betts Computer World, July 14, 2003.

15. Dr. Marianne Broadbent, "A Security State of Mind," *CSO Online* (Australia), July 25, 2003. Available from http://www.csoonline.com .au/index.phpid=468304772.

16. Ibid. (emphasis added).

Chapter 9   Testing Your METL: Or What to Do When the Mission Really Is Essential

1. Peter Senge, *The Fifth Discipline: The Art and Practice of the Learning Organization* (New York: Currency Doubleday, 1990).

2. Adrian Savage (President, Somerville, NJ: PNA Inc.), "Organizational Blackouts," PNA Inc. (2003).

3. Chaim Herzog, *The War of Atonement* (Boston: Little, Brown, 1975), p. 114. Chapter 8 of Herzog's book recounts the battlefield feats of Yossi's unit as "The Epic of the 7th Brigade."

4. U.S. Army, Field Manual 100–5, *Operations,* July 1, 1976, chapters 1 and 2.

5. Kenneth Allard, *Somalia Operations: Lessons Learned* (Washington, DC: National Defense University Press, 1995), pp. 77–82.

Chapter 10   Putting It All Together

1. Robert Fulmer and Marshall Goldsmith, *Leadership Investment—How the World's Best Organizations Gain Strategic Advantage through Leadership Development* (New York: American Management Association, 2001), p. 13.

2. Ibid., p. 14.

3. Ibid., pp. 303–304.

4. Don't blame him: but I am deeply grateful to my friend Tom Petrie, West Point graduate, rancher extraordinaire, and CEO of Petrie-Parkman, Inc. (Denver, CO) for being my guide on these points.

Epilogue

1. Joel Achenbach, "They're Jumping Out of Building One," *Washington Post,* August 29, 2003.

Index